The English Way
of Death

Long regarded as England's authority on funeral customs, Dr
Julian Litten was on the curatorial staff of the Victoria and Albert
Museum, London, between 1966 and 1999, and is now visiting
lecturer in built-heritage conservation at Canterbury Christ
Church University College, Kent.

As a funerary historian and antiquary, he was instrumental in
setting up and invigilating the recording of the contents of the
vaults beneath Christ Church, Spitalfields between 1983 and
1986. He assisted in the organization of the interment of the
Unknown Mariner from the *Mary Rose* at Portsmouth Cathedral
in 1984, was consultant to Westminster Abbey for the
reorganization of its undercroft museum in 1987, and in-house
collaborator for the V&A's 1992 exhibition, *The Art of Death*.

Dr Litten is a fellow of the Society of Antiquaries of London, a
fellow of the Society of Antiquaries of Scotland, and a member of
the Royal Archaeological Institute's Council. A commissioner of
the Cathedrals Fabric Commission for England since 1985, he was
chairman of Portsmouth Cathedral Fabric Advisory Committee
between 1989 and 1999, during which time he steered the
completion and re-ordering of the building. A member of the
Westminster Abbey Fabric Commission since 1993, the
Westminster Abbey Ornaments Committee since 1996, and the
Ely Cathedral Fabric Advisory Committee since 1999, he is also
president of the Church Monuments Society, and a trustee of the
Mausolea & Monuments Trust.

SHILLIBEER'S PATENT FUNERAL CARRIAGES.

SINGLE HORSE FUNERAL

FOUR HORSE FUNERAL

HEARSE & MOURNING COACH FUNERAL, OLD STYLE.

CEMETERY & GENERAL FUNERAL COMPANY.

CITY ROAD FINSBURY,

Next Bunhill Fields Burial Ground.

The Manager of the above Establishment will feel obliged by the necessary Instructions relative to the Interment of Mrs Murray in order that every requirement may be supplied, and the least trouble possible, given to the surviving Relatives.— The annexed Form of Instructions is requested to be filled up, and forwarded by Post to the City Road, as early as possible.

The English Way of Death

The Common Funeral Since 1450

JULIAN LITTEN

ROBERT HALE · LONDON

© *Julian Litten 1991*
First published in Great Britain 1991
Reprinted 1992
Paperback edition 1992
Reprinted in paperback with corrections 2002

ISBN 0 7090 7097 7

Robert Hale Limited
Clerkenwell House
Clerkenwell Green
London EC1R 0HT

The right of Julian Litten to be identified as
author of this work has been asserted by him
in accordance with the Copyright, Designs and
Patents Act 1988

A catalogue record for this book is available from the British Library

2 4 6 8 10 9 7 5 3 1

*Frontispiece: Shillibeer's Funeral Omnibus of
1842, though hailed by some as a marked
improvement in the standard cortège, was
unpopular with the general public.*

Printed in China through Bookbuilders

Contents

Illustrations

Black-and-white Illustrations

Illustrations

Colour Plates

Between pages 46 and 47

Photo Credits

Black-and-white Illustrations

Colour Plates

Life a right shadow is,
For if it long appear,
Then it is spent, and death's long night draws near:
Shadows are moving, light,
And is there aught so moving as is this?
When it is most in sight,
It steals away, and none can tell how, where,
So near our cradles to our coffins are.

William Drummond

Acknowledgements

Original research takes one down many avenues and it would be impossible to list everyone who has helped me on my journey or mapped out my route over the past twenty years. My primary thanks have to go to Sir Roy Strong and Elizabeth Esteve-Coll, the past and present directors of the Victoria and Albert Museum, not only for encouraging me in my work but also for allowing me to pursue field trips, attend seminars and execute research during what would normally be considered as 'working hours'. I owe them both an enormous debt of gratitude.

In the archaeological world I have been assisted by many scholars, notably Dr Richard Morris and Dr Warwick Rodwell, and my particular thanks are due to Max Adams, David Andrews, Hal Bishop, Eric J. Boore, David Caldwell, Frank Clark, Dr Henry Cleere, David Dawson, Ray Fremmer, Charlotte Harding, Carolyn Heighway, Dr Audrey Hume, Dr Ivor Noël Hume, Robert Jannaway, Professor Michael Jarrett, Professor Philip Rahtz, Dr Mark Redknap, Jez Reeve, Hazel Stickings and Pat Wilkinson.

Colleagues at the Victoria and Albert Museum have been particularly patient with my numerous enquiries and endless questions, and special thanks are due to Anne Buddle, Marion Campbell, Martin Chapman, Rosie Eager, Philippa Glanville, Charles Saumarez-Smith, Isobel Sinden, Michael Snodin, Christopher Titterington, Rowan Watson, David Wright and Hilary Young; and also former colleagues Claude Blair, Stephen Calloway, Howard Coutts, Simon Jervis, Professor Michael Kauffmann, Michael Keen and John Morley. I owe a particular debt of gratitude to Ken Jackson for the enormous amount of photography he undertook on my behalf.

It is the privilege of any researcher to come into contact with many academics other than those within one's own institution, and amongst the many who have assisted me are Professor Edzard Baumann (who read the text), Dr John Blair, Mark Lister Bowis, Canon Brian Carne, Stuart Davies, Dr James Dickie, John Fraser, Dr Paul Fritz, Christopher Harrold, Canon Dr Anthony Harvey, Dr Thomas Lacquer, Hon. Christopher Lennox-Boyd, the late Nicholas McMichael, Theya Molleson, Dr Richard Mortimer, Tessa Murdoch, the late John Nevinson, Enid Nixon, A.J.V.B. Norman, Richard Robson, Elizabeth Sellers, Colin Sorensen and Dr Susan Young. Peter A.T.I. Burman, Dr Richard Gem and Professor Lady Pamela Wedgwood have been exceptionally generous with their comments. Stanley Halls of West Kent College has given much advice on building construction in relation to burial vaults.

Acknowledgements

Amongst those involved in the cemetery preservation movement who have given me advice throughout the compilation of this work I am indebted to Professor James Stevens Curl, the doyen of funerary studies, as well as Ashley Barker, Sylvia Barnard, Roderick Bennett, Dr Christopher Brooks, Dr Paul Coones, Dr Brent Elliott, Jennifer Freeman, Peter Howell, Dora Kneebone, Jean Pateman, Kenneth Powell, Dr Benedict Read and Matthew Saunders. Michael Nodes and David Burkett, respectively Chairman and Secretary of the General Cemetery Company, Kensal Green, have afforded me unlimited access to their records over a number of years and have provided me with much information on the formation of private cemeteries.

Access to burial vaults is limited and I am indebted to those many owners and clergy who, over the last twenty years, have afforded me entry to numerous subterranean chambers within their care. I am especially grateful to the Earl De La Warr and the Countess Poulett, to Revd Michael Berry, Revd John Flory, Revd Bryan Roberts, Revd John Whitwell and Revd Brian Macdonald-Milne. I am particularly grateful to the owner of the vault in south-east Leicestershire for allowing me to publish. My thanks are also due to François Jones for drawing the Exton St Peter coffin to my attention.

Within the funeral furnishing trade I would like to record my thanks to Frank Bull (Enfield Co-Op), Messrs Crowsons of Peterborough, Graham and John Harris (T. Cribb & Sons), Colin Field (Great Southern Group), Howard Hodgson (PHK Group), Michael Kenyon (PHK Group), Ivor Leverton, Pamela Maas (former Secretary of the National Association of Funeral Directors), Richard Putt (Leverton's), Lesley White and to Roger Arber, Secretary to the Cremation Society of Great Britain. I also owe a debt of gratitude to the Board of Governors of the British Institute of Funeral Directors for bestowing an honorary membership on me in 1987 in recognition of services rendered to the history of the trade.

Two people deserve to be singled out. Dr Nigel Llewellyn, University of East Sussex, has been exceptionally helpful; as co-organizer and guest curator of the Art of Death exhibition at the Victoria and Albert Museum I could not have asked for a better colleague. His lively stimulation has led me to pastures new, and I recall with pleasure the field trips on which we sought out items for loan. John Pawsey, my literary agent, has shown great patience with me; he has advised, suggested and, on occasions, cajoled me – I've only got this far because of him.

My late parents shared and encouraged my interest in ecclesiastical art; my father drove me to many churches, churchyards and cemeteries and his advice laid the foundation of this work. My gratitude to them is profound, and I thank them most warmly, wherever they are now.

Throughout the four years that it has taken for this book to get off the ground I have been constantly encouraged by my friend Fr Anthony Couchman. He has accompanied me on field trips, given advice on style and content, read the chapters for me, and supplied endless cups of coffee well into the small hours. He has grown up with the book, made numerous telephone calls on my behalf, run off the xeroxes and made sure that I kept to my deadline. One could not have a more stalwart friend; and it is to him, with my deepest gratitude and thanks, that this book is dedicated.

Introduction

In May 1987 I purchased a batch of pristine art deco mourning cards from a stationer's close to where I live in East London. On taking them to the sales assistant, she said: 'We got them when we bought up the stock of an old shop. We used to get asked for them, but not now. I think they're morbid. Anything to do with death is morbid. They don't use them now, do they?'

Many people erect fences whenever conversation turns towards death, heaven and eternity, manœuvring the discussion towards lighter topics. We all know that we shall die, yet our real fear is the process of dying itself: the possible physical pain, the mental confusion, the inability to make our farewells, dying alone or of a sudden, unprepared death as the result of a road accident, an airline disaster or a tragedy at sea.

Continuing advancements in medical science, together with greater prosperity, improved living conditions and a balanced diet have all contributed to a marked increase in longevity; consequently, it is rare for anyone below the age of, say, thirty-five to have attended even a family funeral. As a result, they are both ill-equipped and inexperienced when the burden of arranging one falls on their shoulders. The decision on the method of disposal of the corpse rests with the executors – the 'owners' of the body in law – or, in a few exceptional cases, with a coroner. However, the executors may delegate the practical negotiations with the funeral director to a relative or close friend of the deceased. The funeral expenses, which since April 1988 may also include a simple headstone or other suitable monument, are met from the estate.

The organization of a funeral is usually contracted out to a funeral director who, having ascertained the type of service required and the preferred time and place, contacts the minister and/or the cemetery/crematorium superintendant for an appointment convenient to all parties. It is at this time that any specific requests are made, such as the wish for printed service cards, rather than leaving anything to chance at a later date. The written quotation provided by the funeral director at the time of receiving his instructions, should take the following into account: removal of the body from a local address in normal working hours; laying-out and hygienic treatment (superficial arterial embalming); the coffin, and the use of the chapel of rest; hire of a funeral car (hearse) and one limousine to local churchyard/cemetery/crematorium; attendance of the funeral director and bearers together with the costs of making all the necessary arrangements subject to instruction. Anything else will be treated as an extra and charged for accordingly. The funeral director is also obliged at this time to inform the client of the specification and charges for a Basic Simple Funeral (BSF) as agreed between the National Association of Funeral Directors (NAFD) and the Office of Fair Trading. In addition, he is obliged to make it clear to the client that the prices quoted, be it for a customized or BSF funeral, do not include transport for the minister, additional funeral car and limousine mileage charges, the cost of the grave/cremation fee, the memorial stone or entry in a book of remembrance, nor any disbursements made on the client's behalf, such as church fees and gravedigger's tips.

What does this mean in terms of hard currency? When researching her book *The American Way of Death*, Jessica Mitford visited Messrs Ashton's of South London in the summer of 1962. The majority of Ashton's funerals then averaged £50, to which had to be added about half as much again for the burial/cremation fee, together with the price of a plot. Following Miss Mitford's example, I visited Messrs Ashton's – then trading as Ashton Ebutt Holdings – in the spring of 1987 to see how prices compared twenty-five years on. Ashton Ebutt's BSF was quoted as £450; for this one acquired a complete funeral service consisting of a simulated oak veneer MDF coffin lined with satinette, the exterior fitted with two pairs of injection-moulded plastic handles and an inscription plate, use of a funeral car and one limousine. But, add some lengths of wooden reed moulding to the lid and the base of the sides of the BSF coffin, upgrade the lining to taffeta, and you have the *Ascot*, Ashton Ebutt's cheapest funeral in their customized range, retailing at £560. Their most expensive coffin, the *Headley*, would set you back by £995: a polished (polyurethane spray, to be precise) solid oak or mahogany coffin of superior finish with routered panelled boards and raised lid, the exterior fitted with three pairs of plastic injection-moulded handles, finished in bronze, silver or gilt, plus a machine-engraved metal depositum plate. The interior 'set' (soft furnishings) consisted of a deep ruffled satin lining, gown (shroud), overlay and ruffled lid panel.

The choice of coffin depends largely on the price one is willing to pay for the complete funeral service – the decisions relating to its finish, fittings and soft furnishings are generally left to the funeral director and, as Ashton Ebutt informed me, they rarely met with requests to waver from the items shown in their illustrated catalogue. It appears to be the accepted practice in Greater London for injection-moulded plastic handles and depositum plates to be used on all coffins, be they for burial or cremation, except for those at the top end of the range destined for the earth-cut grave in which case metal fittings are used, though it would be wrong to infer that a funeral director would not provide metal fittings if it were requested.

Since the establishment of the trade in the seventeenth century it has always been the funeral furnisher who selected the fittings, ordering his supplies from trade catalogues – as is done today – and taking items from stock according to the quality of the funeral he has been contracted to undertake, with little or no interference in the matter from his client. This could sometimes lead to ghastly results, especially when money was no object to the client and the undertaker was not imbued with a sense of the aesthetic.

Certainly there is now a wider choice of coffin furniture, though as 'selection rooms' displaying the available merchandise are rare in this country, the client has little idea of the extent of the range. It is still possible to acquire a framed and panelled solid 1¼-inch mahogany coffin with butt joints, wax polished, with solid cast-brass gothic handles and stirrup stops, tapered brass depositum plate with enamelled hand-cut lettering, square-headed cast-brass side and lid bolts, cast lid motifs, the interior caulked and lined with wadding and double domette, ruched silk side sheets with deep flounce, buttoned silk cushion and full silk gown. Not that many funeral directors could provide this, arguing that such merchandise is now no longer available. To them this might be true; however, the reason behind this is a basic lack of knowledge as to the extent of the merchandise available and the history of the trade. It is still possible, believe it or not, to acquire a triple-shell coffin, the outer case upholstered with wadding and rich Genoese silk velvet.

Very few families now have the body of a 'loved one' at home on the night preceding the funeral, and numerous funeral directors tell me of the noticeable decline in those viewing remains in the chapel of rest. The secularization of society has diminished the pomp and panoply of the English funeral: they have become cold, clinical rituals – almost harsh, one might say – and it is not difficult in such a climate to envisage the introduction of a Municipal Funeral Service when, in response to a notification of death, operatives will remove the body from the place of demise and privately dispose of it without any representative of the deceased being present. Again, mourning dress is rarely worn nowadays, its place having been superseded by grey or dark blue for the ladies and a lounge suit for gentlemen; indeed, even some funeral directors are moving away from black, adopting grey or midnight blue livery. To see full mourning one now has to attend either a society or a West Indian funeral; we have much to learn from these, especially the human element so prominently displayed by the Caribbeans. It is a sad indictment of a society which has made every effort to simplify all ritual to its lowest common denominator.

Few funerals now take place in church. Too often one is asked to meet at the crematorium, and what then ensues is dismal: an unaccompanied funeral car glides noiselessly under the *porte-cochère*, the coffin is transferred to a stainless steel 'hors-d'œuvre' trolley and wheeled into the chapel, which looks more like a waiting-room in a university college hospital than a dignified setting for the disposal of the dead. Ten minutes later, to the accompaniment of slurred canned music, the curtains jerk their way noisily round the catafalque as the coffin sinks slowly through the floor, like a Würlitzer organ at the Roxy Kinema, to the furnace below. We have only ourselves to blame for putting up with such banalities. Outside, as the mourners exchange greetings and inspect the wreaths, a plume of black acrid smoke rises from the ill-disguised chimney, bearing its load of burnt plastic and Terylene up, up and away to make its contribution to the 'greenhouse' effect. Cremation may be 'clean' but it's certainly not 'green'.

It has to be said that the trade has done little to improve the situation, apparently happy to tolerate the decline in standards, arguing that they provide only what is wanted. For my own part, I have no intention of being dispatched in a multi-density fibreboard veneered coffin with plastic handles and Terylene lining. Most funeral directors I have spoken to over the last ten years assure me that the public are 'generally satisfied' with the funeral service they buy; an argument difficult to test within a virtual monopoly. However, I would be doing a grave and serious injustice were I to imply that all operatives are themselves 'generally satisfied' with the present state of affairs, or that there are not those who pride themselves on the very high quality of merchandise they provide. My criticism relates to the metropolitan areas; we seem to do things better in the smaller towns and villages.

Funerals are certainly cheaper now in relative terms than at any other time since the eighteenth century. There is no longer a hard-sell approach on the part of the funeral director and neither is there a set scale of charges dependent on the social status of the deceased. It seems odd to me that whilst some do not baulk at spending upwards of £5,000 on a wedding reception, they protest over the expenditure of £500 on a funeral.

The biggest mistake within the trade during the last ten years has been, in my opinion, the 'customizing' of funerals as a result of the corporate image promoted by some of the conglomerate holding companies. Funerals are not commodities; rather they are highly important and emotional social events forming the final ritual in the calendar of life. They should not be marketed as though they were package holidays – even though there is an element of journeying into the unknown – and the offer of fringe benefits and insurance policies somehow cheapens the service further. If we want to rescue the funeral from the quicksand of commercialism we need to ensure that we, the clients, get what we want: a wider choice of merchandise, a better ritual, a proper cremation format (rather than a poorly doctored version of the 1662 Order for the Burial of the Dead), and the latitude to express our grief openly without fear of criticism.

In the pages that follow I have tried to show the development of the trade over the past 500 years. Sixty years ago Bertram Puckle endeavoured to do the same; he was writing as a dedicated cremationist with a futuristic outlook: an Alphaville where cremation reigns supreme and the land is left for the living. I make no such statement, leaving the reader to decide into which lobby I shall be casting my cap. Suffice it to say that it is my earnest wish that a re-evaluation of the English funeral takes place soon, incorporating the best of the past and the best – if there is any – of today; there, conjoined, refined and purified we may well have a ritual which suitably expresses those caring and loving attributes so jealously guarded in the past which now seem, sadly, to be dormant within the nation's soul.

Julian W.S. Litten
Walthamstow, 1990

1

The Trade

The essayist and poet Sir Richard Steel had a poor opinion of undertakers, writing in 1702:

> Where the brass knocker, wrapt in flannel band,
> Forbids the thunder of the footman's hand;
> The upholder, rueful harbinger of death,
> Waits with impatience for the dying breath;
> As vultures o'er a camp, with hovering flight,
> Snuff up the future carnage of the flight.[1]

What had the trade done to deserve such harsh treatment? Were they not merely carrying out a required social service? Had not the medieval burial guilds done precisely the same? So why should he, the late seventeenth-century undertaker, be treated with such disdain? The answer is complex. 'Generally speaking most tradesmen have some ways peculiar to themselves which they either derived from masters who taught them or from the experience of things or from something in the course of business',[2] but this did not strictly apply to undertakers,

> ... a set of men who live by death and never care to appear but at the End of Man's Life ... their Business is to watch Death, and to furnish out the Funeral Solemnity, with as much pomp and feigned sorrow as the Heirs or Successors of the Deceased chose to purchase: They are a hard-hearted Generation, and require more money than Brains to conduct their Business; I know no one

Qualification peculiarly necessary to them, except that is a steady, demure and melancholy Countenance at Command: I do not know, that they take Apprentices in their Capacity as Undertakers, for they are generally Carpenters, or Herald-Painters besides; and they only employ, as Journeymen, a set of Men whom they have picked up, possessed of a sober Countenance, and a solemn melancholy Face, whom they pay at so much a Jobb.[3]

How would the undertaker have defended his position? Probably by saying that he only supplied what custom dictated as appropriate to the social status of the deceased, and that everything was done for the complete satisfaction of his client. The argument advanced by the 1747 author of *The London Tradesman* is a little unfair, for 'undertaking' was at that time a relatively new trade, barely a century old. Its aims and objective were more complex than, and entirely different to, those of the late medieval guilds which had, until their dissolution under the Chantries Act of 1547, taken under their wing the organization of the last of the Christian 'Seven Acts of Mercy', the burial of the dead. We need, therefore, to examine the role of these guilds to see how and why the trade of undertaker came into being before deciding whether or not to cast our lot with *The London Tradesman*.

By the beginning of the thirteenth century there was a widely held belief within the Church that masses said on behalf of the dead would shorten the length of time a soul spent in purgatory. The funeral liturgy included a mass for the dead, but to take full advantage of the memorial rite, masses had also to be sung on the third, seventh and thirtieth days following burial and, to complete the calendar of commemoration, the 'obit': a mass sung on the first anniversary of the death. In some instances the masses did not stop with the obit but went on with the annual 'year's mind' for up to ten years or more. As each subsequent requiem repeated the ritual exhibited at the primary mass, the cycle proved an expensive way of praying for the repose of the dead. There were fresh candles to buy, the hire – or outright purchase – of mourning cloaks; the poor had again to be invited – it was considered worthy and laudable to remember them at one's death – and had to receive a further portion of the largesse exhibited at the funeral. Some of the poor made quite a good living from these services and one can imagine an efficient 'bush telegraph' system to alert others of forthcoming requiems. Not only did the mourners expect a meal but there was also the priest's fee, plus an appropriate 'donation' to church funds.

The endowment fund for such masses was enormous and in the thirteenth century some system of regulation was required. In the larger towns many parish priests were singing the majority of their masses for the dead with no family member present and with only an altar server to chant the responses. This was especially so regarding endowed perpetuity masses. The solution was a simple one: employ priests with the sole responsibility of singing the memorial requiems so as to allow the parish priests to go about their customary role of caring for the spiritual needs of the living. Those taken on from endowment income were known as chantry priests – 'chantry' because such masses were chanted rather than said.

The Black Death exacerbated the situation; whilst there was no shortage of souls to pray for, endowments slackened off, owing to some of the wealthy dying intestate. In addition, parish priests were feeling the pinch through reduced income from alms and tithes. Some villages – such as Little Gaddesden in Hertfordshire – were totally wiped out, whilst others were very badly hit, with as much as a third of the population dying. William of Dene, a monk based at Rochester, wrote in 1349: 'To our great grief the plague carried off so vast a multitude of people of both sexes that nobody could be found who would bear the corpses to the grave. Men and women carried their own children on their shoulders to the church and threw them into a common pit. From these pits such an appalling stench was given off that scarcely anyone dared even to walk beside the churchyards.'[4] A Latin graffito on the north wall of the church tower at Ashwell, Hertfordshire, records the plight there in 1350: 'Wretched, terrible, violent. Only the remnants of the people are left to tell the tale.'[5]

That the rich did not escape the scourge is evident at Crich in Derbyshire when, in October 1349, William de Wakebridge added a small chantry chapel to the parish church in memory of his wife, his father, his two sisters and three brothers, all of whom had died of the plague in the summer of that year. Though enough was provided for requiem masses to be chanted 'for ever', this lapsed 200 years later with the introduction of the Chantries Act. One of the more unprofessional results of the plague was that some priests latched on to the idea of leaving the parochial ministry and becoming chantry priests – often, in the process, gaining a lucrative return for very little work. So notorious was this practice that Chaucer used the antithesis of the chase as a template of virtue for the poor Parson in his *Canterbury Tales*:

> He sette nat his befice to hire,
> And leet his sheepe encombred in the mire,
> And ran to Londoun, unto Seint Poules,
> To seken his a chauntry for soules,
> Or with a bretherhed to been withhold.[6]

There was little social justice in a system whereby simony could dictate the duration of one's time in purgatory; was it right that only the rich could secure such release? It was this feeling of injustice on the part of the poor that brought into being the guilds, secular organizations of the laity whose members' contributions were pooled to endow masses to be sung for the souls of the poor. It was their way of expressing the saying, 'If you can't beat them, join them.'

Some of the guilds were quite large, especially in the greater towns and cities, and wealthy enough to have not only their own chantry priest but also their own altars within the church, and there were even instances when funds allowed for the building of an additional aisle as a guild chapel.

Before we romanticize the size, wealth and power of these guilds, it should be pointed out that in the main they were fairly small. Meade cites the membership of the 'little company of four men and four women who, in 1379, could afford to provide only a candle to burn during the daily mass at the church of St Nicholas, Great Yarmouth'.[7] Those slightly better off could organize an annual requiem for past guild members at All Souls' – 2 November – or on the occasion of the anniversary of the death of their main benefactor, and it was quite in order for bequests to be made to the guild in addition to the contributions given to it during one's lifetime. In many parish churches a parchment scroll or tablet of wood, inscribed with the names of those who had requested obits or provided chantries, was kept on the wall near to the high altar.[8]

One of the duties occasionally assumed by the guilds was the maintenance of a charnel, a subterranean chamber into which were placed the bones of the dead disturbed when interments took place in the churchyard. The charnel at Howden, Yorkshire, was maintained by the Guild of the Holy Trinity. Many so-called crypts beneath churches are nothing more than empty charnels – G.H. Cook gives at least twenty such examples[9] – though those at Hythe in Kent and Rothwell in Northamptonshire are still full. After the Reformation it was not unusual for these charnels to be cleared and taken over by prominent local families as their burial vault, as happened at Saffron Walden and Thaxted, both in Essex. Occasionally chantries were founded within the charnel itself, as at Norwich Cathedral (now the undercroft of the hall of the Grammar School), Grantham and St Nicholas, Bristol. Here altars would be set up within the charnel and the priest would sing the mass in the company of a silent and skeletal congregation – or bits of them, depending on how much had been retrieved from the disturbed graves. At High Wycombe a more sanitary state of affairs persisted with the erection of several guild altars in the Chapel of the Trinity and Our Lady, built over the bone-hole and served by two chantry priests. In the churchyard of St Peter's, St Albans, are the remains of the charnel chapel of the Fraternity of All Saints, also known as the Charnel Brotherhood.

Chantries were not limited to the laity; some of the more senior clergy certainly availed themselves of the system and numerous chantry chapels survive in most of the monastic-foundation cathedrals to abbots and priors. Regardless of their sacerdotal status they, too, had to provide sufficient funds for their endowment but, as they were often as wealthy and powerful as the nobility, this was no hardship. And this did not stop with the Reformation for, 'by virtue of the very generous pensions they were granted when they surrendered their houses to the Crown, ex-abbots possessed ample means to found chantries ... or to make bequests for soul-masses after death'.[10]

Chantries were more popular in London than elsewhere and every City church could boast at least one. Excluding the lay fraternities, 280 private chantries were set up in London during the fourteenth century, the heyday of the movement. Between 1403 and 1502 the number of new foundations fell to 120 and the downward trend continued into the sixteenth century with only thirteen new foundations between 1503 and 1547, the year of the Chantries Act. A closer examination of the figures shows that of those founded during the fourteenth and fifteenth centuries, excluding those of the guilds and fraternities, one-fifth were perpetual. By the end of the fifteenth century many chantries had served their term: some had dissolved through lack of maintenance on the part of the families concerned,[11] while others disappeared through amalgamation; so that by the time of the suppression there were not more than 200 spread among the City churches.[12] Though the Act of 1547 provided that the surrendered endowments of the remaining 2,374 chantries be applied to public and charitable purposes nationally, much of it merely went into the pockets of Edward VI's advisers.

The chantry system was not introduced into the Anglican Communion until

1873 when three laymen of the parish of St James, Hatcham, formed the Guild of All Souls, whose objective was to maintain intercessory prayers for the dying and the repose of the souls of its deceased members and all the faithful departed. It remains today the largest Chantry Guild within the Church of England with its own chantry priest, and survives on the contributions of its members, gifts and bequests. It also holds the advowson of forty-one livings.[13]

Apart from maintaining the cycle of requiem masses, the most important role of the parochial guilds and fraternities was the organization and servicing of the funeral procession. It was they who maintained the parish coffin, the pall, the cloaks, the candles, the hearse and – in those instances when poverty made it necessary – the mass fee. Of the trade guilds, the livery companies in the cities undertook to provide all that was customary for the performance of the obsequies of their deceased members, the street processions often reflecting in size and panoply the funerals of the nobility. Knowing that nearly every parish in the country had their own guild or fraternity at one time, it is all the more frustrating to learn that little exists from the once vast stock of pre-Reformation funerary artefacts. The exceptions are: a mid fifteenth-century embroidered pall from St Peter's, Sudbury, Suffolk (now in Ipswich Museum); two magnificent hearse cloths of 1509, one in the Ashmolean Museum at Oxford and the other in Great St Mary's at Cambridge, provided for the varsities' annual commemoration service for Henry VII; a pall of 1516 belonging to the Guild of St John at Dunstable Priory (*Col. 1*);[14] and six palls of the period *c*.1490–1525 belonging to various livery companies in the City of London.[15] It is doubtful whether these palls would have been considered for outdoor use, their materials being too precious to risk inclement weather and inconsiderate birds. The Cripps-Day mourning hood, the only surviving 'late sixteenth-century' item of its kind,[16] has in recent years proved to be little more than a nineteenth-century pastiche (*1*).[17]

As seemingly no contemporary guild records exist it is impossible to state with accuracy the role played by guild members immediately a death had taken place. However, as the laying-out and preparation of the body was at that time the responsibility of the family, it would appear that the guild limited themselves to three actions: the marshalling of their members to attend, and the selection from that company of those to carry the coffin (though it would have been a strong guild able to command more than half a dozen of its members during a weekday); to see the coffin safely into the church and to ensure that the burial equipment was in place; and to attend the full obsequies on the following day, including the funeral feast. Obviously someone in the guild's hierarchy – perhaps the clerk – would have acted as 'master of ceremonies', informing guild members of their required attendance and possibly liaising with the parish priest and sexton on behalf of the family. Matters would have been made that much simpler had the guild clerk also been the parish clerk and it might well have been the case in some instances. Indeed, this person's role would not have been dissimilar to that undertaken by the present-day funeral director. Be that as it may, the precise chain is not known; somehow the guild was informed and the train of events set in motion.

Neither is it known where the accoutrements were kept. For example, did the guild have storage space within the church or was it expected that they make

1 *Based on mourning hoods as shown in de Bray's panorama of the funeral of Sir Philip Sidney in 1586, the Cripps-Day hood published in 1933 as 'late sixteenth century', now appears to be early nineteenth century, possibly related to the Eglinton Tournament, 1839.*

provision elsewhere? Did the guild members look after their own coats or was there a central wardrobe at the church, or guild-hall in the case of the trade guilds? Who was responsible for getting the coffin ready, the coffin stools and hearse in position and distributing the candles? If we look to existing trends for advice, it seems likely that the coffin stools, hearse and candles would have been kept at the church and put into place by the parish clerk and/or sexton. In the case of the small parish guilds the coffin itself was probably kept somewhere in the church as well, as would have been the 'reserved stock' of unbleached beeswax candles. Again, the trade guilds probably had enough storage space in their own guild-halls for the coffin and cloaks, they might even have had a private stock of candles. It should not be forgotten that only the endowed chantries were confiscated under the Chantries Act; the guilds still continued but more as funeral clubs than intercessionary fraternities. As it was, the chantry duties of the guilds had been in steady decline since the early fifteenth century, so that by 1547 the majority had for many years been looked upon as burial societies. This was not to say that organized and structured prayers for the dead had ceased, for the Roman Rite included plenary intercessions for the living and the dead at every mass; the annual mass for the departed was on All Souls' Day, a standard event in the Church's calendar, set apart for the benefit of souls in purgatory.

In the country towns the gradual decline in status undergone by the guilds also saw a reduction in the number of trappings provided for the funeral. For example, the hearse around the coffin was practically unseen after the third quarter of the fifteenth century, though it survived for the greater obsequies. In Westminster Abbey Museum is a fragment of a funerary taper found in Abbot Thomas Mylling's tomb, which is presumed to have been placed there at the time of his funeral in 1492 and probably came off the hearse. The last two recorded

2 *Raised up in front of the High Altar at Westminster Abbey in 1532 for the funeral of Abbot Islip, this magnificent hearse was made of wood, plaster and wax.*

instances of hearses of any size relate to those at Westminster Abbey provided for Abbot John Islip (2)[18] and Henry VIII (d.1547).

Within parish churches the use of coffin stools was, in some areas, being overtaken by the bier, and the custom of issuing mourners with wax tapers – slender candles some two or three feet in length and between half and 1½ inches in diameter – was already in decline, not to be reintroduced until the late sixteenth century when the tapers reappeared in their new capacity as flambeaus for night-time funerals; in the eighteenth century a more elaborate form of triple candle, twisted to resemble a three-branched candlestick and very much like the Easter Vigil candle once used in the Roman Rite, was carried by one of the undertaker's men preceding the cortège (3).

An improved economic climate during the reign of Elizabeth I saw an increase in those able to afford their own coffins, and no longer was this presumed a luxury limited to the middle and upper classes. By the middle of the seventeenth century the parish coffin was regarded as fit only for transporting the corpses of the poor to the grave. Coffin shapes themselves were beginning to change too. The tapered-sided gable-lidded coffin was being challenged by the new single-break flat-lidded shell, though it appears only to have been the middle classes who focused attention on style. Palls were getting larger: no more the short-hemmed highly embroidered creature; a huge sheet of black velvet twelve by fifteen feet,

3   Richard Chandles' trade card c. 1750 itemizes what was provided for a 'decent' funeral. The side vignettes show how funeral processions were ordered.

sometimes lined with white silk or a lesser-quality material of the same colour, and thrown right over the coffin and its bearers.

Mourning dress, too, was witnessing a change. By the last quarter of the sixteenth century the issue of 'official mourning' was on the wane. The tailored long-sleeved calf-length black coat with tight wristbands and single-button or tape fastenings at the neck was in a decline, as in came the fashionable three-quarter length cloak – of black, certainly, but heavily embroidered and trimmed with braid. The chief mourner continued to wear a coat with train, together with the mourning hood, but even the manner of wearing the hood changed: draped round the shoulders like a short scarf rather than being worn over the head. By the seventeenth century the hood disappeared as an item of mourning and in its place came sashes and scarves. The short cloak had three advantages over the coat: it need not be tailored and so was available 'off the peg'; it was more fashionable; and it allowed unhindered access to the sword. Armourers knew this and they, too, jumped on the funerary bandwagon, producing black-hilted and pommelled mourning swords with black scabbards. Indeed, it was not at all unusual for civic authorities to have a mourning sword which, on the death of a monarch, alderman or council member, was carried in the procession before the mayor in place of the civic sword. A number of these ceremonial mourning swords survive, those of the lord mayors of London and Exeter both having black velvet hilts and scabbards.

The new economic climate of the late sixteenth century brought advantages and disadvantages so far as the funeral was concerned. On the negative side, funerals were becoming so much more secular in outlook, appearance and context that the surviving guilds and fraternities found themselves hard-pressed to provide all that made for an average funeral of the new type; the rules were being rewritten by a public which no longer wished to perpetuate the simple ritual hitherto provided and which were looking for a pageantry close to that of the great baronial funerals as performed by the College of Arms, a corporation of heralds and part of the Royal Household. There was no alternative for the guilds than for them to go out to trade for assistance, passing on their additional expenditure to the client. Of course, had the guilds and fraternities included a handling charge in their reckoning they might have attracted an income allowing them the freedom to purchase for themselves those 'extras' now being clamoured for. But they did not and this was to be their downfall. Indeed, the new economy, the concomitant increase in the standard of living and the purchasing power which it gave to the individual sounded the death-knell for the minor guilds. For the client, the advantage was that he could go direct to those various tradesmen who, collectively, could provide all that made for an average funeral. As for the tradesmen, some saw an opening into what could be a vastly lucrative enterprise. And so it was that the guilds and fraternities melted away and commerce took the lead, as will shortly be seen.

Not everyone desired to mimic the magnificent pomp of the College of Arms; others knew what a risky business this could be, for the College maintained a rigid overview of funerary practices countrywide, taking to task any family which emulated that type of funeral reserved by the rules of etiquette for those of nobler birth. Nevertheless, the College could not have informants everywhere and though some funerals were based on the College's formularies, the client ensured that the most important hallmarks of a College of Arms funeral – the funerary 'achievements' – were substituted by objects loosely indicative of them. The funeral was now becoming a public display of private wealth – a statement of status – rather than a dignified journey to the grave, and there were any number of tradesmen in the private sector eager to cater for the demand and, thereby, to profit from it.

In 1631 the antiquary John Weever lamented this emulation:

> Now howsoever the procuration of funeral, the manner of buriall, the pompe of obsequies, bee rather comforts to the living, then helpes to the dead; and although all these ceremonies be despised by our parents on their death-beds, yet should they not be neglected by us their children, or nearest of kindred, upon their interments. But funerals in any expensive way here with us, are now accounted but as a fruitlesse vanitie, insomuch that almost all the ceremoniall rites of obsequies heretofore used, are altogether laid aside: for we see daily that Noblemen, and Gentlemen of eminent ranke, office, and qualitie, are either silently buried in the night time, with a Torch, a two-penie Linke,[19] and a Lanterne; or parsimoniously interred in the day-time, by the helpe of some ignorant countrey-painter, without the attendance of any one of the Officers of Armes, whose chiefest support, and maintenance, hath ever depended upon the performance of such funerall rites, and exequies.[20]

It would be misleading to imply that there were only three strata of funeral existing at the end of the sixteenth century – monarchial, noble and guild; what one had depended entirely on one's status. For example the clergy, the landed gentry and freemen of livery companies and trade guilds would qualify for a funeral similar in style to those organized by the College of Arms for members of the peerage. It was quite possible for someone to start from relatively humble beginnings and work one's way up in society through trade guild or livery company affiliation to become a member of the town council. Councillors and aldermen commanded grander funerals than those of guild liverymen, for their status was higher. The town council arranged the funeral and the guild members attended in a secondary role.

The College of Arms set and maintained a rigid scale of funerary etiquette: the obsequies of a royal duke would have been more complicated – and costly – than that of an earl, whilst a viscount's cortège would have exceeded in complexity that of a baron. So it was that the trade emulated this sliding scale system for the populace at large. A person of 'quality' – such as a member of the landed gentry or the clergy – would be at the top of their scale, commanding a funeral similar to that organized by the College of Arms for a knight bachelor, with paupers and wayfarers coming in at the bottom. This system was adhered to throughout the seventeenth century. The inflated snobbery of purchasing a ritual traditionally reserved for those of a higher social rank did not appear until the very end of the eighteenth century; conversely, it was a dissatisfied middle class which, towards the close of the nineteenth century, ushered in a less complicated and confusing street procession.

The trade also regulated on the matter of pall-bearers; usually six in number. In general, the rule of thumb was that one's peers were seconded to perform the

4   *Paul Sandby's c. 1795 sketch of a spinster's funeral indicates a*
white pall and white-clad female pall-bearers, probably friends
of the deceased.

role. A married man's pall was expected to be supported by his married friends; if single then bachelor colleagues would perform the duty; likewise for spinsters (*4*) – but not so for children (except in certain rural areas), married women or widows, when the responsibility was delegated either to adult male relatives of the deceased or the undertaker's own men. In the country it was the custom for the estate workers or tenants to act as both coffin- and pall-bearers, this was a necessity as the local builder often doubled up as undertaker and would not have had so many men at his command as the full-time town undertaker. In 1898 four parties of bearers – colliers, estate workmen, tenants and labourers – were detailed to wheel Gladstone's bier from Hawarden church to Broughton Hall railway station, and in 1952 estate workers formed the guard of honour in Sandringham church around the coffin of George VI.

Sometimes the accepted etiquette was dispensed with. William Pitt, First Earl of Chatham, should have had pall-bearers equal in rank to himself, but this was not to be and in a letter written in 1778 following the funeral in Westminster Abbey, the nineteen-year-old Pitt the Younger said to his mother, 'The Court did not honour us with their countenance, nor did they suffer the procession to be as magnificent as it ought; but it had, notwithstanding everything essential to the great object, the attendance being most remarkable. The Duke of Gloucester was in the Abbey. The pall-bearers were Sir G. Saville, Mr Townshend, Dunnin and Burke.'[21]

It was a simple duty to perform, walking alongside the coffin holding the hem of the pall. For the average funeral the pall-bearer was expected to perform his duties *en route* as well as within the church; whereas at the funerals of the great, the pall-bearers were only called into service once the coffin was at the church

*5   Classical symbolism provides the source for this 1746 design by
Gravelot for a funeral ticket. This example was commissioned
by a commercial stationer's.*

and ready to proceed up the nave.

Undertakers rarely advertised, for theirs was – and remains – a trade where discretion took precedence over high-profile marketing and one would not see an undertaker publishing testimonials from satisfied customers. Nevertheless they did issue trade cards and it is from such items and other related mercantile ephemera that we are able to reconstruct a reliable overview of the trade, their connection with other business houses and their livery company affiliations. Seventeenth- and eighteenth-century trade cards were quite large items, a far cry from the small visiting cards issued today, being single sheets of paper ranging from 4×6 to 8×12 inches in folio size. How they were used is not generally agreed upon,[22] for, whilst the obverse of some of these cards – 'shopkeepers' bills' as they were known by the eighteenth-century tradesmen – were sometimes utilized as an invoice to the purchaser, the majority surviving in public and private collections were not. Were they left on the shop counter for the client to take, distributed on the street or pasted up on to street notice-boards? They were certainly not affixed to the merchandise as labels in the same way that some furniture makers and picture framers did, as a recent examination of some one thousand coffins in the vaults at Christchurch, Spitalfields, has proved. Nevertheless, trade cards seem to have been regarded as an important form of advertising and during the eighteenth century a number of well-known artists were commissioned to design such items (5).

The first recorded person trading as an undertaker *per se* is William Boyce, who opened a shop in *c.*1675 'at ye WHIGHT HART & COFFIN, in ye Grate Ould Bayley, near Newgeat' (6). Almost at the same time William Russell, a painter and coffin-maker, opened his London shop; far more ingenious than Boyce, Russell entered into an agreement with the College of Arms in 1689 whereby, for a fee, its members would attend certain funerals which he had arranged. This was a shrewd move on his part for it meant that he not only had the blessing, and guidance, of the College, but also avoided their censure. For Russell, this was an exceptional opening into the mysteries of the craft, whilst for the College of Arms it was a great mistake as their involvement in funerals quickly declined, the embers briefly coming to life with the public obsequies of Queen Mary in 1695. It is in any case debatable whether the College could have survived in the face of such rapid growth in the private sector; their lawsuits against usurping trade

6   *Most of the early trade cards incorporated a representation of a sign-board. William Boyce, trading in c. 1680, could be found 'at ye WHIGHT HART & COFFIN'.*

At ij lower Corner of Fleet-lane al ij Signe of ij Naked Boy
& Coffin you may be Accomodated wᵗʰ all things for a
Funeral as well ij meanest as those of greater Ability
upon Reasonable Terms more particularly Coffins shrou[d]
Palls Cloaks Sconces Stans Hangings for Rooms
Heraldry Hearse & Coaches Gloves wᵗʰ all other things
not here mentioned by Wᵐ Grinly Coffin Maker.

7 William Grinly, though advertising himself as a coffin-maker
in c. 1710, provided a complete funeral service, thereby marking
him out as an undertaker.

diminished once they realized that they had priced themselves out of the market and had little extra to offer than the trade apart from kudos and tradition. Yet even the nobility were loath to pay for such intangibles when they could obtain a similar ritual at less outlay and with greater speed from within the trade. However, the College of Arms remained in charge of the obsequies of royal funerals until 1751 when a private undertaker, a Mr Harcourt, supplied and organized the funeral of Frederick, Prince of Wales. Although this is the first recorded instance of a private undertaker being used by the royal household, it is possible that they had been previously involved in some small way in royal funerals, for it is doubtful that the College of Arms provided coffins and it would seem probable that they contracted this out to the trade, to people such as William Russell – indeed, could it have been Russell who provided the coffin for Queen Mary in late December 1694?

There must have been many jealous eyes directed towards Russell who, owing to his association with the College of Arms, was able to attract a fair proportion of the up-market trade within London. But neither he nor Boyce enjoyed an absolute monopoly, for there were others in business as undertakers at that time, such as Eleazar Malory of Whitechapel, well established by 1700, and John Clarke of Jermyn Street, who was advertising in 1725.

There were no written rules or code of practice in the early years of the trade, and anyone could set themselves up as a coffin-maker or undertaker. An examination of extant trade cards shows that the furnishing of funerals in the early eighteenth century was, in the main, limited to those already involved in the cabinet-making and upholstery trades.[23] Territorial boundaries seem also to have been tacitly adhered to, and it was usual, especially in London, for funeral furnishers to limit their operations to the confines of the parish in which they were situated, and though many of the late eighteenth-century trade cards include the words 'Funerals performed to all parts of Great Britain', it is doubtful that this offer was ever taken up. Fourteen trade cards issued by London undertakers during the period *c.*1680 to *c.*1760 survive,[24] and as none indicate any other craft-affiliation it must be assumed that they were able to furnish from stock all that went to provide for a funeral.

The undertaker's trade card was explicit and left no one in doubt as to the range of items available from any one merchant. William Grinly's *c.*1730 card was concise:

> At yᵉ lower Corner of Fleet lane at yᵉ Sign of yᵉ Naked Boy & Coffin you may be Accomodated wᵗʰ all things for a Funeral as well yᵉ meanest as those of greater Ability upon Reasonable Terms more particularly Coffins Shrouds Palls Cloaks Sconces Stans Hangings for Rooms Heraldry Hearse & Coaches Gloves wᵗʰ all other things not mentioned by Wm. Grinly, Coffin Maker.[25] (7)

Robert Green's card of 1752 (8) is more explicit, leaving nothing to chance; but he had a reason, for not only was he in business as a furnishing undertaker but also provided a wholesale service to the trade in general. Unlike Grinly, Green did not own his own hearse and mourning coaches and was probably more at home performing in-parish funerals similar to that shown in a contemporary engraving by William Hogarth (9) on a funeral ticket issued between 1730 and 1750 by

8 In 1752 Robert Green of London was using a rococo design to frame the printed text on his trade card.

Humphrey Drew, the King Street, Westminster, undertaker.

From surviving pattern books, trade cards, bill headings, contemporary written accounts and livery company admission lists we learn that Southwark and Whitechapel were the two main areas in London accommodating funeral furnishing houses during the eighteenth and early nineteenth centuries. Southwark specialized in coffin furniture – the nomenclature given to the metal fittings found on coffins – while Whitechapel developed a particular expertise in the production of coffins and fabric-covered outer cases. Yet this is not surprising when one realizes that both were close to the docks and that the iron foundries in their areas were more conveniently situated for the timber yards and wharfs along the north bank. Moreover, Whitechapel neighboured on to Spitalfields, whose centre housed what was known as the 'black stuff' industry, the manufacture of the rich and expensive silks and velvets reserved for the exclusive use of the funerary trade. Yet whilst certain cabinet-makers and upholsterers occasionally furnished funerals there is no evidence to show that iron founders did likewise. It seems, then, that the average undertaker was little more than a speculative cabinet-maker and joiner who, either by direct contact with the metalworking trades, or via such funeral houses as Richard Green's, was able to buy in at wholesale all that was required for a funeral. Again, the undertaker offered two choices to the client: outright purchase of all the accoutrements or the hire thereof. Obviously the hearse and mourning coaches were rented, but certainly not the coffin. Reading through Robert Green's trade card it seems highly unlikely that a client would want to purchase outright such items as the velvet pall, the room hangings, the large silvered candlesticks and sconces, or the feathers and cloaks, for these objects would be of little or no use to the purchaser once the funeral had taken place. Indeed, their hire was taken for

9   *Designed by Hogarth in c.1720 for the Westminster
undertaker, Humphrey Drew, this ticket shows the street
procession of a middle-class funeral.*

granted, and it would have been deemed a curious request had a client expressed a view to buy them. Robert Green went further in his services to the trade, hiring out to the smaller undertaker those items required for an up-market funeral. This enabled the humblest of tradesmen to furnish all varieties of funeral, rather than having to turn down trade owing to the paucity of his stock.

The investment made by such wholesale funeral furnishers would have been fairly steep, yet they were able to recoup on their capital outlay through hire charges, which were in turn passed on by the undertaker to the client. This was – and, in some instances, remains – a standard system and an accepted one throughout the trade. In 1843 Edwin Chadwick asked Mr Dix, a successful London undertaker performing upwards of 800 funerals a year, to explain how it worked:

MR DIX:	I frequently perform funerals three deep: that is, I do it for one person, who does it for another, who does it for the relatives of the deceased, he being the first person applied to.
CHADWICK:	The people, then, generally apply to the nearest person?
MR DIX:	Yes, they do. Everybody calls himself an undertaker. The numerous men employed as bearers become undertakers, although they have never done anything until they have got the job. I have known one of these men get a new suit of clothes out of a funeral of one decent mechanic.[26]

When Chadwick's comments on the trade are examined it becomes abundantly clear why hire companies such as Robert Green's were required: 'The number of persons whose sole business is that of undertaker, whose names are enumerated in the post-office directory for the year 1843 for the metropolis, is 275. It is stated that much larger numbers than are named in the Directory retain the insignia of undertakers in their shop-windows, for the sake of the profits of one or two funerals a year. They merely transmit the orders to the furnishing undertakers, who supply materials and men at a comparatively low rate.'[27] The impression given is that anyone involved in woodworking would turn his hand to coffin-making and funeral-furnishing if the opportunity arose. Such were the dangers of a trade not protected by its own guild. In the countryside, matters were no better; the smaller shops in the villages and towns often produced insufficient income to support a family, so that the wife or daughter often looked after it while the man pursued another occupation. Where the latter did keep shop, he might also double up as the local undertaker, as was the case in Essex between 1770–88 at Great Clacton, Thorpe, Toppesfield and Weeley, whilst the London precedent of upholders furnishing funerals (in addition to their established role of auctioneers and general tradesmen) was evident at Chelmsford and Halstead.[28]

With the College of Arms hindering the grant of a new charter to the Upholders' Company in 1722, some London undertakers attempted to form their own livery company. A contemporary trade card by George Bickham Jnr for the United Company of Undertakers survives (*10*).[29] It is quite an elaborate item: Youth and Age sit on an oval cartouche flanked by Time and Eternity. The inscription on the cartouche reads: 'Funerals Performed/To & from all parts of

10   *The United Company of Undertakers had a short life in the eighteenth century, as Guild Hall consistently refused to grant them livery status.*

Great Britain; in y^e/Best, & most Reasonable Manner;/By y^e United Company of UNDERTAKERS;/At their House, the Corner of Southampton Street/Bloomsbury, in Holborn/LONDON'. But was this nothing more than a co-operative of neighbourhood tradesmen? Probably, for the United Company of Undertakers was never admitted at the Guildhall, and their 'house' was none other than the business premises of Robert Legg Snr, upholder, appraiser and undertaker. Could it have been that the upholders contested the undertakers' application to join their guild, on the pretext that the furnishing of funerals was the prerogative of their members? Whatever ensued, the United Company of Undertakers did not receive livery status, though they did excite sufficient interest to merit a sarcastic caricature from William Hogarth entitled 'The Company of Undertakers', and with the motto *'Et Plurima Mortis Imago'* – 'The Very Picture of Death'. This engraving was erroneously published by Bertram Puckle in 1926 as the 'sign of the now extinct "Company of Undertakers" '.[30]

Whilst Robert Legg Snr and his cronies were enjoying a short-lived grandeur within the ill-fated United Company of Undertakers, the Upholders' Company continued to support those members who furnished funerals as part of their everyday trade, though their list of admissions does not identify persons trading as coffin-makers or undertakers though they did admit upholders and mercers, who included funeral furnishing as a sideline to their main trade. By the mid-1730s the Upholders Company saw fit to make available to their members

*11   Coypel, as with Gravelot, relied on classical mythology for his
funeral ticket of c. 1740. Only those items in the left foreground
suggest a Christian affinity.*

blank funeral invitation tickets for overprinting, affiliation to the company being
shown by an inscription on the plate-mark beneath the illustration, reading
'Perform'd by the Company of Upholders at Exeter Change & at their Hall in
Leaden Hall Street.' This copper engraving, designed by A.N. Coypel and cut by J.
Chereau, was an up-market plagiarism of the more primitive original issued by the
United Company of Undertakers. In front of a tall classical tomb – the centre panel
left blank for overprinting – reclines a shrouded skeleton, representing Death, who
leans to the viewer's left to stop Youth from detaining Time who is shown flying off
to his next assignment. On the right, Age addresses her gaze towards Death,
thereby distracting her from cutting the Thread of Life joining Eternity to a
representation of Clotho, seen resting on a cloud to the upper right corner of the
plate (*11*).[31] The silent war between the United Company of Undertakers and the
Worshipful Company of Upholders did not last long, for by 1748 the imprimatur
had been dropped from the Upholders' blank funeral invitations and we no longer
hear from the United Company of Undertakers again.[32]

Few illustrations survive of the interiors of funeral furnishing establishments
prior to the introduction of the camera. Trade cards tend to show stylized street
processions with, perhaps, the occasional spurious hatchment and draped mute's
stave. The Victoria and Albert Museum holds a proof engraving of the 1730s
trade card of the Strand upholsterer and cabinet-maker, Christopher Gibson
(*12*). Here Gibson is shown attending to clients, whilst to the left of the shop can
be seen two painted hatchments of the type offered up on the house of the

deceased, with two smaller shields above of painted canvas mounted on black velvet, as applied to the palls of the nobility and others entitled to bear arms. In the back of the shop, beyond the shelves of material and the cutting bench, are five more hatchments. Judging from his stock, funerals must have held some position of importance to have merited such an impressive display of hatchments.

Conversely, views showing the exteriors of undertakers' and funeral furnishers' are less rare, probably the most well-known image being the shop sign appearing in Hogarth's engraving, *Gin Lane*, showing a suspended coffin and figure of Time. An engraving from 1737 by John Kip (private collection) of St Clement Danes, Strand shows a shop-front of a furnishing undertaker not dissimilar to that of Messrs Barnard's premises in an anonymous water-colour (*c*.1850) in Brighton Museum (*13*). Are we, therefore, to understand that the trade preferred to maintain a low-profile presence on the high street, in much the same way as it does now? From the various addresses given on the trade cards of coffin-makers it appears that many were sited off the high streets, yet not so far away as to be inaccessible to their clients. Barnard's shop would have had shutters, whilst the pavement-level trapdoor allowed for the delivery of ready-made coffins.

12   Most upmarket cabinet-makers could perform funerals for their clients. Christopher Gibson of St Paul's Churchyard did so, and hence the display of hatchments throughout his premises.

*13   The trade maintained a low
profile in the high street, preferring simple shop fronts and
minimal advertising. Note the
hatchments in the window.*

   The trade had three branches: coffin-making, undertaking and funeral
furnishing. The coffin-maker did as the title suggests: he made coffins. He might
also have performed funerals, but not necessarily so. The undertaker was a
coffin-maker and performer of funerals, whereas the funeral furnisher did not
make his own coffins, but bought them in ready-made, dressed them and in
addition performed the funeral. This, then, was the hierarchy of the trade. A
coffin-maker could look up to a funeral furnisher rather than to an undertaker;
an undertaker might have respected the funeral furnisher in as much as he could
afford to buy in his coffins; whereas the funeral furnisher, whilst relying on the
coffin-maker, looked down on the undertaker (*Col. 2*).
   Mr Sowerberry, the undertaker in Charles Dickens's *Oliver Twist*, was in the
middle of the funeral hierarchy, but towards the bottom end as he only catered
for parish funerals – that is to say those from the workhouse or those receiving

outdoor relief. His shop would have been in a back street, probably in a run-down part of the town, amongst the dwellings of those whom he catered for; indeed, Sowerberry himself was only just above the bread-line. It was to this 'salubrious' emporium that Oliver Twist was brought and, after a meagre meal of dog's scraps, shown to his bed: a mattress beneath the counter.

> Oliver, being left to himself in the undertaker's shop, set the lamp down on a workman's bench, and gazed timidly about him with a feeling of awe and dread, which many people a good deal older than he will be at no loss to understand. An unfinished coffin on black tressels, which stood in the middle of the shop, looked so gloomy and death-like that a cold tremble came over him, every time his eyes wandered in the direction of the dismal object: from which he almost expected to see some frightful form slowly rear its head, to drive him mad with terror. Against the wall were ranged, in regular array, a long row of elm boards cut into the same shape: looking, in the dim light, like high-shouldered ghosts with their hands in their breeches-pockets. Coffin-plates, elm-chips, bright-headed nails, and shreds of black cloth, lay scattered on the floor; and the wall behind the counter was ornamented with a lively representation of two mutes in very stiff neckcloths, on duty at a large private door, with a hearse drawn by four black steeds, approaching in the distance. The shop was close and hot. The atmosphere seemed tainted with the smell of coffins. The recess beneath the counter in which his flock mattress was thrust looked like a grave.[33]

The 1895 workshop of Alfred Morgan, undertaker and funeral furnisher of 2 Craven Buildings, Wych Street, Strand (*14*) was not such a far cry from the confusion witnessed fifty years earlier by Oliver Twist in Mr Sowerberry's establishment. Here, a recently polished elm coffin sits on padded woodworking trestles; it is in the process of having its chevroned starched linen fringe gimped to the upper edge of the inner lining, a length of which hangs outside the coffin awaiting turning-in, the lid having been temporarily replaced for the purpose of photography. Against the left-hand wall nearest to the camera are three storage shelves; a lidless unvarnished coffin in the process of construction sits on the middle shelf. To the left of the sash window and to the far right of the plate are stacked more coffin boards, probably of elm or oak, whilst the four half-lids are templates, as is the kerf-guide on the wall to the left of the chimney-breast. In the corner farthest from the camera are propped lengths of beading with, to the right, a bracketed shelf on which sit a bottle and stone jars containing french polish. The brick floor is exceptionally tidy, having doubtless been swept for the photographer's benefit. The photograph itself is marred by the double-exposure of a dining-room laid out for a party, subconsciously reminding us to 'eat, drink and be merry, for tomorrow we die'. Morgan's coffins are of quality, towards the upper-middle range of the trade. His workshop seems to have been situated in the basement of his house, with his office on the ground floor (*15*). Morgan must have done quite well out of his business, being able to afford the rent on the entire house. The house next door, Number 3, was let out as three flats, as can be seen from the three bell-pulls and the much worn doorstep.

Not every funeral furnisher was able to go independent, and relied on the wholesalers to provide items for which he was rarely asked and consequently had

14 *Alfred Morgan's c. 1895 London premises were situated off the Strand, London. This photograph was probably made for archival, rather than advertising, purposes.*

no need to stock. One such nineteenth-century wholesaler was J. Turner of Farringdon Street, a 'Coffin Maker, Plate Chaser, Furnishing Undertaker and Funeral Featherman'. His nine-page catalogue from 1838[34] contains a wealth of information for the funerary historian, listing 111 coffins of thirty differing types, twenty sizes of shroud (each available in four different qualities of material), fifteen types of ruffling, winding-sheets, mattresses, coffin furniture and palls. He even provides quotations for bearers' and attendants' fittings together with the hire charges for hearses, coaches and horses.

Taking items at random, for 17 shillings one got a 'good inch elm Coffin, smoothed, oiled, and finished with one row round of black or white nails, a plate of inscription, four handles, lined and pillow'; whilst for £9 one could buy the *pièce de résistance*, a '1½ inch Oak Case, covered with superfine cloth, finished three rows all round, and six ornamental diamonds, with best nails, lead or brass plate, glory and urn, four pairs of cherub handles, and four dozen rays or stars'. This, together with an 'Elm Shell, covered with 4lb lead, lined, ruffled, and pillow' would provide a creature fit for the grandest vault. His hearse and coach hire depended on whether the funeral was to be held in town, 'on the stones', or in the country. For a town funeral he charged from £2 3s. for a hearse and pair to £6 9s. for a hearse and six; the cost was doubled if the funeral was to be out of town.

To get an idea of the profit made, let us compare Turner's prices against those actually charged by the funeral furnisher in Chadwick's 1843 Report[35] for a simple earth-burial funeral in the metropolis.

28

ITEM	CHADWICK			TURNER		
Covered coffin, lined, ruffled, plate of inscription, mattress, sheet and pillow	4	19	0	2	0	0
Pall		7	6		3	6
2 porters' gowns, staves, bands and gloves	1	12	0		12	0
Four cloaks, crape bands and gloves	1	18	0		5	8
Hearse and coach, pairs; velvets for ditto	4	13	0	2	11	0
2 cloaks and bands		11	0		1	6
6 pages' bands, gloves, truncheons, wands	1	15	0		5	6
TOTAL	£15	16	6	£5	19	2

Taking into account only those items bought from a wholesaler, Chadwick's undertaker was making a 175 per cent profit on his original outlay. This mark-up would have been greater – almost 500 per cent – had the funeral in question been at the top of the market.

Turner also supplied establishments out of town, advertising 'a Conveyance kept for the purpose of sending Coffins, Goods, &c. to any part of Town or

15   Morgan's coffins are of reasonable quality, suitable for the upper-middle-class range. His workshop appears to have been sited in the basement of his premises.

Country, with Dispatch'. But by the third quarter of the nineteenth century, with an efficient railway service and a telegraphic system, road transport was no longer relied on and the two largest funeral furnishing houses, Messrs Dottridge of London and Ingall, Parsons & Clive of Birmingham, were dealing with telegraphic orders dispatched by rail, to reach any part of Great Britain within two days.

The funerals performed by the trade in the middle of the nineteenth century were anything but simple. However, the question arises whether the undertaker was aware of the significance of the many trappings he insisted on providing. The following embarrassing conversation ensued between Edwin Chadwick and a London tradesman:

CHADWICK: Are you aware that the array of funerals, commonly made by undertakers, is strictly the heraldic array of a baronial funeral, the two men who stand at the doors being supposed to be the two porters of the castle, with their staves, in black; the man who heads the procession, wearing a scarf, being a representative of a herald-at-arms; the man who carries a plume of feathers on his head being an esquire, who bears the shield and casque, with its plume of feathers; the pall-bearers, with batons, being representatives of knights-companions-at-arms; the men walking with wands being supposed to represent gentlemen-ushers, with their wands: are you aware that this is said to be the origin and type of the common array usually provided by those who undertake to perform funerals?

UNDERTAKER: No, I am not aware of it.

CHADWICK: It may be presumed that those who order funerals are equally unaware of the incongruity for which such expense is incurred?

UNDERTAKER: Undoubtedly they are.[36]

It was the undertaker, to give him his common nomenclature, who provided what was considered 'correct' in a given situation, and he alone decided on the trappings. There was little individual choice of coffin, linings or handles; all was left to the aesthetic judgement of the undertaker, and the client was rarely asked to express his views. The usual instruction was to 'provide what is customary', though this attitude led to extreme financial hardship for the poorer classes, though it would not be unreasonable to say that it was they who helped to perpetuate the meaningless and elaborate ritual well into the early decades of the twentieth century.

The later Victorian undertakers were arguably the most backward-looking tradesmen of their day. There were many openings they might have exploited, but it never occurred to them to do so. The manufacture of coffin furniture and soft furnishings were independent trades; here was a golden opportunity for the business to effect a take-over, but they did not. Only Dottridge Brothers and Ingall, Parsons & Clive made any attempt at competing with the individual concerns. Again, there was no assault made on mourning stationery or the extremely lucrative trade in mourning jewellery. Both Courtauld's and Messrs Jay's of Regent Street could rest assured, for not one undertaker concerned himself with buying-in to the mourning warehouses, thereby turning the tables on the mercers and upholders. Nor did any undertaker take advantage of private cemetery ownership, Kensal Green and Highgate, for example, employing appointed 'official' undertakers from within the trade.

The trade in the nineteenth century does not stand up to close examination. In the main they were a semi-educated band with neither trade nor union affiliation, and greedy – the occasional client was brought to financial ruin by undertakers charging over-inflated and extortionate prices for an unnecessary spectacle that few could either afford or understand. This was especially heinous, as items charged for were often put back into stock to be 'sold' time after time until they wore out. No wonder that the myth of handles being removed from coffins at the time of cremation perpetuates. The opinion of the trade given by Campbell in 1747 applied equally to 1897.

By the close of the nineteenth century funeral furnishers had amalgamated the individual trades of coffin-maker, undertaker and funeral furnisher. The time was coming for a change of name to describe the craft. It was Banting, the crown undertaker, who provided the model for the future; for he rarely saw a corpse, contracting out at every stage of the proceedings. He was a funeral 'director' rather than a furnisher, and it was to this practice that a number of top-rank funeral furnishers working in London looked – Ballard, Dowbiggin & Holland, J.D. Field, A. France & Son, J. Kenyon, Leverton's and John Nodes – though they were never quite to match his mastery. In about 1895 the trade began to raise the popular image of the 'undertaker' from being a person who merely disposed of the dead to a funeral director whose main object is service to the public. A London funeral furnisher, H.A. Sherry, encouraged colleagues in Liverpool, London, Manchester and Preston to establish local associations. By 1898 national interest had been aroused and the British Institute of Undertakers was formed, succeeding where the United Company of Undertakers had failed 160 years previously.

The British Institute re-formed in 1905 under the new title of the British Undertakers' Association, changing its name in 1935 to the National Association of Funeral Directors, whose prime objectives were to maintain, promote and protect the rights and interests of its members. A separate organization, the British Institute of Funeral Directors, founded in 1982, exists to improve and develop the technical and general knowledge of those engaged in funeral directing. Cross-membership between the Association and the Institute flourishes. It is a pity that the same could not have been said of the United Company of Undertakers and the Worshipful Company of Upholders.

2

Taintless and Pure:
Embalming Techniques

About the year 1737, were found in St Margaret's church-yard, Westminster, in a dry gravelly soil, at the depth of about 18 feet, or less, which had not been broken up for above fifty years before, three entire fir coffins; the two largest clampt together with iron, as boxes sometimes are. In one was a fat, broad-faced man; the body perfect and soft, as if just dead; the lid had been glewed together, lengthways, and the weight of the earth had prest down his nose; his beard was about half an inch long; the winding-sheet was crape, tied with black ribbons; and the thumbs and toes with the like; the date was composed of small nails (1665) by which it appeared he had been dead seventy-two years; as were also the figure of an hour-glass, death's head, and cross bones. In the second coffin was a female body, in the same state, in a white crape winding-sheet, date 1673. And in the third a male child, perfect and beautiful as wax-work; the eyes open and clear, but no date on the coffin. In one of the larger coffins was a dry nosegay of bay and other leaves and flowers, which appeared like a nosegay that had lain a year among linen. These bodies changed within twelve hours after they were exposed.[1]

The historian Kirkpatrick was recalling an incident fourteen years earlier when he included the above in his 1751 treatise 'Reflections on the Causes that may retard Putrefaction of dead Bodies'. If nothing else, he has provided us with an excellent description of coffin-making, coffin furniture and grave clothes of the mid seventeenth century. But was what he saw the result of embalming? Unfortunately not; and there are numerous recorded incidents of the discovery of corpses all owing their 'preservation' to natural causes rather than the influence

32

of man. Had the bodies viewed by Kirkpatrick been embalmed then they would not have 'changed within twelve hours after they were exposed'.

I was present in 1983 during the clearance of the vaults beneath St Marylebone parish church when the coffin of a two-year-old boy, who had died in 1815, was opened. Once the lids of the outer case and the leaden shell had been removed, the workman prised off the lid of the inner coffin; the slightly yellowed silk sheets were drawn back and there lay the body of the child, looking as if he had gone off to sleep but a few moments before. This child had not been embalmed and his preservation was due to nothing more than the construction of the coffin, for the wood was no less thick – 1½ inches – than that of an adult's coffin, and the lead was likewise no different in gauge. The thickness of the wood gave a quality of robustness to the small coffin, whilst the lead made it airtight. The funerary archaeologist has to be certain of the differences between desiccation and chemical preservation: embalming.

Mention embalming to any child and they will immediately conjure up visions of Egyptian mummies: Rameses II, Tutankhamun, pussy-cats and baby crocodiles in latticed bandages. Similar images might occur to adults, too. To medieval man it meant a process reserved for the preservation of the corpses of the important, so that they might sleep uncorrupted in their tombs until the Last Day, when body and soul would be reunited to appear before God for His judgement. Even the humblest peasant probably knew that embalming entailed mutilation and evisceration of the corpse, and that such a 'privilege' was reserved for kings and queens and certain high officers and nobles of the land.

The originator of modern embalming techniques was the eminent eighteenth-century Scottish surgeon and anatomist, William Hunter (*16*). He was dismissive of the Egyptian method of embalming, saying in 1776:

> With regard to the embalming of the Egyptians, whatever they might say was their motive, it appears that it was a catch upon the public. I saw a Mummy examined that had been embalmed for 2,000 years; the embalmer had taken out all the Viscera of the head, Thorax and Abdomen and cut all the flesh off the bones, and the cavities of the Thorax & Abdomen were filled up with Tar, Pitch &c and the form of the leg, Thigh &c were altogether made up of linen Rags dipp'd in Tar, Pitch, &c so that I have an Opinion that they were allow'd to carry the dead Body home by pretending to embalm it to preserve the Flesh &c, but you see they either buried or burnt the Flesh: this art always 'till lately appeared to me ridiculous as I know how soon putrefaction took place after Death; since that time I have often thought it would be pleasing if we could fall upon a method of preserving dead Bodies & I thought that mankind in general would wish to have the Bodies of their Friends &c Preserved. I conceive many People would be happy with an Art of this kind or at least it would be useful to those who die abroad and are brought back home: I often used to talk of embalming but never seriously took it in hand 'til the year before last, which to this time is well preserved.[2]

Although it is perfectly possible for Hunter to have acquired his own Egyptian mummy for dissection, it appears from the above that he did not. So where did it come from? It is quite likely that the source lay with the antiquarian, Smart Lethieullier of Aldersbrook, 'a gentleman of polite literature and elegant taste'.[3]

16 William Hunter (1718–83) is considered as the originator of modern injection embalming. He considered ancient Egyptian embalming as 'a catch upon the public'.

The son of a wealthy London merchant, Lethieullier was a Fellow of the Royal Society and a Fellow of the Society of Antiquaries; he knew both William and John Hunter, who in turn must have been aware of his collection of Egyptian antiquities, amongst which were some mummies brought back from Egypt to Aldersbrook by Lethieullier's cousin, Colonel William Lethieullier. Could it have been one of these specimens that succumbed to the examining blade of the paleopathologist's knife? We know that Lethieullier was also interested in anatomy, for in 1734 he had offered to the Royal Society three infants preserved in spirit, ' ... of which one Elizabeth Baggs, a hard labouring woman in Oxford, was delivered at one birth in 1714'[4] and who lived for but a few hours afterwards. What sealed the knot between Hunter and Lethieullier was the latter's curiosity in all things funereal, including embalming, as will be seen later.

E.F. Scudamore interprets present-day embalming as 'a treatment consisting fundamentally of the injection of some suitable disinfecting preservative into the vascular system, augmented by the relieving of the blood from the superficial vein, and such cavity, cosmetic, and derma-surgery treatment necessary to achieve a pre-mortem appearance, aseptic condition and preservation'.[5] Yet Scudamore concerns himself only with temporary preservation related to the needs and requirements of the modern funeral director. Hunter would have gone further; to him, 'embalming' meant a technique more sophisticated than that practised by the Egyptians, a technique ensuring perpetual preservation of the corpse's remains, involving permanent chemical arrest of decomposition whilst allowing for a pre-mortem appearance. The bodies in Hunter's care were to last.

Warton, in his book *The History of English Poetry*, published in the 1680s, wrote, 'Antient chemistry made people fancy that bodies could be preserved with the resemblance of real life, by means of a precious liquor circulating through every part in golden tubes artificially disposed, and operating on the principles of vegetation.'[6]

When Jeremy Bentham, the radical jurist, philosopher and founder of University College, London, died in 1832 at the age of eighty-four he bequeathed his body to Dr Southwood Smith, an anatomist and author of *Uses of the Dead to the Living*,[7] in which it was suggested that the difficulties experienced by medical schools in acquiring bodies for dissection could be alleviated if people chose to bequeath their bodies to them. The terms of the bequest might seem bizarre, yet they were in keeping with Bentham's philosophical attitudes. The body was to be dissected at a public lecture by Southwood Smith to be entitled 'The Structures and Functions of the Human Frame',[8] after which the skeleton was to be used as the armature of an image – an 'auto-icon' – of himself, to be attired in his own clothes and placed in University College. It is still there, in a glass-fronted cupboard. The head of the 'effigy' is a wax portrait – Bentham's own head was removed, desiccated, provided with glass eyes and placed under a glass dome to sit between the feet of the auto-icon; it, too, is now on public display – a little start-eyed, yet nevertheless recognizable (*Col. 3*). Hunter, one can assume, would have advocated chemical treatment of the entire body. It is, perhaps, a good thing that Bentham's eccentricity did not catch on, for 'disposal of the dead' might have become 'dissection prior to auto-iconism' with nineteenth-century British cemeteries having galleries of the dead, as at Palermo, Rome and Toulouse.

Hunter's known subjects are few – two, to be precise, and both private commissions – and intended as practical examples of his research, related more to improving contemporary methods of preserving anatomical specimens for the medical student than as a deliberate contribution to the undertaking trade. He should not, therefore, be regarded in any way as an up-market embalmer, but a serious scientist, extending his knowledge, and private curiosity, in perfecting a way to arrest the post-mortem decomposition of the human body by the balanced use of chemicals, spices and herbs. Prior to describing his method, and that perfected by his brother John, it is necessary to examine in detail the state of the art that led to the seventeenth- and eighteenth-century experiments, culminating in the most celebrated of the Hunterian 'mummies', Mrs Maria Van Butchell.

It was not an uncommon practice in the Middle Ages, where the corpses of the rich and powerful were concerned, to remove one or more of the organs – usually the heart – for burial at the place of death, such as the monastery which had cared for the person in their infirmary during the final illness. Indeed, some religious houses demanded the deposit as a prerequisite for their care. Over the years these monastic institutions acquired a particular expertise in the embalming of bodies, an example of their handiwork being discovered in 1969 when the coffin of Archbishop Godfrey de Ludham (d. 1265) was opened in York Minster (*17*).[9] Meanwhile, the encoffined, eviscerated cadaver itself was returned to the family for burial in the deceased's parish church.

35

17   The body of Archbishop Godfrey de Ludham (d. 1265) was
exposed in 1969 during restoration work at York Minster. He
had probably been embalmed, for a considerable amount of
tissue remained.

Apart from preserving the body for the sake of the Day of Judgement, two more important facts have to be taken into consideration, delayed burials and monarchial deaths. When a person of rank died far from home, and it was known that the funeral would therefore be delayed, embalming allowed the body to remain recognizable long enough for the relatives to make a positive identification on its arrival home. Embalming a monarch allowed for public examination of the corpse, not only to prove to all and sundry that the monarch was indeed dead but also to let the rightful heir be acclaimed and to deter any pretenders.

The information we have on early techniques comes from contemporary and later chronicles and, during the eighteenth and nineteenth centuries, from antiquarian curiosity in the examination of coffin contents during cathedral and church restorations. The technique during the fourteenth and fifteenth centuries had four stages. To prevent putrefaction the soft organs were removed via an incision in the trunk, and then buried either at the place of death or separately with the body. Then the inner cavities were sluiced out with various aromatic and disinfecting fluids prior to sewing up. The third stage involved the treatment of the exterior of the body with preserving spices, applied either as an ointment or a paste, the latter probably being used in the case of Archbishop Godfrey de Ludham. Finally, the corpse was tightly wrapped in cerecloth, a waxed linen, and the seams further sealed with beeswax so as to establish a near airtight condition. This done, the cocoon was enclosed in a leaden coffin, very much like a mummy case, before being lodged in its outer wooden case.

If death had occurred abroad, the *mos teutonicus* method was sometimes employed. This consisted of cutting up the body into pieces and boiling it in wine or vinegar until fat and flesh separated from the bones. The skeleton was then shipped home for burial and the remainder deposited at the place of death. It was a technique applied to anyone sufficiently important to warrant the effort, such as the Bishop of Hereford, who died in Italy in 1282. But at the end of the thirteenth century Pope Boniface VIII tried to condemn the practice, especially as it was sometimes carried out in the side chapels of churches, which were deemed appropriate 'kitchens'. When Henry V died in Normandy in 1422 *mos teutonicus* was employed, as it was thought that conventional embalming would not hold out for the journey back to England. Rather than bury the flesh and fat in France, it was sealed up with the bones in a leaden case, together with an enormous quantity of spices. After a short lying-in-state at the Abbey of St Denis the remains were shipped back for eventual burial at Westminster, some two months after the death had taken place.[10] It seems unlikely, especially in the light of the papal prohibition, that monks would have had either the inclination or the experience to have practised *mos teutonicus*, and it has been suggested that butchers were called in to perform the grisly deeds. That the usual embalming techniques bore a close similarity to the methods used in the preservation of meat for human consumption one does wonder what involvement butchers had in giving advice in the early experimental years of embalming.

One of the most curious and inexplicable methods of preservation was recorded by the antiquary, John Weever, in Chapter 6 of his *Ancient Funerall Monuments*.

In the North Isle of the Parish church of Newport painell in Buckinghamshire, in the yeare 1619 was found the body of a man whole and perfect; laid downe, or rather leaning downe, North, and South: all the concauous parts of his body, and the hollownesse of euery bone, as well ribs as other, were filled vp with sollid lead. The skull with the lead in it doth weigh thirty pounds and sixe ounces, which with the neck-bone, and some other bones (in like manner full of lead) are reserued, and kept in a little chest in the said Church, neare to the place where the corps were found; there to bee showne to strangers as reliques of admiration. The rest of all the parts of his body are taken away by Gentlemen neare dwellers, or such as take delight in rare Antiquities. This I saw.[11]

Was it possible for the corpse to have been so treated, with the 'hollownesse' of every bone to be filled up with solid lead?

Three royal coffins disturbed by workmen during the eighteenth century give credence to the fact that the corpses of the royal family were also subjected to embalming. In 1703, at St Alban's Abbey, the small vault beneath the tomb of Humphrey, Duke of Gloucester (d.1447), was entered; antiquarian curiosity led to the opening of the anthropoid coffin, wherein, the body was found to be well preserved, '... except for the legs from which the flesh is wasted, the pickle at that end having dried up'.[12] In 1986 I too entered the tomb; the anthropoid leaden shell was resealed after the 1703 examination and placed in a new rectangular elm shell *sans* fittings. It is doubtful that the 1703 visitors were looking at 'pickle' since the anthropoid shell fits so tightly that no additional liquid could have been introduced. However, it is possible that the fluid seen during that visitation once saturated the body but had leaked from the cadaver during the intervening 250 years and thence from the coffin, owing to seasonal fluctuations in the humidity within the vault.

Some workmen digging for stone in the ruins of Bury St Edmunds Abbey in 1773 came across a wooden coffin containing a lead anthropoid shell. Again, curiosity won the day and, as recorded by C. Collingnon in a paper delivered to the Royal Society,[13] the body was that of Thomas Beaufort, Duke of Exeter, who had died in 1424. That the body had been embalmed was established by the nature of the incisions, and its having been 'soaked in pickle'. Unlike the St Albans relic (the remains of Beaufort's nephew), the Duke of Exeter's face had been covered with cerecloth; the hair was in perfect condition, as was the flesh in general.

The discovery of the St Albans and Bury St Edmunds remains were certainly exciting, especially to the examiners, but they pale into insignificance when compared with the results of the research undertaken after the opening of the coffin of Edward IV (d.1483) in 1788, whose funeral was the subject of a paper read to the Society of Antiquaries on 26 January 1769.[14] When the coffin was examined in St George's Chapel, Windsor, the body was found to be in a sufficiently good condition to recognize the features; some of the yellow-gold velvet of the outer shroud was also present.[15] One wonders how close the cost of Edward's interment was to the £15 3s. 4½d. paid to Hugh Brice in 1471 for the cerecloth and spices used to embalm his predecessor, Henry VI.[16]

To discover how these embalmed bodies were wrapped after the completion of the process we need to turn to the report of the examination of the 'mummy' of William Lyndewode, Bishop of St David's (d.1446), discovered in 1852 during the reconstruction of St Stephen's Chapel at the Palace of Westminster. The body 'was swathed in cerements of strong, coarse, thick cloth or canvas ... Around this swathing, for about two-thirds of the length of the trunk from the hips upward, were several turns of a well-made twisted cord, fastened in what is called the half-hitch, in good preservation.'[17] Once the 'mummy' had been removed from its grave, a proper examination was carried out by a Dr W.V. Pettigrew:

> The cere-cloth, which consisted of nine, and in some places of ten distinct layers, was originally dipped in wax. It had become, as it were, welded into one thick compact mass, nearly as hard as wood, and which it was impossible to separate, unrole, or divide in any other way than by cutting ... The head had an extra covering of cloth or canvas beyond that of the rest of the body, forming a kind of mask. On removal of that ... the front part of the head was found swathed and tied round with cord in the same manner as the rest of the body ... On removal of the mask ... the face was at once seen ... When first uncovered, a pledget of tow, imbued with wax, protruding from the mouth, forming a mass soft, black, and pliable, and producing some distortion in the countenance ... The colour of the countenance was dark brown, or chocolate.[18]

The report continues to say that the body was entire and that no viscera had been removed. Neither was there evidence of anything more than superficial surface treatment.

W.J. White tells us that the 'decline of the embalming practice may be seen as one aspect of transitional funerary modes in fifteenth century England'.[19] However, the technique was still employed for monarchial corpses. John Strype, the eighteenth-century antiquarian, gives an account of the care given to the corpse of Henry VIII immediately after his death at Westminster on or around midnight on 28 January 1547. Once the body had been viewed by members of the Privy Council and others to confirm that life had ceased and that the king was dead, word went out to summon the surgeons, apothecaries and wax chandlers 'to do their duties in spurging, cleansing, bowelling, searing, embalming, furnishing and dressing with spices the said corpse'.[20] Knowing the complications and expense involved in getting together the various unguents required, one can assume that these items had already been accumulated by those to whom the task of embalming the royal remains had been devolved. As shall soon be seen, both plumber and carpenter were also alert to their requirements. Casting discretion to the wind, there seems little point in not describing in small detail each stage of the given instructions. 'Spurging' entailed the general washing of the body with spiced and aromatic water to remove the sweat of the death-bed and generally to clean the corpse; 'cleansing' was the euphemism given to the assisted emptying of the bowels and the plugging of the rectum; the removal of the soft organs, following an incision made from the bottom of the rib cage to the pelvic region, was known as 'bowelling'; 'searing' was the cauterizing of the cavity blood vessels after the removal of the soft organs as a precaution against post-mortem haemorrhaging; whilst the purification of the inner cavity was the technical 'embalming'; the outer surface of the body was 'dressed' by the application of balms, a mixture of resins in volatile oils; whilst 'furnishing' implied nothing more than the positioning of the *sudarium* (a linen square covering the face) and the close wrapping of the corpse in layers of cerecloth and waxed twine. This complete, the body was further wrapped in fine velvet, a sheet of linen having first been placed between it and the cerecloth to stop staining of the finer fabric, and tied with silk cord. The plumber then set to work encasing the 'mummy' in its close-fitting anthropoid shell after which the carpenter's men put it into its outer wooden case, upholstered in rich blue velvet. The household's final act was to arrange for the immediate disposal of the viscera which, like the body, were almost certainly placed in a lead box within a velvet-upholstered outer case. Here again we are assisted by Strype: 'The entrails and bowels were honourably buried in the [St George's, Windsor] chapel',[21] for it was not usual for the viscera chest to take any part in the state obsequies; the coffin was reunited with it nineteen days later.

Katherine Parr, the widow of Henry VIII, saw out her last years at Sudeley Castle in Gloucestershire, dying there on 5 September 1548. A letter of 29 April 1777 from J.C. Brooke of the College of Arms to the editor of *Archaeologia* gave an account of her funeral: 'As the funeral of this princess has been hitherto unpublished, I have sent, for your entertainment, the procession, from my collection of ceremonials, Nᵒ. VI. originally copied from a book in the Cotton library.'[22] The manuscript reads: 'Item, on Wenysdaye the vth of Septembre, between ij and iij of the Clocke in the morninge died the aforesaid Ladye, late Quene Dowager at the Castle of Sudley in Glocestreshyre, 1548, and lyeth buried in the Chapell of the seid Castle. Item, she was cearid and chestid in leade accordinglie, and so remaynid in her pryvie Chambre untill things were in a readyness.'[23] It was not beyond the wit of any surgeon worthy of his calling or apothecary worthy of his phial to have been able to perform superficial embalming, and it is highly unlikely that assistance was asked for at the London end. The above account was later reported in Rudder's *History of Gloucestershire*, which

> raised the curiosity of some ladies, who happened to be at the Castle in May 1782, to examine the ruined Chapel, and observing a large block of alabaster, fixed in the North wall of the Chapel, they imagined it might be the back of a monument formerly placed there. Led by this hint they opened the ground not far from the wall; and not much more than a foot away from the surface they found a leaden envelope which they opened in two places, on the face and breast, and found it contained a human body wrapped in cerecloth. Upon removing what covered the face, they discovered the features, and particularly the eyes, in perfect preservation. Alarmed at this sight, and with the smell, which came principally from the cerecloth, they ordered the ground to be thrown in immediately without judiciously closing up the cerecloth and lead, which covered the face: only observing enough of the inscription to convince them that it was the body of Queen Katherine.[24]

Four years later, in October 1786, the Revd Treadway Nash DD FSA went along to Sudeley Castle in the company of the Hon. John Sommers Cox and a Mr John Skipp of Ledbury to examine the coffin, having first obtained leave of the owner, Lord Rivers. Unfortunately the hasty infilling of 1782 had caused the face to decay. Nash, a scrupulous and sensitive antiquarian, tells us what happened next: 'The body, I believe, is perfect, as it has never been opened: we thought it indelicate and indecent to uncover it; but observing the left hand to lie at a small distance from the body, we took off the cerecloth, and found the hand and nails perfect, but of a brownish colour: the cerecloth consisted of many folds of coarse linen, dipped in wax, tar, and perhaps some gums: over this was wrapt a sheet of lead fitted exactly close to the body.'[25] The multi-layered cerecloth implies that she was embalmed in a manner similar to that of her husband. A human touch was added to Nash's report: 'I could heartily wish more respect were paid to the remains of this amiable though unfortunate Queen, and would willingly, with proper leave, have them wrapt in another sheet of lead and coffin, and decently interred in some proper place, that at least after her death her body might remain in peace; whereas the Chapel where she now lies is used for the keeping of rabbits, which make holes and scratch very indecently about her Royal corpse.'[26] Between 1859 and 1863 Sir George Gilbert Scott restored the chapel for its new owners, William and John Dent, at which time Scott designed a canopied tomb for Katherine Parr with a recumbent white marble effigy by John Birnie Philip; Nash would have been pleased.

A particularly gruesome tale is appended to the embalming of Queen Katherine de Valois, wife of Henry V.[27] Katherine died at Bermondsey Abbey (by whose monks she was presumably embalmed) on 3 January 1437 and eventually buried on 8 or 9 February 1437 in front of the high altar of the Lady Chapel at Westminster Abbey – indeed hers was the first royal body to be buried there. When Henry VII demolished the chapel in 1502, 'her body was taken up, and, the coffin being decayed, it was put in a wooden chest, and placed near her husband's tomb in the east end of the Friars' (as Stowe calls it).[28] Henry VII intended to have the remains reinterred in the new chapel but he himself died the day after its consecration and no one else bothered themselves with Queen Katherine's corpse. In 1631 John Weever observed: 'Katherine, Queen of England, lieth here, in a chest or coffin with a loose cover, to be seen and handled of any who will much desire it.'[29] The miserable mummy was to stay above ground for many more years yet; in the mean time it remained an object of spectacle. Even Samuel Pepys went for an audience: '23 February, 1668–9. To Westminster Abbey, and there did see all the tombs very finely, having one with us alone, there being other company this day to see the tombs, it being Shrove Tuesday. And here we did see, by particular favour, the body of Queen Katherine of Valois; and I had the upper part of her body in my hands, and I did kiss her mouth, reflecting upon it that I did kiss a Queene, and this was my birthday, thirty-six years old, that I did kiss a Queene.'[30] The embalming had held out; but so numerous were the numbers of visitors that the body began to decay, and reports of 1711, 1723 and 1773[31] all allude to its degenerate state. But this was probably more because of interference than natural decay: 'The bones [are] firmly united and the flesh and skin dried up like tanned leather. Of late years the Westminster scholars amused themselves with tearing it to pieces; and one in particular, who bore a principal character in the police of India, lies under the imputation of having contributed in an especial manner to that havoc. I can just remember seeing some shapeless mass of mummy of a whitish colour. It is now under lock and key near her husband's tomb, waiting for the next opening of the royal vault for her last repose.'[32] Anon she was not placed in the royal vault; rather the opportunity was taken to put her in the Villiers vault in 1776 when the neighbouring Percy vault was opened for the reception of the remains of the First Duchess of Northumberland. However, the nineteenth-century antiquarian dean, Arthur Penrhyn Stanley, had her removed in 1877 and the subsequent examination showed that although both torso and head had become skeletal, the legs remained entire, enclosed within twelve layers of cerecloth, whilst the left arm and hand were quite perfect. She was eventually deposited, within a new coffin, beneath the altar-slab in her husband's chantry chapel in the Abbey in 1878.

As has already been seen, embalming was not a cheap process. Moreover, no two surgeons were alike and the success ratio of the treatment was mixed – Henry VI's corpse leaked embalming fluid profusely during the lying-in-state. Much primary research into the cost of embalming of the nobility and landed gentry of sixteenth- and seventeenth-century England was published in 1984 by Clare Gittings,[33] the majority of which was based on family documents of Kentish and East Anglian families. For example, when Nicholas Bacon of Stiffkey, Norfolk, died in 1578 three doctors were present at the embalming, though the primary incisions were undertaken by two surgeons; yet regardless of their importance and status, each was paid £2 for their services. Even so, the process was not yet over. A further five surgeons were required to sear and embalm the cadaver; they were paid a total of £7 8s. 4d., with the bill for the spices and perfumes for the balm amounting to the then enormous sum of £9. Four women then dressed and trimmed the body – i.e. shaved the face and washed the hair – prior to its being wrapped in 8¾ yards of cerecloth and then placed in the anthropoid lead case. But was this really necessary? Could not the job have been done by a doctor, a surgeon and one attendant? Certainly, but there was a particular status to be gained by the family in employing so many; it also gave a certain degree of importance to the corpse itself. The total bill for Bacon's embalming came to £26 8s. 4d. which, when compared with the £28 4s. 1d. paid in 1596 for the embalming of Henry, Earl of Huntingdon, seems to have been a fairly standard cost.

There is some confusion as to whether or not Queen Elizabeth I's body was embalmed. The contemporary historian John Manningham relates that it was the Queen's wish not to be so treated and that this was obeyed, her body being '... wrapt up in cerecloth, and that very ill too'.[34] It is difficult to believe that she was not embalmed and Elizabeth Southwell, a minor courtier, relates how Lord Cecil ordered it to be done and Clapham, in his *Elizabeth of England*, states that 'The Queen's body was left in a manner alone a day or two after her death and meane persons [embalmers] had access to it.'[35] W.J. White confuses matters more by saying that 'the body of Elizabeth I was so poorly embalmed that during the funeral the coffin exploded, owing to the accumulation of the gaseous products of decomposition'.[36]

Whom are we to believe? The only person to whom we can give any credence is Manningham; doubtless any delay in embalming the body was caused by Cecil's dilemma whether to obey the late Queen's wishes or not. At no time did Elizabeth I's coffin explode. The best refutation of this is given by Olivia Bland: ' ... such a cataclysmic event could never have been hushed up and yet, it does not appear in any of the other memoirs of the time. Mistress Southwell was a Roman Catholic and with several others sought to surround the events of the Queen Elizabeth's last illness and death with ill-omens and to suggest that she had not died in a state of grace'.[37] Queen Elizabeth's vault in Westminster Abbey was examined in 1868 by Dean Stanley: 'There was no disorder or decay, except that the centring wood had fallen over the head of Elizabeth's coffin, and that the wood case had crumbled away at the sides, and had drawn away part of the decaying lid.'[38] The cereclothed corpse itself was enclosed within an anthropoid lead shell. Elizabeth Southwell's tale can be confidently disregarded.

Queen Elizabeth I was not the only person to have her 'no embalming' request repealed by enthusiastic relatives. James Montague, Bishop of Winchester, had decreed the same shortly before his death in 1618, stating that not more than £400 be spent on his funeral – an incredibly large amount even by early seventeenth-century standards. Montague's brother chose to ignore the request and commissioned a Mr Rowland, surgeon, to perform the task for £2, assisted by two other surgeons at twelve shillings a piece; there was a further outlay of ten shillings for 'a woman to attend the surgeons with water, mops, cloths and other things'.[39] The viscera were removed, encased and buried at night by torchlight. But before the funeral of the body itself took place, the embalming failed and Mr Montague had to recruit others to repair Rowland's blundering, costing Montague £1 for the surgeon and ten shillings for his assistant. In all the funeral exceeded the bishop's estimate by over £540, amounting to £940 18s. 11d. The embalming of an ordinary gentleman of the period cost, by comparison, a mere £5, spices included, with the services of a surgeon for 'ripping the corpse', as it was so graphically described, being available for five shillings.[40]

Clare Gittings suggests that one of the many reasons why embalming decreased during the late sixteenth and early seventeenth centuries was distaste on the part of the nobility – not so much with the practice itself as with the thought of having so many surgeons, apothecaries and wax-chandlers poring over a body at any one time. She proceeds to give an illustration relating to Mary, Countess of Northumberland, who, dying in 1572, left the following comment in her will: 'Do not in any wise let me be opened after I am dead. I have not loved to be very bold afore women, much more would I loathe to come into the hands of any living man, be he physician or surgeon.'[41]

Nor did the general public have a very high regard of embalming, believing it to be another unnecessary luxury meted out to the corpses of the rich. The process is satirically described by Nashe in the *Anatomie* of Martin Marprelate: 'Having bestowed his bowels in a ditch ... and filled his hungry belly ... with coal dust, for spice they could not bestow (his carrion being not worth it) and sawdust they could have none; they wrapped him in a blanket ... for that all others are lapped in sheets.'[42]

By the end of the seventeenth century the high-street undertaker was trying his hand at the technique, much to the chagrin of the surgeons and the apothecaries. Thomas Greenhill was such a one. In the preface to his 1705 treatise on the *Art of Embalming*, he says, 'Some have spared no means to render themselves immortal ... It may be justly said of embalming, that it is undeniably the most considerable and efficacious means to answer their intentions.' Was he touting for custom from his readers? Probably, for we later read that 'want of opportunity has been in some respect a prejudice to my business', and, 'the noble act of embalming has been entirely ruined by the undertakers'.[43]

The clearest single advance in technique was the introduction in the mid seventeenth century of preservation in spirits of wine. The scientist Robert Boyle was looking for a method of preserving corpses so that they could be used for summer as well as winter tutorials. His first experiment, shown at the Royal Society in September 1662, featured a puppy preserved in spirits of wine throughout the summer months. Its good reception encouraged Boyle to set pen to paper, publishing his results in June 1663, at which time he observed, 'Nor is it only by dissection of various animals that the naturalist may promote the anatomist's knowledge, but perhaps he may do it by devising ways to make the dead bodies of man and other animals keep longer than naturally they would do.' His basic idea was to empty arteries and veins of their blood and replace it by something 'fluid enough when it is injected to run into the branches of the vessels, will afterwards quickly grow hard'.[44] He exhibited a number of specimens to the Royal Society in 1664, and two years later published an account of another successful experiment in preserving 'Birds taken out of the Egge', so as to observe 'the Process of Nature in the Formation of a Chick'. Other systems also being tried at the same time included dehydration and injection techniques, the latter to be perfected by a surgeon called Ruysch (1665–1717), Professor of Anatomy at Amsterdam. Ruysch, a member of the Royal Society, devised an arterial technique for human embalming; although a master of the art he was extremely secretive and never divulged his recipe. He embalmed a child in 1717 so skilfully that he deceived Peter the Great, who thought the infant was alive yet in a state of normal repose. When asked how it was done, Ruysch simply said that the corpse had been put in cold water for a day or so, the aorta and venae cavae were then opened, the blood cleared out and the whole put in hot water for four to six hours; for the injection he had used suet or tallow in the winter, and added wax, turpentine and resin in summer.[45]

In eighteenth-century England, as a consequence of the demand for better preservation of anatomical specimens, many scientists and anatomists experimented with a number of techniques, including spirits of wine. Few complete bodies were subjected to this treatment as it was a time-consuming and expensive exercise. The Earl of Moira was one candidate who, having been so treated, was wrapped and bound in pseudo-Egyptian fashion prior to being deposited in his ancestral vault.

Charles White, the celebrated Manchester surgeon, was born in 1728 and received his anatomical training in London at William Hunter's academy in 1748. It was there that he met up with William's younger brother John – they were contemporaries, having both been born in the same year – and began a friendship that ended only with John's death in 1793. On leaving Hunter's, White returned to Manchester to continue his studies, developing his interests in surgery and obstetrics. However, he never relinquished his passion for anatomy and, urged on by John Hunter, amassed an amazing collection of specimens, the most celebrated of which was the body of Miss Hannah Beswick, later known as the Manchester Mummy.

Hannah Beswick was the daughter of John Beswick of Failsworth – a small village between Manchester and Oldham – a man of considerable wealth, most of which his daughter inherited. Charles White acted as her medical adviser for the last eight years or so of her life, until she died in February 1758 at the age of seventy. Whatever the circumstances – and they are conflicting – White acquired Hannah Beswick's body and embalmed her, almost certainly by methods recommended by William Hunter, his former tutor. It seems most odd that a genteel seventy-year-old spinster, or her executors, would want to have the body embalmed by a newly hatched 29-year-old surgeon. Be that as it may, she was embalmed and formed the centre-piece of White's 'Cabinet of Curiosities' at Sale Priory, his Manchester home. Amongst one of Thomas de Quincey's earliest recollections is a visit to Sale Priory to see Charles White's museum and, of course, Miss Hannah Beswick. In his *Autobiography* de Quincey records that Miss Beswick had been placed 'in a common English clock case, having the usual glass face; but a veil of white velvet obscured from all profane eyes the silent features behind'.[46] White died in 1813 and his collection was transferred to the Manchester Natural History Museum; Miss Beswick went too. And here she stayed on public display until 1868 when it was decided not only to close the museum but also to lay Hannah Beswick to rest. She now lies in Harpurhey Cemetery, Manchester, ' ... without stone or tablet to indicate the spot',[47] though a search through the cemetery ledgers of 1868 would soon reveal the whereabouts of the plot. It would be interesting to see what state of preservation she is in, always assuming that the Manchester Natural History Museum had her properly encoffined.[48]

Eighteen years after the production of the Manchester Mummy, William Hunter wrote:

> With respect to the embalming [of] Bodies, the methods that were commonly practised could, I know, have no effect; at that time I read a good many Books upon 'Balsamation'[49] but got very little instruction from reading these: according to my own Idea the best way would be to preserve the Body for some time that putrefaction should hardly be able to take place, & that it should gradually get rid of its moisture, & that, when it dried, it should have such imbalming juices in it, that it should resist putrefaction, & the insects at the same time be either kept off or destroyed: I set out with this Opinion & thought that something must be thrown thro' the whole Body: the when the Body was preserved, my Idea of getting rid of moisture was, to place the Body in some strong absorbent substance, & that substance which proved best I thought was Paris Plaister & I thought I could lay in a common Coffin such a quantity of Paris Plaister as would take out all the moisture & then I thought the Body should be rather in a wooden case than a leaden one because the Wood would assist the Absorption. This was the plan I laid down, and the first time I had occasion to try it in practice was the Summer before the last [1774] & I then did it in the case of a Lady and in the hottest weather: the next Body I tried these experiments upon was Jan.[y] 13 1775 & that Body is vastly improv'd the longer it is kept & the little remains of fat shine a little more thro' & it is now very much the colour of Indian Copper, i.e. it is very near the colour of finished work'd mahogany & is really a beautiful mass, the Legs are now perfectly dry and from the Beginning to the end there is nothing of putrefaction.[50]

The identity of the 1774 specimen is not known. But his 1775 candidate is well known – indeed she was better known and more celebrated after death than at any other time in her existence.

> 14th January 1775. At half past two this morning my wife died. At eight this morning the statuary took off her face in plaister.[51] At half past two this afternoon Mr Cruikshanks injected at the crural arteries 5 pints of Oil of Turpentine mixed with Venice Turpentine and Vermillion.[52]

Who was this lady, and what was her importance? She was Maria, the wife of the empiric, Martin Van Butchell (1735–1812), son of Martin Van Butchell, tapestry-maker to George II. A pupil of the anatomist John Hunter, Van Butchell later practised as a highly successful dentist before becoming an eminent truss-maker, specializing in the treatment of fistula. Arguably he was known to Londoners less for his medical expertise than for his incredible eccentricity, which was exaggerated by a long beard, a predilection for extraordinary costume and his habit of riding about in the streets and Hyde Park on a white pony, which he sometimes painted all purple or, when the mood took him, purple with black spots. He carried a most unusual weapon at all times, namely a large white bone which, he proclaimed, had once been used as an item of warfare in the island of Otaheite (*18*). Despite his outer appearance and his bizarre equestrian habits, he was a highly respected practitioner residing first at St James's and then in Mount Street, off Berkeley Square.

Van Butchell kept a diary of the embalming of his 36-year-old wife, which took a month to perfect. His second entry reads:

> 15th January 1775. At nine this morning Dr Hunter and Mr Cruikshanks began to open and embalm the body of my Wife. Her deseases were a large Empyema of the left lung (which would not receive any air), accompanied with Pleuropneumony, and much adhesion: the right lung was also beginning to decay, and had some Pus in it. The spleen hard and much contracted; the Liver disease called Rata Malpigi. The stomach very sound, the kidneys, uterus, bladder and intestine in good order.
>
> 17th January 1775. I opened the abdomen and put in the remainder of the powders ... [And on the next day] Dr Hunter and Mr Cruikshanks came at 9 this morning and put my wife into the Box on and in 130 lb weight of Paris plaister at 18d a bag. I put inbetween the thighs three Arquesbusade bottles, one full of Camphorated Spirits very rich of the Gum; one containing 8 oz of Oil of Rosemary; and in the other 2 oz Oil of Lavender.
>
> 11th February 1775. I unluted the glasses to clean the face and legs with Spirits of Wine and Oil of Lavender.
>
> 12th February 1775. Dr Hunter came to look at the neck and shoulders.[53]

William Hunter kept a complete record of the process,[54] occupying eighteen sheets of foolscap in a hurried hand. The embalming involved three stages, a précis of which was published by Jessie Dobson in 1953 in the *Journal of the History of Medicine*.[55] The first stage featured the injection of turpentine and vermillion ' ... to fill the Arteries and Veins and even go further to produce extravasation to every part of the Body, i.e. til the face and all the flesh swell

1   Given by Henry Fayrey
in 1516 to the Guild of St
John at Dunstable Priory, the
Dunstable Pall is one of the more
accomplished of the ten surviving
pre-Reformation palls.

2   'Paying one's respects' was an important part of the funerary ritual, though
in James Hayllar's 1883 painting, The Old Master, the eye is drawn towards
the mourning widow.

3 *Jeremy Bentham (d.1832). This auto-icon is not an embalmed body;*
rather, Bentham's skeleton was used as an armature,
the head being made entirely of wax.

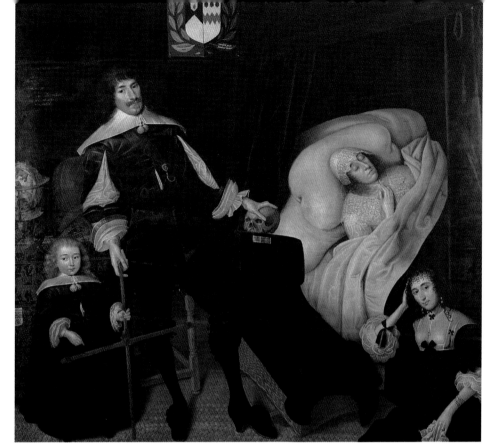

4   In the Aston Portrait of 1635 by John Souch of Chester,
Thomas Aston and his family are gathered round the corpse of
his wife, who had died in childbirth.

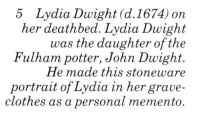

5   Lydia Dwight (d.1674) on
her deathbed. Lydia Dwight
was the daughter of the
Fulham potter, John Dwight.
He made this stoneware
portrait of Lydia in her grave-
clothes as a personal memento.

6 *Figures mourning over an open coffin. It was usual in the eighteenth century for coffins to be taken home, so the trade had to be particularly vigilant over presentation of the corpse and its grave-clothes.*

7 *Though not a coffin* per se, *this c.1500 painted oak mortuary chest in Winchester Cathedral was based on coffins of the period. Note the placement of the lifting ring.*

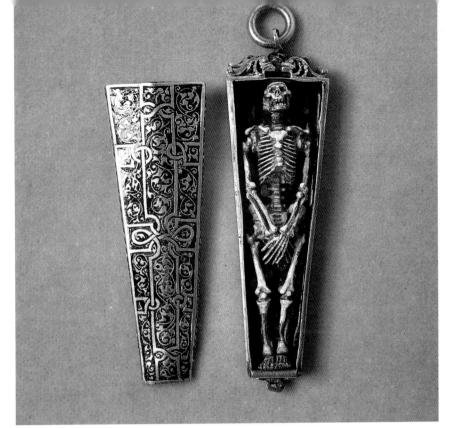

8   *The Tor Abbey Jewel of c.1546 confirms the shape of the English coffin at that time. The design on the lid is a jeweller's fantasy and should not be taken as indicative of coffin decoration.*

9   *The c.1574–80 Poulett Vault at Hinton St George, Somerset, showing three lead shells of c.1700–20 with decorative borders to the lids. Lead shells of this design would not have been provided with outer wooden cases.*

10   The 1615 St John Triptych at Lydiard Tregoz, Wiltshire. The central
sarcophagus is supported on three gable-lidded wooden coffins of the period.

11   The c.1645 parish coffin at Easingwold, Yorkshire, is the earliest and only lidded example to survive. This shape of coffin was in vogue between c.1600–75.

12   The coffin on the 1655 Allestry monument in Derby Cathedral, though little more than a sculptor's component, is important as far as coffin construction is concerned.

13 A velvet-covered outer case of 1795 from the Sackville Vault at Withyham, Sussex. This represents top-quality undertaking of the eighteenth century, the velvet having been backed with shoddy to obtain a luxurious finish.

14 A Grave Idea: An Apartment for a Single Gentleman. This 1828 caricature by T. Jones, a warning to youth to guard against the pleasures of the flesh, indicates the use of fabric-covered coffins for earth burial.

18   Martin Van Butchell (1735–
1812), empiric, truss-maker
and eccentric of St James's,
London, kept a diary on the
embalming of his first wife in
1775.

which will be a proof of extravasation and the more there is so much the better'. The body was left in an open state for several hours prior to the second stage, when the thorax and abdomen were removed and placed in water. Hunter observed that ' ... the whole viscera when all the Blood is press'd out goes into a very little bulk, even the Liver will lose vastly of its bulk and in short the whole viscera will come into a small compass when they are well clean'd and put into dry cloths; you are then to go to the trunk of the Body and empty it of Blood as well as you can and *press* the Blood out from the Face, Hands, etc. as well as Arms, and the more Blood is pressed out the better'. Regarding the bladder and rectum, Hunter was especially precise: 'Instead of being only 10 minutes about this Process you must be ½ an Hour to an Hour about it.' All parts of the body were then to be carefully washed in spirits of wine before proceeding to the third stage, which consisted in the injection of the body a second time – his system being an amalgam of that advocated by Robert Boyle and Ruysch – and the viscera, should it be considered necessary. Unlike the Egyptians, with whose process Hunter was not impressed, he did not remove the brain, implying that it could be sufficiently well treated *in situ* by general injection. The viscera were then returned to the cavity together with a substantial quantity of camphor,

47

nitre and resin. Then, having sewn up the body and filled the outlets with camphor, it was well washed, thoroughly dried and rubbed with fragrant oils – in the case of Maria Van Butchell this last act was done by her husband on 12 February 1775.

The final stage in the process was to make sure that the box provided was filled to half-way with plaster of Paris to absorb moisture, though he gives no guidelines as to how deep such a box should be; 'after this, the cover and two windows were put down'. Hunter ended his description with a comment on Maria and a hint as to his charges to Martin Van Butchell: 'This body … yet promises exceedingly well, nor do I see any great improvement to be made; a number of experiments must be made before I embalm any other body, such as finding the exact proportion of moisture Paris Plaister will take up etc. but at present I know of no other Process at all useful and considering the trouble you must have during all these Processes now laid down, you ought not to undertake it under 100 Guineas.'

And of Mrs Van Butchell herself? Well, she was the subject of much interest and became one of the sights of London (*19*). Indeed, so pressing were the requests to see her, and no doubt her eccentric widower as well, that Martin Van Butchell was obliged to place an announcement in the *St James's Chronicle* on 21 October 1775, restricting the hours for viewing and putting conditions on those who wished to view. Mrs Van Butchell was not to be gawped at. The general public might have been disappointed but they needed only refer to a contemporary poem then available:

19   Van Butchell limited visitations to view his embalmed wife's remains by means of a press announcement. She remained on view until presented to the Royal College of Surgeons in 1812.

St. James's Chronicle, Oct. 21, 1775.

VANBUT·CHELL (not willing to be unpleasantly circumftanced, and wifhing to convince fome good Minds they have been mifinformed) acquaints the Curious, no Stranger can fee his embalmed Wife, unlefs (by a Friend perfonally) introduced to himfelf, any Day, between Nine and One, *Sundays* excepted.

EPITAPH on Mrs Vanbutchel whose remains, preserved by a curious and newly invented method of embalment, are the object of her husband's daily attention.

Here, unentombed, Vanbutchel's consort lies
To feed a husband's grief, or charm his eyes;
Taintless and pure her body still remains,
And all its former elegance retains.
Long had disease been preying on her charms,
'Till slow she sunk in Death's expecting arms;
When HUNTER's skill in spite of Nature's laws,
Her beauty rescued from Corruption's jaws;
Bade the pale roses of her cheeks revive
And her shrunk features seem again to live;
– Hunter, who first conceived the happy thought,
And here at length to full perfection brought.
O! Lucky husband! Blest of Heav'n
To thee the privilege is given,
A much loved wife at home to keep,
Caress, touch, talk to, even sleep
Close by her side, when e'er you will
As quiet as if living still;
And, strange to tell, that fairer she,
And sweeter, than alive should be;
Firm, plump and juicy as before
And full as tractable, or more –
Thrice happy mortal! Envied lot;
What a rare treasure thou hast got!
Who to a woman can lay claim
Whose temper's every day the same![56]

What the second Mrs Van Butchell thought of having her predecessor in the house is not recorded, neither was Hunter's opinion. But Hunter must surely have known that Van Butchell, famed for his eccentricities, had no intention of burying his wife once the embalming had been done. And why did he do it when it was perfectly possible for him to have experimented on any cadaver purchased by him for his medical academy? Could it be that he was aware of Van Butchell's intentions and saw this as a means of bringing his technique to the notice of the public, being able, at the same time, to lay any charge of indecency at Van Butchell's door, if it arose? That Van Butchell was willing to pay the 100 guineas is interesting and suggests that there were no bounds to his eccentricities.

Van Butchell died on 30 October 1814. No record exists as to whether or not he was embalmed. However, in August 1815 Van Butchell's son presented the embalmed body of his mother to the Royal College of Surgeons where it was placed in the Curio Room. In 1857 C. Cobbe saw it, remarking that

> ... no doubt extraordinary pains were taken to preserve both form and feature; and yet, what a wretched mockery of a once lovely woman it now appears, with its shrunken and rotten-looking bust, its hideous, mahogany-coloured face, and its remarkably fine set of teeth. Between the feet are the remains of a green parrot – whether immolated or not at the death of his mistress is

uncertain – but it still retains its plumage; it is a far less repulsive-looking object than the larger bi-ped. By the side of Mrs Van Butchell is the body of another woman, embalmed by a different process about the same period: she is even more ugly than her neighbour. As curiosities, these few loathsome relics are no doubt both valuable and interesting, but were there a heap of such dry rubbish, one would feel strongly disposed to make a bonfire of the whole, for it looks nothing fit for anything else.[57]

Cobbe was to have his way, for Maria Van Butchell, the green parrot and the 'ugly neighbour' were all destroyed during an air raid in 1941.

The second body seen by Cobbe in 1857 was that of a Miss Johnson who had died of phthisis aged twenty-four at the Lock Hospital in 1774. The embalmer was John Sheldon, a recently qualified surgeon not much older than Miss Johnson herself. Sheldon had become much attached to her during his time at the Lock Hospital and it is said that she asked him to embalm her body after her death, which he did. And that was Mrs Sheldon's side of the story as related forty-one years later after the death of her husband. The true identity of the corpse was made known in 1838 by William Sweeting, Sheldon's nephew: the body was none other than Sarah Stone, a medical artist who had worked for both Sheldon and Hunter's assistant, Cruikshank. Sweeting also confirmed that the Miss Johnson story originated from his aunt who, as he wittily put it, 'could only know what was told her!' Sheldon himself never lied to his friends about the mummy and we have to be grateful to Faujas Saint-Fond for the following account written shortly after a visit he had made on Sheldon: 'It is [said Sheldon] a mistress whom I tenderly loved. I paid every attention to her during a long sickness and, a short time before her death, she requested that I should make a mummy of her body, and keep her beside me – I have kept my word.'[58]

Were we able to exhume the body of the Earl of Moira then we would see an example of John Hunter's technique, as performed by his two assistants John Doratt and Everard Hone. Moira died in 1793 leaving instructions that his corpse be fully embalmed prior to its being deposited in the family vault. John Hunter's system was similar to that performed by his brother on Maria Van Butchell. The most important difference was the protection given to the embalmed body itself. The limbs were individually wrapped, similar to the bandaging as perfected by the ancient Egyptians, prior to the whole being enveloped in cerecloth after the fashion of the late medieval English embalmer.

London was not the only place where such experiments were going on. Sir John Pryce (1698–1761) of Newton, Glamorgan, was so distressed when his first wife died that he had the body embalmed and placed next to his bed. He soon remarried and it appears that his second wife had no qualms about sharing the bedchamber with her predecessor. Misfortune struck Sir John when his second wife died; she received the same treatment as his first spouse. Sporting Sir John married for a third time but the new Lady Pryce refused to play second – or, perhaps, third – fiddle and insisted that the embalmed bodies in the moribund harem be removed. They were, and the Pryces spent a few years in married bliss before the third Lady Pryce died in 1748. No embalming this time – rather Sir John summoned the services of Bridget Bostock, known as the 'Cheshire Pythoness', who claimed that she could cure all known diseases. Sir John's

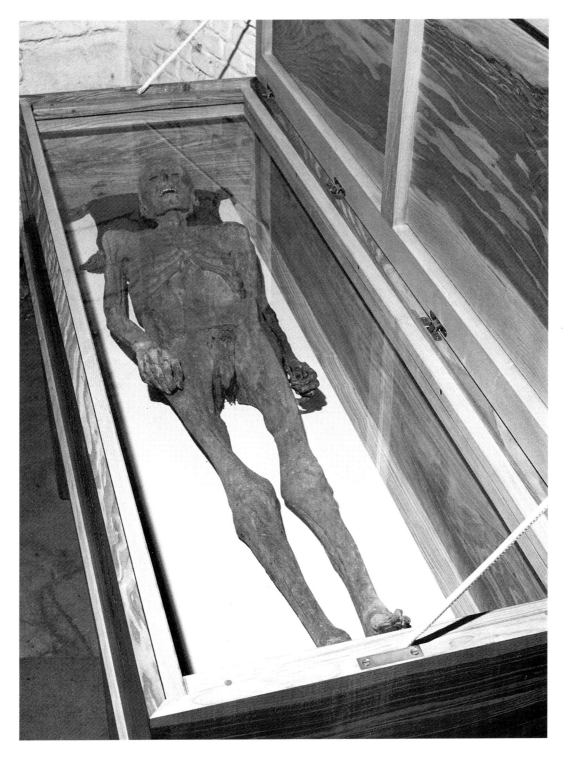

20   Discovered during vault clearances at St James Garlickhythe
in 1855, Jimmy Garlick is probably Seagrave Chamberlain
(1659–75), one of the first burials in Wren's rebuilt church of 1675.

request was a simple one: that Bridget Bostock raise the third Lady Pryce from the dead. Mrs Bostock did visit Newton, but failed in her mission. There was nothing else for Sir John to do but marry again; unfortunately, he died before he could accomplish this.[59]

As has already been stated, the great majority of bodies were not embalmed, but put into a lined coffin, whose mattress overlaid a quantity of sawdust, wood shavings and bran to soak up any leakage associated with putrefaction (*20*). Misson, in his commentary on the English funeral, tells us what happened next, and why: 'They let it [the corpse] lye three of four Days ... which Time they allow, as well to give the dead Person an Opportunity of Coming to Life again, if his Soul has not quite left his Body, as to prepare Mourning, and the Ceremonies of the Funeral.'[60] Embalming would not have allowed for this and, had the person not been dead prior to the beginning of the operation, he certainly would be once it was all over. Arguably the only practical advantage in embalming was that it could reveal whether or not a person had been suffering from catalepsy.

An interesting discovery which would certainly have brought the Hunters running was unearthed at Danbury, Essex, in October 1779. Some workmen digging a grave inside the parish church uncovered a lead anthropoid coffin inside of which was the body of a lad ' ... laying in a liquor, or pickle, somewhat resembling mushroom catchup, but of a paler complexion, and somewhat thicker in consistance', according to Dr T. White of Colchester who, together with Dr Gower of Chelmsford, had been invited by the rector, the Revd de l'Angle, and the churchwarden, Lewis Disney Ffytche of Danbury Place, to examine the coffin. White continues, 'As I never possessed the sense of smelling, and was willing to ascertain the flavour of the liquor, I tasted and found it to be aromatic, tho' not very pungent, partaking of the taste of catchup and of the pickle of Spanish olives.' The body itself was late medieval, not wrapped in cerecloth but in a long linen shift with a narrow hem of lace; the features were discernible, though bald, whilst the 'inside of the body seemed to be filled with some substance which rendered it very hard.' As to the liquor, it filled about half the coffin and in it 'feathers, flowers, and herbs in abundance were floating, the leaves and stalks of which appeared quite perfect, but totally discoloured'. The body itself was not much more than five feet tall, the coffin measuring five foot 6 inches in length. Once examined, the church was opened for a short time so that the locals could view the remains prior to the coffin being resealed and put back 'as near as circumstances would admit, in status quo'.[61]

A similar scenario had been enacted a little more than 100 years previously at St Paul's Cathedral, London, concerning the corpse of John Colet, Dean of St Paul's, who died in 1519. In about 1680 John Aubrey retold the following story:

John Colet, D.D., Deane of St Paule's, London. After the Conflagration (his Monument being broken) somebody made a little hole towards the upper edge of his Coffin, which was closed like the coffin of a Pye and was full of a Liquour which conserved the body. Mr Wyld and Ralph Greatorex tasted it and 'twas of a kind of insipid tast, something of an Ironish tast. The Coffin was of Lead, and layd in the Wall about 2 foot ½ above the surface of the Floore. This was a strange rare way of conserving a Corps: perhaps it was a Pickle, as for Beefe, whose Saltness in so many years the Lead might sweeten and render insipid. The body felt, to the probe of a stick which they thrust into a chinke, like boyld Brawne.[62]

How much of the liquor in this anthropoid coffin was body fluid will have to be left to the imagination; suffice it to say that owing to the construction of such coffins it would have been practically impossible to have introduced much liquid preservatives.

In about 1724 John Lethieullier obtained a faculty (that is, a licence from the ecclesiastical authorities) to construct a mausoleum with subterranean burial vault on to St Mary's, Little Ilford. He left instructions regarding the disposal of his remains, directing that his body should 'be first opened' and decently deposited in a leaden coffin at Little Ilford with his late wife; this was so done in 1737. The 1984 reordering of the church provided the opportunity to examine the contents, and amongst the eight coffins was that of Charles Lethieullier, brother of the celebrated antiquarian, Smart Lethieullier, whose coffin also lay in the vault, though it had lost its outer wooden case and the inner lead shell had split along the joint where left flank and lid met (*21*). The lead coffin itself was filled to within one inch of the brim with a tacky ochre-coloured liquid, somewhat the colour of heather honey but not quite so solid. Only by touch was it possible to

21 Although evisceration waned during the eighteenth century, Charles Lethieullier (d. 1759) was so treated, and his soft organs were subsequently encased in the viscera chest atop his coffin.

22 When John, Duke of Lauderdale (d. Tunbridge Wells, 1682) was embalmed, the viscera were 'potted' prior to encasement in their own chest for the journey to Haddington, East Lothian.

establish that the body inside was entire, though it was not practical either to drain the liquid or to lift the remains. The viscera chest was, however, opened. Beneath the wooden lid and at the bottom of the still damp aromatic bran lay the soft organs and the heart, still elastic and resistant to the touch (22).

The Hunters' techniques cannot, alas, be regarded as contributions to the state of the art as it then existed. Embalming was rarely practised during the eighteenth century and it had almost entirely disappeared during the nineteenth century. However, in the 1890s an attempt was made by the trade to introduce arterial embalming as practised in the United States, the leading campaigners for this being the funeral furnishing firm of Dottridge Brothers. It soon received the acclamation of the trade and by the 1920s the majority of undertakers in this country were offering hygienic treatment of the dead to their clients. Part of this success must have been due to the Dottridges' persuasive advertising (23):

It is now becoming a generally acknowledged fact that the Undertakers in England have too long neglected the importance of sanitation as applied to their own profession. No doubt the neglect has been due to the absence of

54

SANITARY PRESERVATION DEPT.

Complete Embalming Outfit

D.B. Preservation Fluid   Vaporiser   Satisfax Fluid

Dottoformol   Ozocone   Dotterello

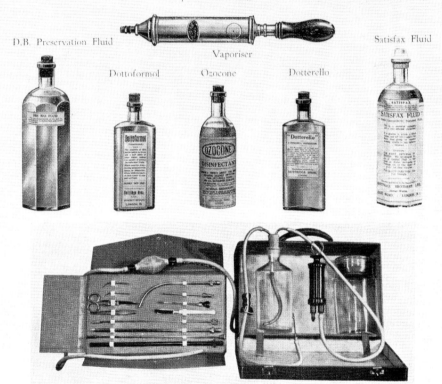

Temporary Preservation Outfit.

These Laboratory equipments have been carefully prepared and will be found invaluable to all engaged in the Sanitary Preservation of the dead.

We are prepared, upon receipt of a telegram, to dispatch immediately a Qualified Operator to any part of the Kingdom.

23   *Dottridge Brothers based their 1922 arterial embalming kit on American precedents, augmenting it with bottles of their own fluids, 'Dottoformol' and 'Dotterello'.*

knowledge in dealing with these matters, and the ignorance of the right methods and necessary articles for use … We all know the prehistoric method of treating the dead, which obtains even to-day in the less enlightened parts of the country – the body hurriedly placed in the coffin, the packing with sawdust, and the necessarily precipitate screwing down of the lid. We know, too, the frequent result of such crude precautions, the often painful unpleasantness – to use a mild term – which results from putrefaction, and which the undertaker assures the family is 'quite inevitable' … whereas when the body has been prepared by the Operator it keeps the appearance of life for an indefinite period, and the last look remains as a pleasant remembrance to their friends. (*24*)[63]

Firm, plump and juicy as Maria Van Butchell, no doubt!

24   Queen Alexandra gave permission for W. & D. Downey to release to the public postcards of Edward VII on his deathbed at Buckingham Palace.

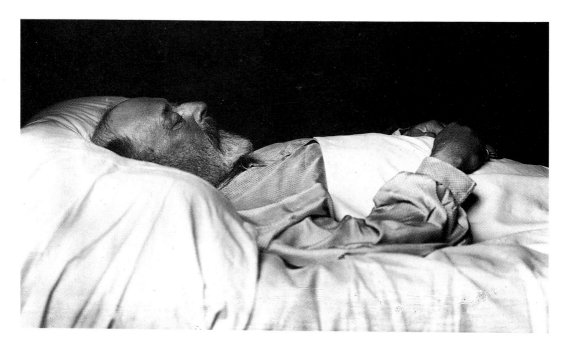

3

Dress'd and Trimm'd:
Winding-Sheets and Shrouds

We went to see a dead man laid out, and it would be a pity not to give you an account of his state. He was dressed in a long flannel shirt edged with lace, with flounces all down the middle, and five or six more on either side of the chest, all sewn with wool, in accordance with an Act of Parliament which forbids the use of linen or cotton for this purpose. The sleeves end in cuffs. This shirt is put on over the head and does not surround the body in one piece but is fastened at the back. The body is laid out in a coffin resting on a bed of bran or sawdust. The face is shaved, the head is dressed in a bonnet, fastened at the top, and a cravat and gloves of flannel are worn. When the lady is laid out, it is in a mob-cap and an embroidered headband, and neatly pressed flounces. The shirt comes right down over the feet, and threaded through with a woollen thread at the ankles, with tassels at the end.[1]

This account, written by a foreigner in London during his travels through England, is a description of 'corpse dressing' current during the first quarter of the eighteenth century. Its author, Antoine-Joseph Dezallier-D'Argenville, writing in 1731, records the then recently introduced fashion for flounces on the front of the shroud.

Until the second and third quarters of the seventeenth century not all bodies were buried in coffins; but they did have shrouds. The sixteenth-century shroud was a voluminous sheet, gathered at the head and foot ends in a knot; those of the eighteenth century were more tailored, with sleeves and draw-strings; whilst in the nineteenth century they were fully fashioned. But it was not always thus.

The illuminated manuscripts known as Books of Hours, produced in the

57

25 *The Bedford Hours, c. 1423. The close-shrouded body is placed
in the grave by the sexton during the Committal; a server
stands to one side with the holy water bucket.*

Lowlands during the fifteenth century, particularly those containing the Office of the Dead, not only show how corpses were dressed at that time but also indicate how the limbs were positioned. In the *Rohan Hours*, produced for Yolande of Aragon between *c*.1418-25 and now in the Bibliothèque Nationale, Paris,[2] the shroud is shown as a loose sheet, almost as if the dead man had been lifted from his bed and placed into his coffin; no attempt has been made to mould the cloth about the body or to position the limbs. By contrast, a small vignette on folio 120 of the *Bedford Hours* in the British Library (*25*)[3] has the corpse closely wrapped in a manner not unlike that of an Egyptian mummy. A very small illumination of about 1450, and not much more than 1½ inches square (*26*), provides an insight into how the body was wrapped. A sheet of cloth has been placed on to a stripped bed, the winding-sheet has been folded over the left-hand side of the corpse, the remainder drawn over the right, whilst the arms have been folded across the body in line with the bottom of the rib-cage.[4] Sometimes the winding-sheet was pinned, at other times it was sewn along the centre; the artist of the *c*.1435 *Heures de Neville*, also in the Bibliothèque Nationale, Paris, shows two corpses with centre-sewn winding-sheets in a larger illumination of monks reading in a bone-yard.

The representation of personages on monuments before the second quarter of

26 In these small vignettes of c. 1475–89 by Simon Marmion, a
widow kneels in prayer as directions are given for sewing the
shroud; the second scene is of the burial.

the fifteenth century showed them in all their might, majesty and power, attired in their finery and dressed to illustrate their status. Thus a king would be shown in full coronation robes, holding the sceptres of estate and with a crown on his head, a bishop in full pontificals, a knight in his finest suit of armour and his lady dressed for Court. However, during the fifteenth century changes were introduced and we see for the first time representations of corpses, cadavers and skeletons, and it is from these – usually to be found on memorial brasses, and particularly on those in East Anglia – that we acquire our first glimpse of the English shroud.

The Revd Herbert Macklin did not like the shroud brasses:

> The custom of engraving shrouded figures and skeletons was introduced shortly before the middle of the fifteenth century and continued until the end of the sixteenth. It was a horrible practice, and became most common in the reign of Henry VII, and especially in the eastern counties. The shroud is usually knotted at the head and feet, and sufficiently open to expose the breast and knees of the deceased. These ghastly memorials were frequently laid down during the lifetime of the persons they were intended to commemorate, in order that they might constantly be reminded that they were but mortal. The emaciated corpse is the form most frequently adopted. Skeletons are rarer, but may be seen at Hildersham, Cambs; Weybridge, Surrey; Margate, Norwich, and other places.[5]

In form, the skeletons are rather crude, looking more like playful chimpanzees than fearful osseous frames, with their wide mouths and eye-sockets being no bigger than chocolate drops. There are, however, two styles of shroud, one all-enveloping with top-knot and flowing drapery at the feet, the fabric pushed apart to exhibit the remains from upper pelvis to forehead and with the arms crossed over the breast so that the fingers touch the shoulders; the other is knotted at top and bottom with the skeleton free-standing, something achieved by sitting the top-knot on the skull and letting the rest fall freely, acting as a backdrop to the ghastly remains, with the arms dangling free and the hands outstretched.

The corpse/cadaver brasses sport shrouds of a type seen on the skeleton examples, though the presence of flesh allowed the cutter to render a more accurate portrayal of human features – often producing a successfully recognizable human being, albeit one in want of a good meal. It is in these brasses that one discovers the three different ways of positioning the arms of a corpse. The more common form shows the hands in an attitude of prayer, centre-chest height, with the fingertips touching and, occasionally, the thumbs crossed; the second position involves the crossing of the arms with fingertips at centre chest, the right arm being placed over the left and the fingers of both hands remaining closed but outstretched; finally, there is the attitude of total repose, legs slightly parted at the knees, the shoulders down and the hands placed over the groin, again with the right hand over the left and the fingers together yet unclasped.

It is extremely difficult to gauge accurately the dimensions of the shroud from these brasses, but a mean average would be twelve inches longer than the length

27 Before the Reformation, it was the custom for children who died before the age of one month to be buried in swaddling clothes.

of the body – to allow for a six-inch knot at top and bottom – and three times its width. The method of forming the top- and bottom-knots was to twist a thin strip of the shroud material into a cord. However, some scholars have maintained that it was not unusual to save a remnant of one's swaddling clothes – particularly the chrysom cloth – for this purpose.

Children do not appear on memorial brasses until the 1420s, though by the 1450s they were a regular occurrence. However, shrouded children had to wait until 1467 before being considered worthy of commemoration, and their introduction is a dramatic one on the 1467 Astley brass at Standon in Hertfordshire where ten swathed infants, four girls and six boys, are shown. Rarer still are chrysom babies. At public baptism the head of the naked infant was anointed, immediately after immersion had taken place, with the chrysom oil, a mixture of olive oil and balsam. To prevent this from running down on to the rest of the body and the swaddling clothes, the head was covered by a rectangle of linen known as the 'chrysom'; and it was the custom, should a child die before it was one month old, that this chrysom was used as the head-covering to the funerary swaddling. On memorial brasses chrysom children are depicted in this outfit, with a cross shown on the forehead. Seven examples of such chrysoms survive, one each in Buckinghamshire, Essex, Middlesex, Suffolk and Surrey, and two in Kent. The finest in the series is that at Stoke d'Abernon, Surrey, to Elyn Bray, who died in 1516 (*27*). Anointing with chrysom oil ceased with the introduction of the Second Prayer Book of Edward VI in 1552. Even so the showing of chrysom babies on brasses went on until the second quarter of the seventeenth century, the last three in the extant series being 1600, 1606 and 1631.

Figures on sepulchral monuments sporting shrouds in place of customary day dress are not so rare as those depicted on memorial brasses. Both the 1431 monument to Bishop Richard Fleming in Lincoln Cathedral and that of 1442 to Sir John Golafre at Fyfield, Buckinghamshire, are of a type known collectively as 'cadaver' tombs, in which a standard effigy clothed as in life, lies on top of the tomb-chest, with a shrouded, sometimes verminous cadaver visible through the pierced side of the tomb-chest. Those two examples, both with shrouds, are little more than three-dimensional renditions of the monumental brass type, the shrouds held in place with a top-knot, the opposite end hanging freely behind the feet.

It is not until the last quarter of the sixteenth century that the shrouded effigy appears as the central sculptural feature on funerary monuments. On the north wall of the chancel of St Mary's Church at Burford, Shropshire, stands a magnificent monument to Richard Cornwall (d.1568) with his parents. It takes the form of a painted triptych, eleven feet high, and is signed by Melchior Salabuss and dated 1588. Beneath the centre panel is a predella which, when opened, displays the corpse of Richard Cornwall in his shroud (*28*). Here we see the usual linen winding-sheet, parted to show not only the face but the entire body, with the arms placed at his side and turned in at the elbows so that the hands meet over the groin. The macabre cadaver is not the chosen depiction – rather we see a fresh corpse, almost as though we are viewing him immediately after his shrouding. At Annesley, Nottinghamshire, is a more discreetly dressed gentleman of similar date, whose loosely wrapped winding-sheet is drawn down, rather than parted, to show the facial features, shoulder-length hair and a delicately embroidered cap.

Two further monuments of the late sixteenth century with shrouded effigies can be seen at Chesterfield and Fenny Bentley, both in Derbyshire. The Chesterfield monument (*c.*1580–90), commemorating an unknown member of the Foljambe family (*29*), has the corpse loosely wrapped in an end-knotted winding-sheet and lying on a bier – the corpse does not lie flat but is slightly concave, as though suffering from a slight rigor mortis. The Fenny Bentley figures, for there are two of them, also wear winding-sheets, but here they are tucked under the feet, secured by linen bands around the calves, and finished off with a neat bow; but the head end displays the standard knot. The male figure of the pair has his arms across his chest, level with the bottom of the rib-cage, whereas the wife has her hands resting on the chest and clasped in an attitude of prayer.[6]

In 1617 the sculptor Nicholas Stone '… mad a pector lieng on a grav ston of gre marbell for Mr Corell of Hatfield for which I had £20'.[7] William Curll still lies flat on the floor of Salisbury Chapel in St Etheldreda's, Hatfield, in his loosely fitting grave-clothes. Gone now is the stylized shroud, for here we see a naturalistic figure, almost a portrait, wrapped in a very convincing linen sheet. The high-relief figure – one could hardly call it a three-dimensional effigy – is placed on a plain black ledger lying on the floor, and appears as a body rising vertically from the grave. A similar monument exists at Bassingbourne, Cambridgeshire, to Henry Buller who died in 1647.

*28 The Cornwall Triptych of 1588 by Melchior Salabuss at
Burford, Shropshire, showing Richard Cornwall (d. 1568) in
his shroud.*

When Mrs Elizabeth Williams died in childbirth in 1622 her father, Bishop Miles Smith, commissioned a magnificent monument from Samuel Baldwin to be set up in Gloucester Cathedral to her memory and that of her child. Mother and baby lie side by side: Mrs Williams, represented as wearing day-clothes, is propped up on her right elbow, staring adoringly at her deceased infant; the latter is wrapped in a fine close-fitting linen shroud, drawn up over the feet rather than under, and tied at the knees with a fairly broad linen band. As to posture, the baby's arms lie flat against its sides but with the hands meeting at the groin, similar to the Cornwall painting at Burford, Salop; its face is wreathed in a supercilious smile. To complete the ensemble, Baldwin carved a small ruffled bib and a stiff cap. The infant on the 1623 Manners tomb at Bakewell, Derbyshire *(30)*, is a less attractive creature than the Williams child, though the grave-clothes are of greater interest. The little dumpling stands to attention with its arms stiffly by its sides, as if being told off by a parent; the shroud appears to be a shift with separate head-cloth but in actuality is nothing more than the usual loosely gathered linen, parted with greater than usual emphasis to show the entire face. The tie, of twisted fabric, is placed around the ankles and the parted shroud displays a small cap with ruffling, this last soon to become one of the standard items of grave-clothing.

63

*30   A shrouded infant on the
1623 Manners tomb at Bak-
ewell, Derbyshire, shows how a
twisted length of shroud-cloth
was used to secure the ankles.*

It is rather difficult accurately to describe the idiosyncratic monument by Maximilian Colt at St Peter's, Edensor, in Derbyshire to the First Earl of Devonshire (d.1625) and his brother, Henry Cavendish (d.1616) – perhaps the closest parallel would be a marble armoire with dressing-table in front, the whole flanked by two fearsome martial figures. Beneath the table, hard up against the back of the monument, is Henry Cavendish's skeleton, executed with some precision in marble, whilst in front is a truly magnificent image of the First Earl in the latest fashion for the grave. Gone are the ties round the feet and in comes a full, loosely fitting single-piece garment, pleated at the neck but still with the top-knot; the face is completely exposed, showing the features in a peaceful attitude of repose, the limbs no longer with a stiff formality but a far more relaxed naturalism. This new fashion for dressing a corpse was to remain in vogue for the next fifty years. Yet, *à la mode* as the Earl's effigy might have been, nothing was to have such a profound effect on the sculptural representation of the shroud than that introduced by Nicholas Stone in his standing effigy of Dr John Donne for Old St Paul's Cathedral.

John Donne wrote freely on the subject of dying in his poems and of the respect he wished to have shown towards his corpse by those who dressed it and those who came to view it. He also knew what he wanted when it came to the matter of his monument. A few years before he died he posed for this effigy, placing the completed picture in his room, adjacent to his bed, as a *memento mori*. Isaac

*29   A loosely wrapped corpse on a c. 1592 monument to a
member of the Foljambe family at Chesterfield, Derbyshire. The
bier is unusual in sepulchral sculpture.*

Walton, Donne's biographer, relates the tale: 'Several charcoal fires being first madde in his large study, he brought with him into that place a winding sheet in his hand, and having put off all his clothes, had this sheet put on him, and so tied with knots at his head and feet, and his hands so placed as dead bodies are usually fitted, to be shrouded and put into their coffin, or grave ... with his eyes shut and with so much of the sheet turned aside as might show his lean, pale and death-like face.'[8] During his last agonies Donne was often to glance towards this fearsome drawing. It was eventually delivered up to Nicholas Stone shortly after Donne's death in March 1631 for transformation into stone. It is, without doubt, one of the masterpieces of English baroque sculpture, the result of an excellent collaboration between an ingenious wit and a highly important sculptor. Donne steps forward, his arms relaxing as if to balance himself during his first few faltering steps after centuries of rest in the tomb. The loose shroud impedes his progress and his feet strain in vain against the tie of the bottom knot, a highly stylized gathering, resembling more a crimped ruff (*31*).

When Amy Moyle, the wife of Josias Clarke, died in 1631 her husband decided to petrify his last memory of her by having cut a supine effigy, which showed his wife in her shroud. Her monument in Boughton Aluph church, Kent, is a majestic *tour de force* and ably illustrates early seventeenth-century female grave-clothes. The shroud is, again, a one-piece creation, sufficiently long to be draped over and under the feet, the sleeves equally full. And here we learn something new, for though the sculptor has chosen to leave the left hand exposed he gives us an indication as to how shrouds were placed once the body had been encoffined: the right sleeve has been pulled down over its hands and gently tucked under the fingers. Yet again we see the draw-string at the neck band, the ruching now turned down, as if a ruff. The head, supported on a tasselled pillow, wears a frilled cap and the winding-sheet again hangs from the head in neat folds, running the length of the body underneath. An identical monument exists at Spaxworth, Norfolk, but here we have two shrouded figures, William Peck (d.1635) and his wife, he lying behind and a little above her. Both wear shrouds of the Boughton Aluph type, though she is *sans* cap and he *sans* ruff; in both cases the winding-sheet with its discreet top-knot, acts as the cap. The Spaxworth monument is by Edward Marshall; that at Boughton Aluph is so similar that it must come from the same workshop.

The Donne monument set a fashion for 'resurrection' figures. William Wright of Charing Cross's 1634 monument to Lady Deane at Great Maplestead, Essex, has a more exaggerated movement than that of Donne, and the hands are now completely liberated from the shroud as she emerges from the black marble recess of the tomb. The top-knot is still in evidence but the bottom tie has yielded due to the 'movement' of the corpse in answering the Resurrection Trump. Less dramatic, but in a similar style of shroud, are the life-size standing figures by Joshua Marshall on the 1664 monument at Chipping Campden, Gloucestershire, to Edward Noel, Viscount Campden and his wife Juliana, whose emergence from a black niche gives added emphasis to the whiteness of the shroud and the posture of the figures. In 1674 Marshall was commissioned to erect a similar monument at East Carlton, Northamptonshire, to Sir Geoffrey and Lady Palmer (*32*). This is more romantic in concept than the Chipping Campden version. Sir

31   *A full-flowing shroud clings to the body of Dr John Donne*
(d.1632) on his magnificent effigy by Nicholas Stone in
St Paul's Cathedral, London.

32 Stepping out from the tomb on hearing the Last Trump, Sir Geoffrey and Lady Palmer wear haute couture *shrouds of the period on their 1674 monument at East Carlton, Northamptonshire.*

Geoffrey, in a fashionable high-necked flannel undershirt leads his wife by the hand out from the niche, he inquisitive and she pensive, but both with their right foot firmly forward. It is a somewhat ridiculous pose, as if they were dancing a gavotte at an exclusive pyjama party. The shrouds are shapeless, almost winding-sheets, and the creases too deliberately crisp to be taken for flannel.

More popular – because they were cheaper – than the Joshua Marshall type of resurrection monument were those produced from the yard of John and Matthias Christmas. These displayed a more immediate response to the Last Trump, with the shrouded figure depicted in the very act of rising from the coffin. Five such monuments were commissioned from the brothers between 1628 and 1651: Constance Whitney (d.1628) in St Giles, Cripplegate (destroyed during the Second World War); Mary Salter (d.1631) at Iver, Buckinghamshire; Sara Colville (d.1631) in All Saints', Chelsea; Temperance Brown (d.1635) at Steane, Northamptonshire; and Mary Calthorpe (d.1640) at East Barsham, Norfolk (*33*). A provincial rendition of the Iver, Bucks., version – and almost certainly not by the Christmas brothers – was erected at Rodney Stoke, Somerset, in 1650 to commemorate George Rodney. All wear the same type of loose shroud, a garment similar to a long nightshirt with draw-strings at the neck and wrists and a cuff deep enough to cover the hand while leaving the fingers exposed. Apart from George Rodney with his distinctive male top-knot, the head-dress of the other five appears to be nothing more than the broad folds of the linen winding-sheet.

John Tradescant Jnr and Elias Ashmole, Windsor herald, were great friends. Tradescant's father, also named John, was an ingenious gentleman gardener, the Gertrude Jekyll of the seventeenth century. He was first employed by the Cecils at Hatfield prior to his becoming arboriculturalist to George Villiers, Duke of Buckingham, and then, in 1630, 'Keeper of his Majesty's Gardens, Vines and Silkworms', being succeeded at his death in 1638 by his son, John. Both travelled widely in their search for new specimen plants and, on their sojourns, amassed an amazing collection of ethnographical curios and shells which they housed at Lambeth in a room known as 'The Ark'. These treasures came to Elias Ashmole in 1678 on the death of Hester, Tradescant Jnr's widow, and eventually formed the nucleus of the Ashmolean Museum, Oxford. Amongst the curiosities was a series of Tradescant portraits, which were hung on the gallery walls. One of these, by an anonymous artist, shows John Tradescant Snr on his death-bed in 1638 (*34*). The pose of the corpse recalls that of Thomas Aston's wife in the celebrated portrait of 1635 by John Souch of Chester (*Col. 4*) and, in a more romantic vein, that of 1633 by van Dyck of Lady Venetia Stanley on her death-bed.[9] Of the three, that showing John Tradescant is the finest, for neither corpse in the other two paintings is shown in shrouds, both women having been painted as if at the moment of death rather than after the laying-out. By contrast, we see Tradescant lying on his newly sheeted bed, washed and with beard neatly trimmed, wearing a superfine linen shroud of the highest quality, the top-knot having now become nothing more than a small tassel attached to the linen itself. It is, arguably, the finest pictorial representation of a seventeenth-century winding-sheet.[10]

In one the vestibules of the rebuilt church of St John, Egham, is a reset monument of 1638 by Maximilian Colt to Sir John Denham. Far more dramatic

33 *The shroud shown on Mrs Calthorpe's 1640 monument at East Barsham, Norfolk, was repeated elsewhere on five similar monuments by the sculptor brothers John and Matthias Christmas.*

than his 1625 Cavendish monument at Edensor, here he has Denham resembling a semi-nude Donne, for the top-knotted winding-sheet has lost its pins and slipped off the body as his reinvigorated corpse steps out of a coffin, his left hand raised as if to shield his eyes from the brillance of the Second Coming.

The particular feeling of revulsion held by certain members of the aristocracy against poor and lowly corpse-dressers gazing on their naked cadavers is more associated with embalming than shrouding. However, Dame Margaret Verney of Claydon gave quite specific instructions in her will, drafted on 2 May 1639 and addressed to her son, Ralph.

Let me be buried in lead at Claydon next to where your father proposes to lie himself, and let no stranger wind me, nor do not let me be stripped, but put a clean smock on me, and let my face be hid and do you stay in the room and see me wound and laid in the first coffin, which must be of wood if I do not die of any infectious disease, else I am so far from desiring it that I forbid you to come near me.[11]

So far we have been looking at the type of grave-clothes provided for the very wealthy. But what about the poor and the lower middle class? *Haute couture* in the tomb did not really preoccupy the majority of the populace and, in the fifteenth and sixteenth centuries, the system of requisitioning a single linen sheet from the household supply seemed to be the norm. In instances where the corpse was to travel to the grave in just a winding-sheet, either palled on the bier or via the parish coffin, one does wonder whether there was an unwritten code that the sheet chosen be one of the best from the linen cupboard, or if the sheet upon which the person died sufficed. Whatever the case, the sheet would have been wrapped around the body in the customary fashion with top- and bottom-knots. Occasionally linen, holland or cerecloth would have been specially bought in for this purpose rather than sacrificing a useful item of domestic furnishing in an age when linen of any appreciable width was a luxury and worthy of bequest ('There are 4 very fine smocks in your father's little linen trunk and one of my four breadth Holland sheets for your own girl Peg ... and I desire your father that he will not let any of my household linen be sold, but that it may go to you and your eldest son and I hope to his son too, only some of my broderies

34   John Tradescant's (d. 1638) one-piece winding-sheet ends with corner tassels, shown here wrapped round the neck and draped across the shoulders.

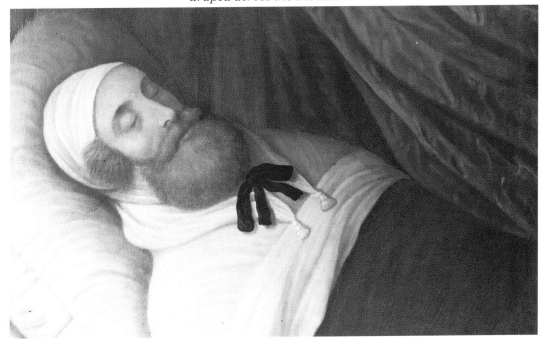

of my own making give to your sister.'[12]). This cloth could be had off the baulk in length by the ell, a measurement approximating forty-four inches, with four and a half ells considered sufficient for the purpose. Certainly it was possible to purchase shrouds ready-made by, at the latest, the second quarter of the seventeenth century, and Gittings makes mention of the body of Reginald Shrawley, a brother of the Hospital of St John, Canterbury, being buried in 'a sheet, shirt and cap', costing, in all, four shillings.[13]

The precise choice of material was important, a status symbol almost. Linen, when new, had a certain quantity of starch applied, thereby making it slightly stiff whilst remaining pliable; wrapped in such material a body would be given a neat, crisp appearance and presentable for viewing, the shroud being drawn away from the features for this purpose. Holland was an unbleached linen with a glazed surface and, though slightly less attractive to the eye than bleached linen, had the same properties, with the addition of being water-resistant, an important matter to be taken into account when dead bodies were concerned. Cerecloth, a waxed unbleached linen – nowadays only seen as the protective sheet between the top of an altar and the fair linen – was rarely used for shrouds and is more associated with the wrapping of embalmed corpses, having been used as an adjunct to such hygienic treatment.

The laying-out and washing of a corpse, the 'dressing and trimming' as it was known, might have been performed by a member of the family, though by the early seventeenth century it was more usual, both in town and country, for this service to be provided by the coffin-maker. He would tend to have a number of lowly women on his books living in the locality whom he could call upon at short notice to attend – the Mrs Gamps of this world. Once washed, the body was dressed in a shirt, cap and winding-sheet if male, or shift, ruffle-edged cap and winding-sheet if female, with the type of material and its finish dependent on the social standing of the deceased, the snobbery of the purchaser or the depth of the purse. Chin-cloths were usually removed before the fitting of the headgear, the tapes of the latter producing the same effect. Occasionally the women dressing the corpse might introduce sprigs of sweet-smelling herbs, such as rosemary, bay or thyme, in between the inner garments and the winding-sheet. This helped to mask the odour of death if the corpse was to stay in the home, especially during the warmer summer months. This appears not to have happened in the case of Samuel Pepys's uncle; writing in his diary for 6 July 1661, he related the incident of 'My uncle's corpse in a coffin standing upon joint stools in the chimney in the hall; but it began to smell so I caused it to be set forth in the yard all night, and watched by my aunt.'[14] Poor aunt!

It was rare for corpses to be committed to the grave wearing day-clothes, items of personal jewellery or any other keepsake. However, fourteenth-century people were sometimes buried with a purchased Indulgence,[15] and there is at the Ashmolean Museum, Oxford,[16] a small latten figure, not much more than four inches high, of a man in a winding-sheet (*35*) which might have been enclosed within the folds of the shroud, in the same way that stamped leaden crosses were used up to the seventeenth century, to foil Satan's attempts to claim the deceased's soul as his own; the date of manufacture of the Ashmolean item is indeterminate, but it seems doubtful that such an item would have been

*35   This small figure in a winding-
sheet was probably inserted
amongst the folds of a shroud to
foil Satan's attempts to steal
the deceased's soul.*

produced much after *c.*1550. Recent vault clearances of over 2,000 coffins of the period 1729-1865 from St Marylebone Parish Church[17] and Christchurch, Spitalfields,[18] exhibit a change in attitude; for here, whilst it was not unusual to find wedding rings and dentures *in situ*, there were two instances – both men – of day-clothes having been used in place of the shroud: one in military uniform, the other an octogenerian *macaroni* with his walking stick, sporting an outfit more suited to a man sixty years his junior, as did the coiffure of his wig.

How long these shrouded corpses lay above ground depended on a number of factors: whether or not an autopsy was required, the undertaker's schedule, the availability of a grave-digger – or the parish coffin if it was needed – the wishes of the family or any specific instruction left by the deceased. Judging from entries made in burial registers it appears that three days was the average length of delay. Misson agrees:

> The Body being thus equipp'd and laid in the Coffin (which Coffin is sometimes very magnificent), it is visited a second time to see that it is bury'd in Flannel, and that nothing about it sowed with Thread. They let it lye three or four days in this Condition; which Time they allowe, as well to give the dead Person an Opportunity of Coming to Life again, if his Soul has not quite left his Body, as to prepare Mourning, and the Ceremonies of the Funerall.[19]

Dezallier-D'Argenville slightly reduces the delay: 'Among the common people it is customary to stay at home for two or three days after death, and to keep the body in a room where friends and relatives are invited to come and see it.'[20]

The year 1660 saw a major revolution in grave-clothes, indirectly leading to the firm establishment of undertaking as a distinct trade, the birth of a new industry and some additional work for the jobbing printer; for in this year an Act came into force, which decreed that all persons had to be buried in shifts, shrouds and winding-sheets made of woollen material, rather than linen, and free from 'Flax, Hemp, Silk, Hair, Gold or Silver, or other than what is made of Sheeps Wooll only'. As it happened, not everyone was willing to kowtow to this woolly Act, so it had to be strengthened in 1678 by another, this time imposing a fine on all defaulters. In addition, this 1678 Act 'for lessening the importation of Linnen from beyond the Seas, and the encouragement of the Woollen and Paper Manufacturers of the Kingdome' further instructed that the curate of every parish keep a register, provided at the expense of the parish, into which had to be entered all burials together with the affidavits taken by the justice of the peace, mayor, 'or such like chief officer' in the parish or, 'if there be no officer, then by any curate within the county where the corpse was buried (except him in whose parish the corpse was buried), who must administer the oath, and set his hand gratis'. Compliance sometimes led to delay in burial, though there was a waiver for anyone dying of the plague. The penalty for not complying with these terms was £5, of which half towards the relief of the poor of the parish. It was a highly unpopular Act; nevertheless it remained on the statute books until 1815.[21]

For the wealthy, the Act for Burying in Woollen imposed but another expense, as £5 was but a small price to pay so as not to be buried in a material proscribed for even the lowliest rustic. John Aubrey records how Thomas Hobbes, the philosopher, was 'put into a Woollen shroud' at his death in 1679, arguing that had Hobbes received the £100 per annum pension granted by Charles II in 1660 – 'At the Restoration, Charles II awarded him a pension of £100 a year – which, however, His Majesty forgot to pay'[22] – then he might not have been buried in such a common shift. Some even went so far as to stipulate the use of linen in their will: Hannah Deane of High Ongar, Essex, took account of the £5 fine when drawing up her instructions in 1784: 'And I do hereby Order and direct that sum of Ten pound shall be paid to the person who shall … see me Inclosed and laid in my Coffin in Linen and shall give Information and make Oath thereof wheereby the Poor of the parish Will be intitled to the sum of fifty shilling …'[23] However, it was an ill wind and some did profit by it, namely the undertakers. If everyone was now to be buried in flannel then what profit could be gained in having ready-made shrouds in stock in a multitude of patterns and sizes and available on demand! Consequently, specialist workshops sprung up, supplying not only off-the-peg shrouds but also coffin linings and other associated items of soft goods. How much of a threat this posed to those drapers who themselves furnished funerals is not recorded, but as none appear to have taken legal action, it can only be assumed that they too had dealings with these manufacturers whilst continuing to offer a funeral service to the general public. The other set of tradesmen to benefit from the Act were the jobbing printers, for it was they – rather than an alternative central source – who provided the blank affidavits. Whilst most of these were quite plain, others had woodblock illustrations of skulls, skeletons, death's heads, crossed bones, spades, hour-glasses, winged cherub heads, shrouded corpses – in flannel, of course – and coffins. There was no set text for the wording, it being left to the printer to ensure that what was asked for complied with the Act.

The acquisition of grave-clothes did not need to wait until death, and many a young bride-to-be, especially in the more remote country areas, included such items in their trousseaus, either buying them ready-made from one of the known outlets, or having them made by a local seamstress, or producing them herself.[24] It was a dismal yet necessary task, and whilst one can imagine a young woman's producing such items for herself and her future husband, it is more difficult for us to accept that she probably also fashioned one or two smaller versions at the same time, for infant mortality was high.

The tradition continued throughout the nineteenth century and well into the twentieth. Alice Shelley (d.1960) and Minnie Shelley (d.1966), two nonagenerian sisters of Cheshunt, Hertfordshire, were buried in shrouds which they had themselves made.[25]

The most moving renditions of late seventeenth-century children's shrouds appear in two works executed by artists in memory of their own infants. The miniaturist John Hoskins the Younger married Grace Beaumont in February 1669/70 and their first child, a boy, was born in 1670/71. He died soon afterwards and Samuel Cooper executed a chalk drawing of the boy on his death-bed (*36*). The bed has been laid with fresh linen, cold and white. The shroud is a one-piece shift with a broad, slightly ruched yoke and, in place of draw-strings, black ribbons have been tied about the wrist over the sleeve; a further black bow has been attached to the neck of the garment. The body has slipped slightly down into the bed, rucking the shroud at the waist and behind the right shoulder. This type of shift was slit

36   Master Hopkins (d. 1670/71) by Samuel Cooper. The infant wears an ensemble of high-quality grave-clothes, the wrist-ties of black ribbon rather than draw-strings.

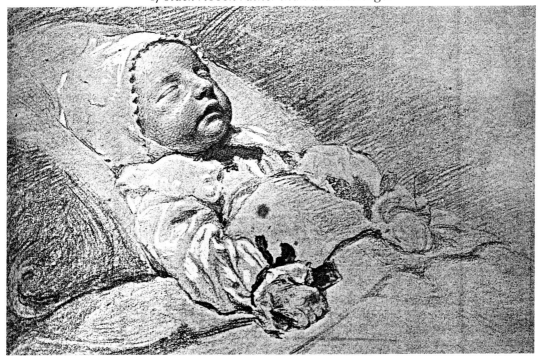

down the back for ease of application and secured with back-tie draw-strings at the neck and waist; such items were, it is assumed, readily available from the undertaker. To complete the ensemble there is a loose-fitting bonnet with pinked edging and a broad white tie-tape. It is a highly accomplished drawing, full of pathos and the grief of the artist.[26]

Lydia Dwight, the daughter of the Fulham potter John Dwight, died in 1674 when she was five years old. Her father, as anxious as Hoskins to possess a memento of the child, executed two stoneware portraits, one a figurine of a small bare-footed child in a loose calf-length shift walking towards the New Horizon, the other a naturalistic representation of the little girl dressed for her coffin (*Col. 5*). Lydia lies more comfortably than baby Hoskins, the angle of the corpse *vis-à-vis* the pillow being less exaggerated. A detailed examination of the linen, the small pillow with its corner tassels and *broderie anglaise* hem and the wrap-over sheet with similar trimmings, appear not to be bedclothes but an exceptionally superior coffin suite. Primarily the body has been dressed in a blouse with long sleeves and tightly buttoned cuffs; over this is a simple shift with integral hood, drawn back to show the features. Beneath the hood Lydia sports a close-fitting cap with broad head-bean of *broderie anglaise* with similar tie-tapes. On encoffining, the hood would be unfolded and drawn over the face, the top sheet turned up and tucked in around the neck, if not higher. Her hands are clasped in the traditional manner, at centre chest with right hand over left, the index finger of the left hand placed between the index finger and thumb of the right, and clasping a bunch of small summer flowers. Her natural expression removes some of the horror of death and, with her floral tribute, looks more like Little Red Riding Hood asleep under the tree;[27] the same cannot be said for the Hoskins child.

One of the more interesting adjuncts to the Act for Burying in Woollen was the introduction of the funeral ticket – whether first suggested by the jobbing printers or a particularly ingenious coffin-maker is not known. The majority of the early tickets, those produced during the last four decades of the seventeenth century, incorporated imagery similar to that found on the printed affidavits (*37*). These tickets were produced *en masse*, though certain coffin-makers and funeral furnishers are known to have commissioned their own designs, with a central cartouche for the printed or hand-written details announcing the name of the deceased and the place, date and time of the funeral. Alternatively, they could be had ready-printed with blanks in the text for completion by the funeral furnisher. Whatever the method chosen, these invitations were issued only for the more important – i.e. expensive – funerals; those of lesser rank had to rely on word of mouth.

By around 1700 grave-clothes changed, probably as a result of the influence of the soft-goods trade in ready-made items, and adopted a form which was to last for the next seventy-five years. The winding-sheet with its top- and bottom-knots had been in steady decline during the last quarter of the seventeenth century, its place being taken by the open-backed long-sleeved shift with draw-strings at wrist and neck, either with or without an integral hood. The cap and bonnet had been a feature of grave-clothes since the 1630s, the under-shirt having been introduced at the same time. However, with the coming of the off-the-peg shroud there was a designer influence coming into force, which resulted in a less

Ou are Defired to Accompany
the Body of Deputy *Lenthall*,
from *Turners* Hall
London, unto the Parifh Church
of St. *Mary Aɗ-Hill*, upon *Wednefday* the
Third day of *September* inftant, at Four of
the Clock in the Afternoon, and to bring
this Tickett with you, Dated the *firft*
day of *September*, Anno Dom. 1679.

37   Two shrouded figures in single-break coffins and a corpse
in a winding-sheet decorate the border of this livery company
funeral ticket of 1679.

voluminous garment with tacked ruching, or gathered pleats, running the length
of the garment, with or without appliqué horizontal bows. For the time being the
knot at the foot end remained. Types of this shroud can be seen on the *c.*1700
trade card of William Grinley and to better effect on the *c.*1720 trade card of
coffin-maker Eleazar Malory (*38*), the latter showing an extremely contented
corpse modelling one of Malory's own creations.

The 1690s saw the end of the formal representation of the shroud in funerary
sculpture with the commissioning in 1694 of the Catesby monument at Whiston,
Northamptonshire. Erected in 1700 it takes the form of two busts on a wide
plinth, flanked by Ionic columns and surmount by a pediment. Thomas Catesby
wears semi-formal day-clothes with a full wig; however, Mrs Catesby sports a
daring shift – loose, and rather too low-cut for decency in the tomb – and an *à la
mode* one-piece shroud with attached top-knotted hood. With eyes open and face
smiling she appears to be unaware of the grave-clothes; it is as if the sculptor
added them against orders, his way of telling the viewer that this attractive lady
was now dead. It is difficult to judge the material of the shroud from its marble
representation, for sculpture does not lend itself easily to such subtleties.

77

ELeazar Malory Joiner at the Coffin in White Chapel. near Red Lion Street end, maketh Coffins, Shrouds. letteth Palls, Cloaks and Furnisheth with all other things neceffary for funerals, at Reasonable Rates, Also Appraiseth and Buyeth all forts of Houshold Goods

38 An early example of the 'night-dress' type of shroud, with vertical ruching and ribbon wrist-ties, appears on a c. 1720 trade card of Eleazar Malory.

However, the thin cut of the marble shift here contrasts with the slightly thicker gauge of the shroud; is the sculptor thus implying that the shift is of linen and the shroud of flannel?

During the seventeenth and early eighteenth centuries the skeleton was a recurring motif in funerary art, appearing not only on trade cards and invitations but also on monuments; its symbolism was profound. When Lady Diana Warburton died in March 1693–94, her executors commissioned a large standing monument for St John's church, Chester, from the sculptor Edward Pierce, the symbolism of which leaving no one in doubt of its meaning. The central figure is a naturalistic marble skeleton holding open a winding-sheet to welcome Lady Warburton. It is a *tour de force*; for the sculptor, who died shortly after its erection,[28] it was to be his last monument.

Two animated skeletons appear on an unusual wall monument of *c*.1710 by Francis Bird to Mrs Elizabeth Benson in St Leonard's, Shoreditch. Having completed the fixing of a winding-sheet to a young oak, they proceed to tear the tree in two – an attempt to destroy the Tree of Life. Less dramatic is Thomas Stayner's 1714 monument to Dr Thomas Turner at Stowe-Nine-Churches, Northamptonshire; large and grand, the inscription appears on an outstretched winding-sheet beneath a central *baldacchino* (or canopy).

Very little was published on coffins and coffin-making before the beginning of this century. However, a detailed examination in the early 1980s of nearly 1,000 coffins of the period 1730-1860 in the vaults of Christchurch, Spitalfields, revealed a wealth of information previously unrecorded. It was noticed that some undertakers dispensed with full-length shrouds, preferring to adapt the coffin lining to serve this purpose. Once the coffin had received its primary lining and edged frill, two rectangular sheets – both the length and width of the coffin – were tacked to the base at its sides. Once the body had been placed in the coffin and the fitted pillow positioned under the head, these 'sheets' were folded over the remains and either pinned together or roughly sewn into place. The upper section of the sheet was left parted to expose the features to view and remained so until the time came to secure the lid. In this way the body was put into the coffin wearing just a shift and bonnet. It was not only a neat way to 'finish' the interior but also gave the dressed corpse the appearance of being in a bed. This would have been more expensive than the winding-sheet but it presented the body in a more natural attitude of repose. Mrs Strutt, the wife of the pioneer mill-owner Jedidiah Strutt, was encoffined in this way, in 'a Suit of Superfine Crape consisting of a Shroud Sheets Cap & Pillow ... £2 2s 0d'.[29]

By the 1770s the winding-sheet had almost disappeared, to be replaced by coffin sheets. The plain or flounced shroud with cap or bonnet became the standard mode of dress for the tomb, with the optional extras of mittens, stockings and, occasionally, slippers. One coffin of the 1780s, examined at Spitalfields, had the remains dressed in gown, chin cloth, cap, mittens, stockings and slippers in addition to fitted side-sheets. In the provinces it took a little time before London fashions were adopted. When Thomas Spackman entered into negotiations with the sculptor John Deval in 1782 regarding his monument for Cliffe Pypard church, Wiltshire, he reverted to a style fashionable in the late seventeenth century: the 'resurrection' model as erected by Joshua Marshall in

1664 at Chipping Campden, Gloucestershire, and that of 1674 to Sir Geoffrey and Lady Palmer at East Carlton, Northamptonshire. Spackman is seen walking out of a black niche, his right leg forward, and the right hand holding the winding-sheet against the outer thigh; underneath he wears an open shirt with broad cuffs from which the draw-strings have been released. Unfortunately we do not know what his chosen undertaker, John Rogers, of Great Tittlefield Street, Oxford Market, London, provided in the way of grave-clothing on Spackman's death in 1786.

But why go to the expense of elaborate shrouds and superfine linen coffin linings; why not just put the naked body into the coffin and have done with it? Dezallier-D'Argenville provides us with the answer: 'Among the common people it is customary to stay at home for two or three days after death, and to keep the body in a room where friends and relatives are invited to come and see it.'[30] No coffin-maker or funeral furnisher worthy of his reputation would have failed to dress a corpse, no matter how lowly his subject might have been. Funeral furnishing was a trade in which the outward and visible signs of his merchandise helped to advertise his craft. It was important, bearing in mind private viewing, that bodies should be not only as wholesome as possible but also as well dressed; and dressed not only in a material according to social status but also in as well upholstered a coffin as funds would permit. Agreed, there was little he could do to

*39   White brushed cotton shroud of the late nineteenth century.
These were unisex, and were provided for children
as well as adults.*

'sweeten' the corpse, but so much depended on how the body was 'dress'd and trimm'd'; few people would be willing to patronize a funeral furnisher who took little care over the presentation of bodies. The women weeping over an open coffin in a Rowlandson drawing of *c.*1760 would have had more reason for grief had the merchandise not come up to their expectations (*Col. 6*).

One particular difficulty experienced by the trade with the single-piece gown related to the positioning of the limbs. The enveloping shroud covered a multitude of sins but, now that the corpse was exposed, greater attention had to be paid to posture. One way of doing this was to tie the ankles together and to pinion the arms against the side of the corpse with the waist-band of the shroud. This was in evidence at Spitalfields and again during Dr Owen Beattie's 1981–6 examination of three seamen from the Franklin Arctic expedition of 1845–8, particularly the corpse of John Torrington (d.1846) which had ties at the elbows, wrist, ankles and big toes.

The majority of eighteenth- and early nineteenth-century grave-clothes were still manufactured in Lancashire and London but by the 1830s more were coming from the Lancashire area. With the repeal of the Act for Burial in Woollen the market was open to a variety of textiles: alpaca, calico, cambric, cashmere, etamine, flannel, holland, linen, muslin, poplin, satin, serge and silk being used for shrouds and winding-sheets; and calico, cambric, flannel, linen, silk and swansdown for linings.

By the end of the eighteenth century ready-made coffins were being supplied lined by the manufacturers but one had to purchase shrouds and winding-sheets separately. From a trade catalogue issued by Turner of Farringdon in 1838[31] omes the following list of prices:

SHROUDS

Feet	Inches	Common Quality		Middle Quality		Fine Rose		Sup. Rose fully trimmed	
		s.	d.	s.	d.	s.	d.	s.	d.
6	0	2	8	3	8	4	9	6	3

WINDING-SHEETS

Feet	Inches	Common		Fine		Superfine	
		s.	d.	s.	d.	s.	d.
6	0	4	0	6	0	9	0

In all, Turner stocked twenty lengths of shroud, from twenty inches to six feet 3 inches and nineteen lengths of winding-sheet, from twenty-two inches to six feet 3 inches. Both the 'Fine Rose' and the 'Superior Rose fully trimmed' would have been provided with buttoned rosettes, similar to those shown on a late nineteenth-century shroud in the Castle Museum, York (*39*).

For those who wished to make their own coffin clothes the 1838 *Workwoman's Guide* came to the rescue:

> A SHROUD, is composed of a peculiar kind of flannel, woven on purpose, and called shrouding flannel; it is made of a breadth and a half, full length, so as to cover the feet; one seam is sewed up, leaving the other open behind, like a pinafore; slits are cut for arm-holes, and plain long sleeves, without gussets set in; the front is gathered at the waist, and drawn up into a narrow piece; this is twice repeated, at intervals of three nails down the skirt, upon each of these gatherings, round the neck and at the wrists, a kind of border of the same flannel, punched at the edge in a pattern, is plaited, and an edging of the same is made at the bottom. For men, the shroud is made exactly the same as the above for women, excepting that there is no gathering in the front.

There were also instructions relating to the head-gear: 'CAP. If the usual cap is not put on, the following is made for a man: it is of flannel, cut exactly like an infant's foundling cap. A quilling of the punched flannel is put round the face, and a band of it laid on behind, and across the top of the head, strings of the same, are also sewed in. CAP FOR A WOMAN. This is of flannel: the round part is plaited up to form the front, and a quilling of the bordering put on, a band of the same laid on at the back, and strings.'[32]

Post-mortem photographic portraiture is extremely rare but in the churchyard at St John's, Bedwardine, Worcestershire, is a small monument by James Forsyth incorporating a positive collodion on glass of John Garmston Hopkins, the son of Thomas Hopkins, hop merchant. John Garmston Hopkins died at Belmont House, Worcester, on 22 January 1871 and his father commissioned Francis Charles Earl of Worcester Broad Street to immortalize the lad in a photograph destined for the churchyard memorial. The finished product was

40 *John Garmston Hopkins (d. 1871) wears a cashmere shroud in this portrait by F.C. Earl of Worcester.*

large, 6 by 13¾ inches, and shows a young man on a draped sofa, his head resting on a pillow. He wears a one-piece cashmere shroud tied at the waist with a twisted silken cord and with rosettes on either side of the turned-down collar. It is an interesting garment which, with its long sleeves, has the flavour more of a monastic habit than a shroud. The arms are placed across the breast, with the hands directed towards the opposite shoulder, a pose not met with in funerary sculpture. Although he was obviously placed carefully on to the sofa, the freshly pomaded hair is awry and could have benefited from a comb prior to being photographed. It is a terrible image; the child is so patently dead and cold. Yet perhaps Thomas Hopkins and his wife took some solace in so commemorating the death of their eldest son (40).[33]

By the close of the nineteenth century the major centre for the manufacture of shrouds had shifted from London to Lancashire, the supplier selling either to the wholesale warehouses or direct to the funeral furnisher. The shroud was beginning to adopt a couture of its own, with distinct styles for boys and girls, men and women; those for males were *sans* bows whilst the female styles had less panel ruching on the torso and a high-neck frill. Stiffer materials such as swansdown and cashmere were replacing silk, whilst flannel and stiffened cotton remained the more popular lines. There was a greater choice in colour and one could now acquire a purple cashmere for one's wife or a navy serge for a deceased child. For the funeral furnisher and the hospital there was a very simple 'manchestered' cotton gown, suitable for laying-out purposes but perhaps too plain for encoffining. There has been little development in style since the 1920s though the range of materials has increased. The present-day funeral director has more choice now than ever before. However, a glance at a catalogue issued in the 1920s (41)[34] illustrates how little the designs have changed over the last seventy years.

No. 2186.

No. 2051.

No. 2222½.

No. 1704.

No. 2181.

No. 200 R

No. 1057 T.
All Sizes.

No. A 231.   Cashmere.

No. X 03.
All Sizes.

41   Shrouds of the early twentieth century bore a close relation to baby clothes. These examples from Dottridge's 1922 catalogue, were backless though with full sleeves.

Lapped in Lead, Encased in Oak: The Coffin

W. PICKARD,
UNDERTAKER, CABINET MAKER, UPHOLSTERER, PAPER HANGER, &C.,
MARKET PLACE, LICHFIELD
Sole AGENT FOR THE
New Patent AIR-TIGHT METALLIC COFFINS,

Answering the purpose of shell, lead, and outside coffin, at less than half the usual cost. An inspection of the Models and the Testimonials of the most eminent of the Medical Profession of the country cannot fail to produce a decided conviction in their superiority. The following are the Testimonials of the Medical Gentlemen of Lichfield. 'Various reasons enable me to form a high estimate of the benefits to be derived from the use of the Air-Tight Metallic Coffins, in all cases of interment. They are cheaper than wooden coffins, lighter than coffins of lead, and as safe as the most expensive contrivance.'

JAMES RAWSON, M.D., &c.

'We consider the Metallic Coffins superior to any we have seen, in a sanitary point of view.'

M.B. MORGAN.
HERBERT M. MORGAN.
C.E.E. WELCHMAN.
W.F. SPOFFORTH.
HALFORD W. HEWITT.
A.C. MORGAN.

85

The foregoing announcement appeared in an 1865 issue of the *Lichfield Advertiser*. Doubtless Mr Pickard was pleased to have the support of the medical men of the town – a great fillip to his trade – though it is questionable whether he would have received like acclamation from the superintendent of Lichfield Cemetery, for iron coffins, as well as lead shells, took a long time to break down if deposited in the soil. The vestry of the City church of St Peter-le-Poore, Broad Street, also had this in mind and, as a result, officials were charging an additional £50 in 1838 for iron coffins deposited in their vaults over and above the standard fee of £1 15s. 2d. as against the extra £20 asked for a lead shell – with all fees double for non-parishioners. A single-shell wooden coffin disintegrated in a shorter time, thereby releasing space within the soil for further deposits, to the financial advantage of the incumbent. Equally, St Paul's, Shadwell, was at the same time looking for a £6 fee for each iron or lead coffin deposited within a brick-lined grave in the churchyard, though their most expensive intramural location commanded a charge of only £4 18s. Convincing as Pickard's advertisement might appear, iron coffins did not capture the imagination of the trade nor that of the populace, being one of the least successful funerary innovations of the nineteenth century. Francis Seymour Haden's 'earth to earth' wicker basket, Dottridge Brothers' lacquered papier-mâché 'earth to earth' coffin, the metallic shell with glass face panel and gutta-percha seal – so convenient for viewing the remains of the repatriated – and the shallow cremation coffin with its combustible metal fittings and recessed lid (tailored to fit Gorini's furnaces at St John's, Woking) were four of the better-known alternatives available at the end of the nineteenth century to those interested in the sanitary disposal of the dead. To the majority, the corpse was putrefying matter which formerly housed the soul and spirit; others were less realistic, seeing in it instead a human being in suspended animation, in a profound sleep beyond our ken, awaiting a miraculous awakening. Whilst most recognized the coffin as a means of transporting the dead to an authorized place of disposal, some viewed it as a receptacle for a precious relic – so precious that the very thought of earth or elements contributing to its destruction should be avoided at all cost.

The coffin was – and, to some extent, still is – a status symbol, its finish and furniture indicative of the social standing of the deceased. No fifteenth-century peasant or artisan expected to be buried in a coffin; by contrast no noble would have been subjected to shroud burial in the churchyard. The introduction of the reusable parish coffin in the sixteenth century signalled a marked improvement in the decoration on coffins supplied for the nobility and gentry: in this way the class differential persisted well after death. The contributing factor to the abandonment of the parish coffin in the seventeenth century was not the new and innovative trade of funeral furnishing – though that did have a profound effect on coffin types – but pestilence and the plague. By the eighteenth century the trade had the total monopoly on the provision of coffins.

In 1668 the dramatist Sir William Davenant died. 'I went to his funerall. He had a coffin of Walnutt-tree; Sir John Denham said 'twas the finest coffin that ever he sawe![1] O rare coffin! The funeral trade furnished funerals in accordance with the rank of the deceased, and it was they who decided on the suitable coffin type, quality of lining and shroud. Sometimes, though certainly not as a general rule, the family had some influence on what was provided. As walnut was both an exceedingly expensive and difficult wood to work, few if any coffin-makers would have kept it in stock or have possessed the expertise to fashion it. On balance it seems reasonable to assume that this coffin was supplied by one of the established London cabinet-makers with a small funeral furnishing interest. But who selected walnut as the medium to be used? Almost certainly it would have been the executors, after consultation with the family, as not even a cabinet-maker used to the undertaking trade would have been so bold as to have proceeded with such an elaborate item without having first enquired of the executors.

Some people, but only a very few, endeavoured to thwart the lucrative customs of the funeral furnisher by specifically requesting a coffin of a type not expected of their situation. Sarah Hare, the youngest daughter of Sir Thomas and Lady Elizabeth Hare of Stow Bardolph, Norfolk, was very specific regarding the simplicity of her grave-clothes and coffin, making her wishes abundantly clear in her will of 1743: '... my coffin to be made of the best Elm lin'd with a thinn lead with a flap of lead sawder'd down over me, not to have a nail or any ornament that is not absolutely necessary, except a plate with my coat of arms and with this inscription: They that humble themselves shall be Exalted.'[2]

Whilst Sarah Hare left a perfect template for a gentlewoman's funeral, Hannah Deane of High Ongar, Essex, went even further when it came to the specification for her coffin. Indeed it would be more to the point had her will of 1784 been retitled 'Funeral Instructions' as most of its wording relates specifically to the funeral.

> ... And my Will is that William Moore (Carpenter if living) shall make my Coffin and that the same shall be covered with Black Cloth and nailed with White Nails and to be of the value of Five Pounds or thereabouts. But in case he shall die in my Lifetime then I desire that my Coffin be made by his Son in like manner as his Father was to have made the same for which I Will he shall be paid the Sum of Ten Pounds and that in such Case the said Legacy of Ten Pounds so given to his father shall cease and not be paid. And my Will is to be Buried in Linen in a Suit which I shall provide for that purpose And I do hereby order and direct that the Sum of Ten Pounds shall be paid to the person who shall be the last in attending me to the time of my expiring and who shall see me Inclosed and laid in my Coffin in Linen.[3]

This eighteenth-century fascination with funerary exactitude was not limited to the distaff side of society. Nathaniel Houlton, a widower living in Bristol, itemized the details of his coffin in a will drafted on 26 May 1767: 'First, It is my Will and Desire (if it can be done without being Offensive) to have my Body kept for the space of One Week at the Least after my Demise, before my Coffin (which I direct shall have a Double or false Lid, as my late Wife's had), be closed up; ... My Coffin I direct to be made by Mr Daniel Millard Carpenter or his partner, of the same Thickness and sort in every Respect as my said late Wife's.'[4]

Bodies wrapped in blankets, linen burial suits, a coffin of the best elm lined with lead, one covered with black cloth and decorated with white nails – indicative of a spinster – and another with a double or false lid. Were they more exacting in the eighteenth century than at any other time? Was this the only way whereby one could exert control over an over-zealous undertaker? Moreover, were things quite so dreadful that such control needed to be exerted? For the answer to these and many other questions we have to look in detail at the items giving rise to so much concern.

Until the appearance in the late eighteenth century of catalogues and pattern books on the types of coffin, linings and coffin furniture provided for the lower-class funeral, the details relating to the upper and middle classes of society have to be gleaned from undertakers' trade cards, eyewitness accounts of funerals and through specific instructions imparted via wills. Much additional information can, however, be learnt from sepulchral sculpture, prints and drawings, paintings and *memento mori* jewellery. Of all the hundreds of trade pattern books issued by manufacturers during the eighteenth and nineteenth centuries it appears that not more than ten survive in public collections, and only one pre-Victorian priced catalogue relating to coffins and lining materials. The majority of information on coffin types comes as a result of the recent introduction of funerary studies in archaeology and vault examinations – much from work carried out in the 1980s at such places as Christchurch, Spitalfields, at Hinton St George, Somerset, and Withyham, Sussex – where opportunities arose to study at first hand coffins dating from the sixteenth century to the present day.

Neither of the two Prayer Books of Edward VI, nor those of Elizabeth I and Charles II, make any reference to coffins. The rubrics in the 1662 Order for the Burial of the Dead only make mention of the 'corpse' or 'body': 'The Priest and Clerks, meeting the Corpse at the entrance of the Church-yard ...'; 'When they come to the Grave, while the Corpse is made ready to be laid into the earth ...'; and 'Then, while the earth shall be cast upon the Body by some standing by ...'. It was enough for the Church that a corpse had been presented for burial. Shrouds and winding-sheets were provided for convenience rather than necessity and, to some extent, to conform to common standards of decency. The private coffin, on the other hand, was an item indicative of status, a luxury unobtainable for the majority and, until the mid sixteenth century, its use in England was limited. However, whilst it should be understood that coffins were generally associated with those whose bodies were destined for intramural burial, it should also be noted that recent archaeology has revealed instances of pre-sixteenth-century encoffined burials in churchyards and intramural shroud burial.[5] This chapter, however, will be looking at coffins and coffin-making from *c*.1450 to *c*.1900.

Coffins and corpses are meant to biodegrade, the acidic content of one assisting the decomposition of the other; they are destined for burial or deposit, hidden away from the eyes of mortal man, and there it is hoped they will remain. Consequently, very little has survived and, apart from a late fourteenth-century rectangular oak coffin in the St Peter Hungate Church Museum at Norwich (*42*), and a *c*.1500 ossuary chest in Winchester Cathedral (*Col. 7*), excavated in 1958 from the site of the Carmelite Friary at Cowgate, Norwich, we have to turn our attention to illuminated manuscripts of the period to see what was provided at the close of the Middle Ages.

Shortly before his 1430 coronation in Paris as King of France, the young Henry

The Coffin

42   A simple plank coffin, in oak, of the fourteenth century found on the site of the Carmelite Friary in Cowgate, Norwich.

VI was given a *manuscrit de luxe* (now known as *The Bedford Hours*) by Anne of Burgundy, Duchess of Bedford.[6] Opened at the Mass for the Dead (*25*) one sees a magnificent hearse within which lies a palled coffin, presumably raised on stools, with a gabled lid and sides tapering towards the feet. This shape of coffin had been in use throughout western Europe since at least the middle of the fourteenth century, as shown by an illuminated manuscript in the Royal Library, Brussels, depicting the burial of victims of the Great Plague of Tournai in 1349. An almost identical coffin as that shown in the *Bedford Hours*, though within a far less elaborate hearse, can be seen in the equally luxurious *London Hours* of René of Anjou[7] from the Egerton Workshop. But both the Bedford and Egerton manuscripts were produced by French artists working in Britain and we have to ask ourselves if what we see in these illuminated manuscripts also existed in this country.

In 1856 the South Kensington Museum (now the Victoria and Albert Museum) acquired a small enamelled gold *memento mori* pendant found at the site of Tor Abbey, Devonshire (*Col. 8*).[8] This sumptuous bauble, appropriately named the Tor Abbey Jewel, was doubtless made for a wealthy patron. The gold is enamelled in white, black, opaque pale blue and white, translucent green and dark blue, with an inscription round the sides of the coffin: THROUGH. THE. RESVRRECTION. OF. CHRISTE. WE. BE. ALL. SANCTIFIED. The detachable lid reveals an enamelled gold skeleton. It is English, probably dating from *c.*1546, and confirms that the type of coffin depicted in the Bedford and Egerton manuscripts was in use in Britain. To the funerary historian the Tor Abbey Jewel is a highly important record. The skeleton, whose hands are placed over the groin in one of the traditional attitudes of repose, is slightly proud of the shell; hence the gable lid, resulting in a close-fitting coffin. From about *c*.1575 a new style appeared: the coffin is angled at the shoulders and the gable lid retained. An early example of this single-break gable-lidded type (containing the remains of Lady Margaret Howard (d.1591)) is in the De La Warr vault at Withyham, Sussex.

It appears that no distinct regional trends in basic coffin style existed. Consequently, in the early modern period, gable-lidded wooden coffins were no more restricted to any one area of the country than, say, the lead anthropoid type used for vault deposit. The same applies to the upholstering of the outer flat-lidded shaped-shouldered velvet-covered cases of the eighteenth and nineteenth centuries, though some coffin-makers and funeral furnishers did have their own patterns when it came to the application of the round-headed upholstery pins[9] – as noticed in the east Gostling vault beneath St John's Church, Egham, Surrey, used from 1817–41, where each of the five coffins had a similar cross motif between the three side panels – whilst others introduced variety through the use of two complementary colours of velvet.

The 'Lancashire' coffin appears not to have made its début until the second quarter of the nineteenth century. Though it had little to differentiate itself from its colleagues, apart from double ring-grips at both head and foot, its construction was more elaborate than the standard framed and panelled model – thus it was more expensive and carried a certain snob value. The casket was an idea introduced from the United States in the 1870s and does not, therefore, make more than the briefest possible appearance in this history of the English trade.

There are at least fourteen types of coffin recorded for the period 1450 to 1900, from the simple gable-lidded single shell, provided for late medieval Everyman, to the hulking triple-shell polished mahogany cases of the late nineteenth century. The traditional wood for coffins is elm, being cross-grained and therefore less prone to splitting; it is also to some extent water-resistant. Oak was occasionally used, but only for exceptionally important interments. Walnut, beech and deal have also been used at different times. However with the introduction of french polishing in the second quarter of the nineteenth century, oak came into its own, as elm could not be so treated. This both pleased and hampered the trade: pleased, because oak was more expensive than the traditional elm; hampered, as it was easier, less time-consuming and required far less skill to cover an elm coffin with baize or velvet than to spend time on french polishing. Waxing, a more traditional English technique employed by those unable or unwilling to undertake french polishing, ousted the latter by the 1920s, having run alongside it for the previous forty years. Veneers appear in the 1880s although an eighteenth-century example was discovered during the 1983–4 excavations at St Augustine-the-Less, Bristol, but this might have been no more than an attempt on the part of the coffin-maker to mask some splits at the shoulder caused by over-zealous saw-cuts when kerfing.

The basic construction of the standard single-break flat-lidded coffin was fairly simple and any able carpenter could have produced one. The corners were neither mitred nor dove-tailed; rather they were butt-jointed, with sides internally kerfed at the shoulders – usually seven saw-cuts – and then bent to

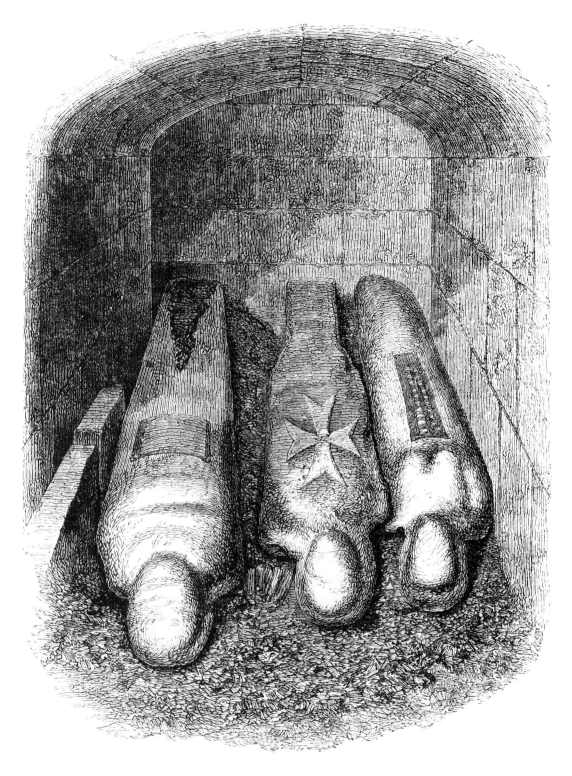

*43   Henry VII's vault in Westminster Abbey showing, from left
to right, the anthropoid coffins of James I (d.1625), Elizabeth of
York (d.1503) and Henry VII (d.1509).*

shape. The base boards fitted within the coffin, screwed into position through the side. This helped to anchor the sides to the base and maximized reliability, for a base board nailed to the underneath of the sides might have failed on lifting. The sides were screwed to the head and foot ends and the lid spanned the sides. In this way the item was immovable, each joint relying on its neighbour for strength and support. The screw holes were countersunk and infilled once the screw had been driven home, though infilling was unnecessary with polished coffins where decorative beading was to be used.

Once formed, the joints were internally sealed with pitch to prevent the escape of any obnoxious gasses or liquids. The type and quality of the inner lining was dependent on the purse of the purchaser. In the eighteenth century it was the practice, as Misson reminds us, to put bran and sawdust at the bottom of the coffin to a depth of about four inches, and extra wood shavings at the head end. Sometimes, rosemary or balm was added to the bran to counteract the smell of decomposition. The undersheet was first tacked into place prior to fixing the side lining, the side-sheets and ruched frill along the visible top edge. Everything had a purpose. The sawdust and bran mixture not only provided a soft base on which to rest the corpse but also acted as a sponge for exuded matter; the side lining masked the bare wood; the side-sheets assisted in the presentation of the corpse; and the frill along the visible top edge formed a seal when the lid was screwed down and helped to keep it all airtight. Occasionally one could dispense with the bran and undersheet and purchase a tailored mattress; likewise the sides could be padded and buttoned and a pillow provided. The permutations were many and varied. In this way were also made the double-shell and triple-shell coffins.

The anthropoid coffin is associated almost exclusively with the burial vault. These coffins, England's response in lead to the Egyptian mummy case, became fashionable in the fifteenth century and were still to be seen in some areas in the last decade of the seventeenth century, though they were beginning to decline in popularity during the 1660s and 1670s. The delay occasioned by the organization of, for example, a heraldic funeral required certain hygienic treatment to the body and it was necessary to encapsulate the corpse within a watertight container to prevent leakage, lead being the accepted material. To aid in the process, the body was eviscerated and wrapped – though 'trussed' would be a more realistic description – in a number of layers of cerecloth, the outer layer being sewn. The anthropoid shell was fashioned to fit this cocoon, and consequently the plumber had to be close at hand and work quickly to bespoke his client. One of the earliest examples is that encasing the remains of Elizabeth of York (d.1503) (*43*) in Westminster Abbey. The lead is unadorned save for an appliqué lead Maltese cross on the breast; the shell follows the contours of the body, highly defined at the head end, and thus provides an indication of the true size of the occupant. From the basic shape it can be deduced that the arms were placed alongside the body, turned in at the elbows, with the hands on the groin. Conversely, Henry VII's shell is more tubular, probably allowing for a more natural appearance of majesty when positioning the funerary sceptres in the hands. Along the right-hand side of the shell is an appliqué lead depositum plate, twenty-four inches long and four inches wide, with a cast inscription in raised letters: *Hic est Henricus, Rex Angliae et Franciae ac Dominus Hiberniae, hujus*

44   Two children's anthropoid coffins in the Sackville Vault at Withyham, Sussex. The upper of 1617, the lower of 1618.

nominis septimus, qui obiit XII. die Aprilis, anno regni sui XXIII et incarnationis dominicae MCVIX. The inscription is preceded by a cross *alisée patée* painted directly on to the lead.

At the east end of the south side of the De La Warr vault at Withyham, Sussex, is a group of children's coffins dating from the early seventeenth century. Amongst them are two very small anthropoid shells (*44*), one of 1617, the other of 1618. The babies have been laid with their arms along their sides and, as small coffins are always better preserved than those of adults, it is possible to ascertain from these undamaged specimens how anthropoid coffins were sealed. It appears that the body was laid on a shallow lead tray with lip, and the upper section was shaped to fit over the body. Once the top section had been put into place and its edge tucked in as close to the body as possible, the lip of the base tray was eased towards the sides of the upper half and the joint soldered. In the case of the Withyham infants the joints were neatly burnished.

A slightly later anthropoid shell of the 1630s in the same vault displays an alternative technique. The base tray is as deep as the corpse is high, the head section having been fashioned from a separate sheet of lead and soldered on to the main body of the shell. With the body encased, the top lid – with the merest ghost of a form – was placed over the lip of the main case, as one would the lid of a shoe-box, and soldered with a ¾-inch iron. Finally, an incised depositum plate was soldered above the chest. Over the years the lead has eased, the lid settling on the contents, highlighting the outline of the corpse within.

93

In south-east Leicestershire two anthropoid shells of local manufacture are to be found in an extensive seventeenth-century vault. Originally ascribed to the 1660s it now seems highly likely that they date from the 1630s and were made within a few years of each other. One, to an unknown female, pays particular attention to the facial features and the posture of the corpse, the other is not so highly detailed. Again we have the standard format of the lower tray having been soldered to the upper shell. The arms positioned alongside the body turn in at the elbows with the hands over the groin. Whilst some attempt has been made to define both stomach and breasts, the hands are wanting. The facial features are those of an elderly woman and, though not a portrait of the deceased, they are in line with standard representational portraiture of the period; viewed from above (*45*) one can almost visualize the parted winding-sheet. The attention paid to posture is most noticeable at the foot end, for rather than having the feet at right-angles to the ankles they are totally relaxed and display a more natural attitude of repose. This would have been a somewhat difficult task for the plumber, but he was probably restricted in any case due to the close cering of the corpse. There is no depositum plate though there are marks to show where one had been.

Depositum details were either cut into the lead or achieved by the imposition of cast lead letters. Rectangular, square and shield-shaped appliqué plaques were also used, the details being either inscribed, cast or appliquéed. The

45　*Most anthropoid coffins provided for adults were fully moulded with defined facial features and arms, legs, hands and feet. This example of c. 1630 was made in London.*

94

*46   Appliqué and incised lettering on the lead shells in the
Culpeper Vault at Hollingbourne, Kent, show the variety of
plumbing techniques available when outer wooden cases were
not provided.*

Barnardiston vaults at Kedington, Suffolk,[10] have a number of anthropoid coffins with appliqué shield depositum plates; two incised shields cut from anthropoid coffins of 1671 and 1676, together with most of the lid of Dame Ann Combe's 1658 lead shell with incised lettering – and four very high-quality cast armorials from the same coffin – can be seen on the walls in St Mary's Church, Hemel Hempstead, Hertfordshire.

Not all lead coffins destined for vaults were provided with outer wooden cases. Those in the Culpeper vault at Hollingbourne, Kent (*46*), fall into this category, though it is just possible that the flat-lidded rectangular shell encasing Elizabeth Culpeper (d.1638) did have an outer case. In south-east Leicestershire is a lead shell of c.1650 with its own lead lion's-head grip-plates and iron stirrup-handles (*47*); a similar coffin of the same date exists in the western St John vault at Lydiard Tregoz in Wiltshire. Princess Elizabeth (d.1650), the second daughter of King Charles I, lies at St Thomas's, Newport, Isle of Wight in a lead shell, which marks the transition from anthropoid to flat-lid single-break (*48*); again, no outer case, rather simple iron grips affixed to the lead. In the east chamber of the Maynard vault at Little Easton, Essex, lies a coffin from the 1660s elaborately appliquéed

47   Outer case or no, carrying rings had to be provided. Sand-cast lead lions' heads appear on a youth's lead shell of c. 1650 in a burial vault in south-east Leicestershire.

with coats-of-arms similar to those at Hemel Hempstead, Hertfordshire; whilst in the eastern Poulett vault at Hinton St George, Somerset, are three children's coffins with delightful stamped filigree fringes around the lid (*Col. 9*) as well as simple iron grips, all three dating from the early 1700s.

By far the rarest type of post-medieval coffin is the gable-lidded tapered shape; this is frustrating, especially as they are so well known in contemporary art from the fourteenth through to the seventeenth centuries. The 1615 St John triptych at Lydiard Tregoz, Wiltshire (*Col. 10*), shows three such coffins beneath their parents' sarcophagus. In 1984, a faculty to examine the St John vault for these items proved that it had been extensively reordered in the early eighteenth century when the decayed earlier coffins were cleared and placed in a charnel cistern within the vault. To date no such coffin has been discovered in spite of their proliferation. This is equally frustrating when one notices that the coffins appearing on a series of five resurrection monuments executed by John and Mathias Christmas between 1628 and 1640[11] are also of this type. A further faculty acquired in 1983 to examine Temperance Brown's vault at Steane, Northamptonshire, also ended in failure, the coffin having disintegrated and she having 'gone to earth'.

Though the single-break flat-lidded coffin had made its entrance in the last quarter of the sixteenth century – the lead shell of Lady Elizabeth Howard

96

(d.1591) with appliqué lettering at Withyham, Sussex, is of this type, as is the pictorial representation of Sir Henry Unton's 1596 coffin in the Unton portrait at the National Portrait Gallery, as well as a small sculptural representation of a coffin on the 1615 mural monument to Susan Kinges at Morston, Norfolk – the single-break gable-lidded shell seems to have been more popular. An example of this type in lead, dated 1648, rests on the children's shelf in the De La Warr vault, but of greater interest are three wooden versions. One is now no longer on view: when the church of St Peter's, Exton, Somerset, was being reordered in 1984 a clay-puddled grave shaft beneath the ledger stone of William Averie (d.1608) was exposed. Within the grave were the remains of a single-break gable-lidded elm coffin, the outer surface covered with pitched cambric or linen and decorated with black-headed upholstery nails. The lid had collapsed on to the remains, the sides had fallen outwards, but the two end pieces remained upright. The clay-puddled cutting itself was of single-break shape and is believed to be the earliest example of the type. Of far greater importance is a little-known parish coffin of *c*.1645 at Easingwold, Yorkshire (*Col. 11*). It is made of ½-inch oak, unlined and with simple iron ring handles, those at the angle of the shoulders being sufficiently high up to fit over a pierced hasp protruding from the lid through which a padlock might be fitted, thereby rendering the contents safe from body-snatchers. The patination of the wood and the delightful patchwork of

48   The change in style from anthropoid to flat-lidded single-break can best be seen in this engraving of Princess Elizabeth's 1650 lead shell at St Thomas's, Newport, Isle of Wight.

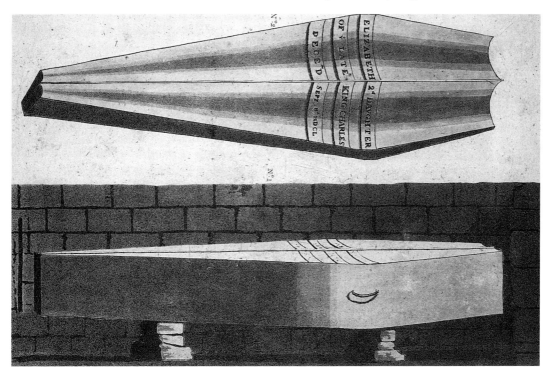

sheet-iron repairs testify to its many years of service. It is the only surviving example of a complete parish coffin. A wooden coffin similar to that at Easingwold forms part of the 1655 Allestry monument in Derby Cathedral (*Col. 12*), though this shell is pure theatricality, a coffin cut in half, lengthways along the ridge of the lid. However, its importance lies within the ½-inch oak boards and the positioning of the nails along the butt-joints as a parallel to the Easingwold model. The lidless 1664 parish coffin at Howden Minster, Yorkshire (*49*), is of ¾-inch oak, better constructed than the Easingwold model, though with identical iron rings and, as there are no nail or screw holes on the upper width of the side panels, it is to be assumed that the lid was of the Easingwold type. The presumed parish coffin at St James, Garlickhythe, City of London, is, in fact, an elm container made in 1855 for the safekeeping of 'Jimmy Garlick', the celebrated seventeenth-century desiccated corpse; he was subsequently recased in the nineteenth century in a glass-fronted mahogany vitrine, erect rather than supine, at which time it must have been decided to keep the coffin rather than discard it.

49 *Of all the thousands produced over the centuries, only two parish coffins survive. This one, at Howden Minster in Yorkshire, was provided by the Churchwardens in 1664.*

During *c.*1660–75 the trapezoidal gable-lidded coffin gave way to the single-break flat-lidded type, shaped at the shoulders. The coffin furniture – the term given to the appliqué metalwork fixed to the black fabric-covered outer case – was usually quite plain, with very simple grip-plates and grips of a type found on most average items of domestic furniture of the period, being of sheet iron and wrought iron respectively. Only in a few instances were brass or copper depositum plates provided, for it was more usual to outline the initials, date of death and age of the occupant on to the lid with black-headed upholstery nails with the possible addition of a skull and crossbones outlined at the head of the lid, whilst the sides were decorated with a single row of close-set nails all round. Decorative angle brackets stamped or cut from thin sheet-iron and spaced along the edge of the lid at intervals of about six inches completed the furniture. In the trade these angle brackets were known as 'hinges'. Cases of this type have been recorded in many vaults whilst another, of 1678 to Francis Osbaston, High Sheriff of Essex, was discovered in an earth-cut grave at Little Ilford, Essex, during excavations in 1984 prior to the site's reordering.[12] News concerning the development in style took a little time to percolate through to the country; a sculptor carving a resurrection scene on a 1707 headstone outside the south door of Uffington church, Oxfordshire, continues to depict the gable-lidded coffin.

By 1700–25 the funeral furnishing trade had become firmly established, providing funerals for all classes of society and at various costs, dependent on the social status of the deceased, basing their street ritual and panoply on that exhibited by the College of Arms during the last quarter of the seventeenth century, diluting or adding to it accordingly. Most of the day-to-day trade came from the man in the street, and it would be wrong to infer that every coffin-maker and funeral furnisher hungered after catering for the top end of the market. Further, many could not afford to undertake such pomp as they had neither the capital, credit facilities, stock, staff nor expertise; some simply did not have the inclination to become involved. They were content to stay in the back-streets of our towns making their own coffins and providing a much needed service to a community which was either unqualified, unwilling or unable to extend to such outrageous luxuries. Whilst the royal funerals continued to be furnished 'in-house' by the Lord Chamberlain via the royal upholders, there were a number of top-quality cabinet-makers, mercers and upholders willing to undertake the organization of funerals for members of the nobility and the landed gentry as an extension to their established clients; so it is not surprising that Chippendale, for example, also furnished funerals if called upon to do so. In the same way that the jobbing funeral furnisher was unable to undertake the obsequies of the nobility, likewise the top cabinet-makers would have refused some of their lesser clients, referring them to one of more able members of the trade.

A number of tradesmen in the timber, textile and tin-plate industries looked upon coffin-making and funeral furnishing as something by which they could profit, and it was not unknown for some to meet with such success that they abandoned their established trade to go into undertaking full time. Most preferred to remain as a supplier to the trade, others advertising their ability to furnish funerals in addition to their daily trade. This increased as the use of the parish coffin began to wane, so that by the end of the seventeenth century and the beginning of the eighteenth, the parish coffin had practically disappeared. It could be argued that this was hastened in London by the Great Plague of 1665 when the familiar sight of cartloads of corpses contrasted with the decency and sanitary advantage of encoffining the dead. Broadsheets issued at the time do not elaborate on the detail of the finish given to the coffin, but show a plain gable-lidded type with or without handles. With the need for speedy disposal of the dead – and that organized by others than the coffin-makers – together with a dwindling supply of wood in the face of more work than they could handle, few involved in the trade were going to do more than fabricate a utilitarian box of standard shape. In the rest of the country, and in post-Plague London, the change was due to social trends more than anything else.

The 'golden age' of the English funeral, as far as undertaking techniques were concerned, was the period from 1725 to 1775 and most of the finest extant coffins in public and private vaults were made during that time. The constituent parts of a top-quality coffin of the period would have been as follows: a 1½-inch inner elm coffin with recessed lid, lined and covered with cambric – no depositum plate; a lead shell of five pounds – i.e. five pounds' weight per square foot – diapered and with lead depositum plate; an outer case of 1½-inch elm or oak, padded and covered with rich scarlet Genoese or black Utrecht velvet; four pairs of gilt grip-plates and grips; two rows round of gilt-headed upholstery nails; and escutcheons, lid motifs and brass or lead depositum plate. When Smart Lethieullier of Aldersbrook had completed his mortuary chapel adjoining St Mary's, Little Ilford, Essex, in *c*.1740 he transferred the remains of his parents into the present vault from elsewhere in the church. He had new cases made for the shells, covered in scarlet Genoese velvet with two rows round of gilt-headed upholstery nails on the lid, the sides and ends blank-panelled with a single row of the same. On examination it transpires that he requested the retention of the original gilt brass depositum plates. The coffins have identical plumbing and outer cases, and it therefore appears that the same funeral furnisher was used throughout, giving a continuity of thirty-one years.

Almost without exception coffins of the period 1725–75 were single-break and flat-lidded, obtainable in four basic types:[13] (1) single case; (2) single case with double lid; (3) double case; (4) triple case, comprising an inner wooden coffin, a lead shell and an outer wooden case. The collective noun for each of these types is 'coffin', but the trade maintained its own nomenclature for the constituent parts. Hence with a double coffin, the inner container was described as the 'coffin', the outer container being the 'case'. Likewise, the triple container comprised an inner wooden 'coffin', a lead 'shell' and an outer wooden 'case'.

The single case was used for the straighforward earth burial and was by far the most common coffin type – and remains so today. However, some did slip the net and get into burial vaults, such as these three nineteenth-century intruders in the Atkyns vault at Sapperton, Gloucestershire. As they were neither wholly water-resistant nor airtight some very unpleasant odours must have arisen from below. In the 1820s the vestry at Christchurch, Spitalfields, had to issue general instructions against the use of the single case in their vaults, advocating the triple case in all instances.

The single-case double lid was a more expensive version of the single-case type, though what service the additional lid rendered appears to be a mystery. It could have been provided as an additional barrier to odour, but this could only have been achieved by the use of waxed paper – as seen in the Lethieullier vault at Little Ilford, Essex – between the top of the sides of the coffin and the lid. Again, what little space there was between the two lids might also have been packed with powdered charcoal.

The unleaded double-case double lid is met with in parochial, rather than private, vaults and both intramural and churchyard brick-lined graves. Having said this, it would appear that this was the least acceptable type for vault and intramural brick-lined grave deposit.

The triple shell was the traditional coffin for the burial vault and brick-lined grave. As they are the most common form met with in burial vaults it is worth looking at their construction in detail.

The inner coffin was usually elm, one or 1½ inches thick, planed and smoothed, butt-joined with recessed lid and covered in cambric. These sections were both glued and screwed together, the base within the sides, the screw holes countersunk and infilled with putty. To support the recessed lid a length of beading was affixed with glue and tacks around the upper inner side, one or 1½

50   One of the most comprehensive collections of lead shells of the period c. 1550–c. 1850 can be seen in the Harvey Vault beneath Hempstead Church, Essex.

inches from the top, dependent on the thickness of the lid. The lid was anchored to the sides by screws through the sides. Prior to fixing this lid the inner joints, base and sides were caulked with swedish pitch, the base covered with a shallow layer of bran and sawdust over which the bottom sheet was tacked – alternatively a fitted buttoned mattress could be supplied – then the side lining and, possibly, a ruched or *broderie anglaise* frill; finally the pillow and the shrouded body. If there was to be no viewing of the remains, the coffin was at once covered with plain or waxed cambric, glued and gimped into place.

The lead shell had to be bespoke. Few coffin-makers had the talent to fashion such an item, so an order would have gone out to a local plumber. Eight different ways of cutting and fitting the lead have been recorded, but the two most commonly used were the 'shoe box' and the 'smooth wrap'. To produce the latter the inner coffin was placed on to a width of lead which was then cut so as to be three inches larger all round than the coffin itself; this was then turned up and tacked to the wood. A similar-sized length was laid on the lid and likewise folded over the edge and tacked into place. Lengths were then cut to go round the head end and one side and the foot end and the other side, and tacked into place. All joints were then soldered and smoothed, the tack-heads soldered so as to maintain the water-resistance and airtight quality of the coffin. A diaper design was then card-wired on to the shell using a template and a straight-edge. Finally, the lead depositum plate was soldered into place. The 'shoe box' type was similarly fashioned, though the sides were affixed before the lid (*50*).

Whether the coffin-maker produced a bespoke outer case or took one from existing stock is not known, though logic argues in favour of the latter. Outer cases of the period 1725 to 1775 and later were sumptuously upholstered and provided with elaborate coffin furniture. Veneers were used only to mask carpentry mistakes.[14] Cases made and upholstered by cabinet-makers, as distinct from coffin-makers, have had greater attention paid to the fitting of the velvet, those in the Poulett vault at Hinton St George, Somerset, and the De La Warr vault at Withyham, Sussex, being examples of this type. The coffin of the Fourth Earl De La Warr (d.1795) (*Col. 13*) was padded with shoddy prior to the fitting of the velvet, shoddy and velvet being gimped to the chamfered base of the sides, with the coffin base itself shamfered along the edge. The velvet – or baize, for the lesser mortal – was always used sparingly, tucked in behind itself at the angles of the coffin and the width of the plank at the top. The lid was similarly fitted though sometimes the velvet did intrude on the surface of the underside.

Occasionally both underside of lid and inside of case were lined with plain cambric. Care had to be taken in fitting the cotter-pins securing the grips, and grooves were cut on the inside of the coffin into which the cotter-pins were bent, so as not to come into contact with the lead shell. The upholstery pins, escutcheons, lid motifs and depositum plate were affixed to the outer case prior to the insertion of the lead shell, their appearance being enhanced if applied to a fully upholstered case.

The positioning of the lead shell was a delicate operation, care being needed to avoid piercing or damaging the lead in any way. Having been placed on to three lengths of webbing, six men would be required to lift the shell and put it into the case; the webs were then cut, as it would not have been possible to withdraw

51 Most coffins after c. 1750 were fabric-covered, whether for earth burial or vault deposit. This example was discovered during the 1984 excavations within St Mary's, Little Ilford, Essex.

them. Finally, the lid was put into position and screwed or bolted down. The trade never solved the problem of the aesthetic positioning of the case-lid screws – too often they either interrupt or abut the upholstery pins around the edge of the lid. Some tradesmen did try to mask the screws by covering the countersunk heads with a small disc of velvet. Whilst coffins of this type were produced for vault and brick-lined shaft deposit they were also required for intramural earth-cut graves; one such example from the 1820s was discovered during the excavations at St Mary's Church, Little Ilford, Essex (*51*) in 1984.

Not all coffin-makers could go to the expense of buying in two-foot widths of wood; some made up their cases from twelve-inch or six-inch planks, relying on the velvet covering to mask their technique. A number of cases of this type were noticed at Christchurch, Spitalfields, and St Marylebone parish church as well as in the vaults beneath St Paul's, Shadwell, and St John's, Wapping. A classic example survives at Hinton St George, Somerset, with the coffin of Colonel William Poulett (d.1805). The black velvet has perished, exposing the side of the case which, on examination, proves not to be a single plank but four six-inch lengths of ½-inch board bonded together by iron straps (*52*). Identical grip-plates and grips were also provided for the case of Lady Harriet Poulett (d.1802).

Not all coffins of this period were put to funerary use. When the medieval roof of St Botolph's, Hadstock, Essex, was being recorded in 1974 a number of eighteenth-century coffin boards were found, having been used for running repairs. Mrs Delany, in her *Autobiography*, records that in *c*.1720:

> Sir William Pendarvis's house was the rendezvous of a very immoral set of
> men. One of his strange exploits among other frolics, was having a coffin made

103

52 The use of fabric to cover the outer case meant that coffin-makers could get away with using planks rather than full-width boards. This only comes to light when the velvet begins to perish.

of copper (which one of his mines had that year produced), and placed in the great hall, and instead of his making use of it as a monitor that might have made him ashamed and terrified at his past life, and induce him to make amends in future, it was filled with punch, and he and his comrades soon made themselves incapable of *any* sort of reflection; this was *often* repeated, and hurried him on to that awful moment he had so much reason to dread.[15]

On 6 February 1771, a Colonel Luttrell turned up at Mrs Cornely's Masquerade at the Pantheon, London, dressed as a coffin (*53*); R.S. Kirby, who was also present, recorded that Luttrell cast such a 'pall of gloom' over the proceedings that he was obliged to leave almost as soon as he had arrived.[16] But none of these incidents could possibly have matched that witnessed at a masquerade organized by Lord Tylney at Wanstead House, Essex, in 1768, as recorded by an Italian noblewoman staying with the Tylneys at the time.

Many lights appear in the trees and on the water. We are off and have great excitement fishing up treasure (fake) tied to bladders. His Lordship is hailed from the shore by a knight, who we are told is King Arthur, have you the sacrifice my Lord, who answers no, then take my sword and smite the water in front of the grot and see what my wizard has done, take also this dove and when asked, give it to the keeper. Off again to some distance from the grotto, the lights are small and water still, the giant eagle appears and asks, have you the sacrifice, no my Lord answers, so be it and disappears in steam.

His Lordship smites the water with King Arthur's sword, all the company are still, a rumble sucking noise comes in front of the opening of the grotto the water as if boiling and to the horror of all the company both on the water and on the shore scream with fright, appearing as though from the depth of hell arose a ghastly coffin covered with slime and other things. Silence as though relief, when suddenly with a creaking and ghostly groaning the lid slid as if off and up sat a terrible apparition with outstretched hand screeching in a hollow voice, give me my gift with such violence, that some of the company fell into the water and had to be saved, and those on the shore scrambled in allways confusion was everywhere. We allmost fainted with fright and was only stayed from the same fate by the hand of his Lordship, who handed the keeper the dove (fake) the keeper shut its hand and with a gurgling noise vanished with a clang of its lid, and all went pitch. Then the roof of the grotto glowed two times lighting the water and the company a little, nothing was to be seen of the keeper or his coffin, as though it did not happen. [*sic!*][17]

This must have been a most amazing sight, coming as it did as the climax of a much longer event staged beforehand outside Wanstead House itself. The idea was obviously Tylney's; but who arranged it? There is a possible hint in 'King Arthur's' words '... see what my wizard has done ...'. King Arthur's wizard was

53 *Arriving dressed as a coffin at Mrs Cornely's Masquerade in 1771, Colonel Luttrell cast such a 'pall of gloom' over the proceedings that he was obliged to leave.*

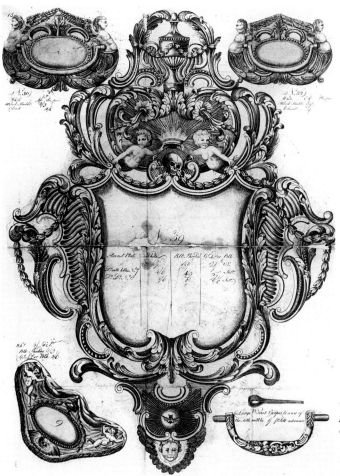

54 *Design for a depositum plate from Tuesby & Cooper's coffin furniture catalogue of 1783. Tuesby & Cooper provided coffin furniture for upmarket funerals only.*

Merlin. In 1760 an ingenious inventor called John Joseph Merlin (1735–1803) arrived in England from Paris in the suite of the Conde de Fuentes on his appointment as Ambassador Extraordinary in London. Merlin was soon known for his fantastic mechanical automata, and it is not inconceivable that Tylney met him at one of the many masquerades then all the rage in London. There seem to be few other candidates for such a mystery.

In 1769 Thomas Pickering, a tin-plate manufacturer in Southwark, patented a method of raising patterns in sheet iron which was to affect the production of coffin furniture. From *c.*1720–30 coffin furniture had been produced by hand-operated die-stamping machines; Pickering's was power-assisted. Nevertheless, some of the coffin furniture produced during the 1730s was of a high standard, though the designs were limited, rococo in style, and copied *ad nauseam* by a multitude of tin-plate manufacturers in London and Birmingham. Some manufacturers could come up trumps and it is regrettable that we do not know the name of the supplier of a truly splendid set of stamped gilt copper grip-plates with integral coronets and a trinity of really charming chinoiserie bells on the 1777 coffin of the Second Earl De La Warr at Withyam, Sussex.

Of the three extant trade catalogues for coffin furniture of the period

1783–1826 – all in the Victoria and Albert Museum[18] – that of 1783 by 'J.B.' issued through Tuesby & Cooper, Coffin Furniture Ironmongery of 221 Borough High Street, Southwark, is by far the finest (*54*). 'A.T.' of *c*.1821–4 is almost as fine, though the plates are not so highly finished, with 'E.L.' of 1826 coming in at a deserved third in the field. Be that as it may, far more items have been discovered on extant coffins matching illustrations in the 'E.L.' catalogue than any other; and either their prices were keener or their distribution and service to the trade better. From these catalogues we learn that coffin furniture has its own terminology: coffin plates are described as 'breast plates' or 'depositum plates'; handle back-plates as 'grip-plates'; handles as 'grips'; lid decorations as 'motifs'; upholstery pins as 'nails'; and side decorations as 'escutcheons' or 'drops'. Stamped iron depositum plates, tin-dipped and designed in the form of a concave oval cartouche encircled by a garland of flowers, first appeared at the end of the seventeenth century; so did grip-plates, which were similarly oval with a repoussé design of winged cherubs' heads. When Tuesby & Cooper published their catalogue there was already a considerable variety of 'finishes' available for coffin furniture: gilt copper, copper, bronze, brass, silver and 'white' (tin-dipped stamped iron, though silver leaf was sometimes applied on top of the tin); black (more expensive than silver, being tin-dipped stamped iron painted with two or more coats of matt black paint); and 'coloured' for children's coffins (tin-dipped stamped iron, painted with two or more coats of matt white with certain details highlighted with water-gilding). Opposite the title page comes some very useful information: 'N.B. A Sett of Coffin Furniture contains a Breast Plate, Flower Pot and Angel, 3 P⸢ of Handles & Pins to fix them. If order'd with 4 P⸢ of Handles & 20 Yds of Lace &c the Price is advanced in Proportion. Large Wr⸢ Cast Gripes to any of the Setts will be 1/- p⸢ Sett advance.' A 'Flower Pot and Angel' was the trade's nickname for certain lid motifs (*55*);[19] an alternative design was the Urn and Angels.

*55   Design for stamped iron 'Flower Pot and Angel' lid motifs –
manufactured by Thomas Pickering, and available from
Tuesby & Cooper's 1783 catalogue.*

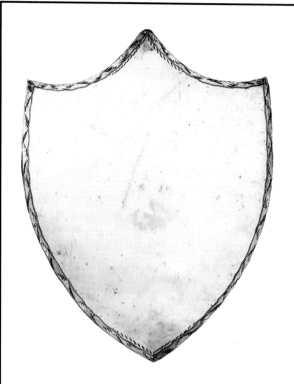

56   *A late eighteenth-century youth's silvered tin depositum plate with bright-cut border. Pure tin coffin furniture was extremely rare, owing to its expense.*

57   *Brass snuff-box in the shape of a coffin, 1792. Mr Sowerberry, the undertaker in Dicken's* Oliver Twist, *took snuff from such a box.*

The tin-dipped stamped iron coffin furniture had one drawback: it was not possible to cut lettering into the depositum plates. This would not have served for vaults, and the stamped lead plate remained the more usual item in such instances. Towards the end of the eighteenth century both pewter and pure tin – natural or silvered (*56*) – were also being used, though the nobility appear to have remained loyal to brass, it being more convenient for the engraver to work, especially if one's coat-of-arms was to appear on it.

The coffin furniture industry moved away from London during the late eighteenth century, transferring itself to Birmingham. Nevertheless, many a London manufacturer had profited by it and was easily able to afford the type of little memento shown in *57*. Coffin furniture was also exported to the colonies, it being so cheap to buy that it was unnecessary to produce it in far-flung corners of the Empire. A very fine set of eighteenth-century coffin furniture of the highest-quality Tuesby & Cooper type was discovered in 1975 in a private vault in Jamaica.

Although the majority of depositum plates were rectangular, a few followed the dictates of heraldry. Thus the plate for a young girl or spinster was lozenge-shaped, shield-shaped for a boy or young man, rectangular with central cartouche for a married woman or widow, and rectangular with central square panel for an adult male, married man or widower. However, it should be pointed out that not every coffin-maker or funeral furnisher knew this and one could end up with the horrendous mismatch of an elderly widower being given a plate intended for a young girl.

One innovation of the eighteenth century was the introduction of the patent self-locking iron coffin to foil body-snatchers. This was really unnecessary, since a body would have been far too decomposed after eight to ten days to be of much use to any medical school. It would have been better to build secure mortuaries rather than putting one's money into an expensive contraption. Nevertheless, Messrs Jarvis (*58*) did produce an ingenious creature which, with its standard outer case, would have fooled even Burke and Hare. Jarvis informs the public that to provide one's relatives or friends with such a container would bring peace of mind. Unfortunately their advertising trade card is too detailed and any Resurrectionist worth his salt could have worked out from the illustration how best to break it open.

Tuesby & Cooper, in their catalogue of 1783 make a passing reference to 'lace'. This had nothing whatsoever to do with fabrics, referring instead to an alternative to upholstery nails: tin-dipped filigree stamped iron available in rolls of – it must be presumed – twenty yards, a length sufficient to outline the lid, sides and ends of a coffin, such as that on the outer case of Lord Vere Bertie (d.1770) in the Wray vault at All Saints', Branston, in Lincolnshire (*59*). His wife's tiny coffin was similarly decorated. Not all lace was quite so decorative; that provided by Dottridge Brothers in 1922 was really rather crude. But lace was nothing new; in the Victoria and Albert Museum, London, is a late seventeenth-century English mirror (*60*)[20] with a delicate border of engraved blue glass in ten sections, each abutment masked by a thin strip of gilt lead coffin lace. Does this mean that we are looking at an item produced by a cabinet-maker who was also able to furnish funerals?

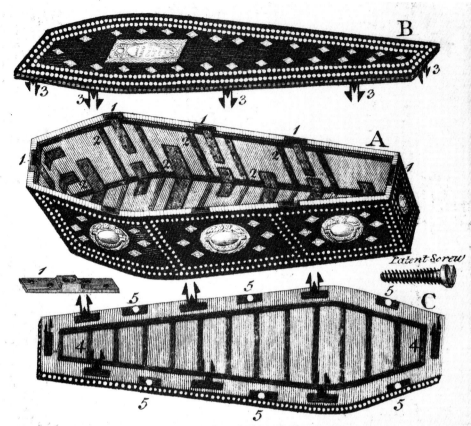

A. The Coffin, with the outside finish'd, & the inside left uncover'd to shew the Patent Apparatus, which consists of eight Iron Boxes (1) & bindings of Iron (2). B. The upper side of the Lid, with Springs (3), which shoot into the Iron Boxes fix'd on the top edge of the Coffin (1). C. The under-side of the Lid, with Iron Bindings (4), & six Iron Boxes (5), to receive the head of the patent Screw, which is on such a construction that after it is screw'd in the Coffin it can not be taken out with any Instrument whatever. The Patent Coffins being made without sawcuts, are considerably stronger than others; & the Screws are case harden'd to prevent them from being cut with Spring Saws.

58   Jarvis's Patent Coffin of c. 1810. 'The fastenings of these
approved receptacles being on such a principle as to render it
impracticable for the Grave Robbers to open them.'

IMPROVED COFFINS.

By his *MAJESTY's ROYAL LETTERS PATENT.*

The fastenings of these approved receptacles being on such a principle as to render it impracticable for the Grave Robbers to open them, those whose friends are buried in the Patent Coffins will have the satisfaction of knowing that their remains cannot be stolen, or their Coffins broken to pieces before they are decayed. This security must afford great consolation at an Æra, when it is a well authenticated fact that nearly one thousand bodies are annually appropriated to the purpose of dissection.

Jarvis and Son,

UNDERTAKERS & COFFIN-MAKERS,

Charing Cross;

and Great Marylebone Street
the corner of Welbeck Street.

The Patent Coffin may be had at an additional charge of three Guineas & a half, & used with, or without Lead. Funerals furnished in the best manner & on the most reasonable terms.

59 Two mid eighteenth-century coffins in the south-west corner of the Bertie Vault at Branston, Lincolnshire, showing (left) strip coffin lace and (right) pierced coffin lace.

One item not supplied by Tuesby & Cooper, nor by the other two warehousemen, were coronets, both the repoussé and the three-dimensional type. Throughout this chapter we have been coming across the coffins of nobles, all of which had repoussé coronets about the grip-plates and three-dimensional gilt copper versions – usually with gilt wooden baubles and remnants of the cap – sitting on the lid(*61*). They begin to appear in the first quarter of the eighteenth century, a remnant of the funerary effigy, though it is not recorded that nobles, apart from those of royal blood, ever had them (Cromwell and General Monck excepted). They were probably introduced as a spin-off from the revived interest in heraldry in the early eighteenth century. Where they do not exist it can be presumed that either the genuine silver-gilt coronet was used at the funeral and then put back into the strongroom after the funeral, or they have disintegrated. One such funerary coronet still sits on its tasselled cushion atop the coffin of the Earl of Clare in the 1837 catacombs at Kensal Green, whilst a very fine, though late, specimen of 1915 sits on the top of the Dowbiggen & Holland coffin of Rosa, Countess Poulett, at Hinton St George.

Colourful velvets for the outer case began to appear in the early nineteenth century. No longer were the sole colours available black and scarlet, for one now had the choice of midnight blue, holly green and turquoise, the latter being usually reserved for infants. And that was not the end of it, for there were permutations. Black with midnight blue, scarlet with holly green and black with turquoise. The predominant colours were black and scarlet, the midnight blue and holly green being used to relieve the border in between the rows of upholstery nails. A very fine light green velvet – almost eau-de-Nil – was seen on a child's coffin in the vaults at St Paul's, Shadwell, and made all the more attractive with its gilt furniture. Coffins for churchyard earth burial were also fabric-covered, though black baize was more the norm than scarlet (*Col. 14*). Arguably the most majestic covering was black Utrecht velvet (*Col. 15*); Nelson's 1806 coffin, furnished by Messrs France of London, with its gilt bronze fittings on padded velvet, was particularly sumptuous (*Col. 16*), but one would expect this of the crown undertaker's work.

From a trade catalogue issued by Turner of Farringdon Street, London, in 1838 we get an overview of the types of coffin used at that time: thirty-three are described, of which fourteen styles were for children's coffins only. The cheapest ready-made coffin for a six-foot adult was a 'Good inch elm Coffin, smoothed, oiled, and finished with one row round of black or white nails, a plate of inscription, four handles, lined and pillow.' Turner's most elaborate case consisted of a 'Double Lid Elm Coffin, lined with 4lb lead, and covered with cloth, finished two rows all round, close drove, best nails, lead or brass plate, angel and flower, four pair cherub handles, with grips and drops, lined and ruffled with fine

60   Strips of gilt lead coffin lace were used to mask the joints of engraved border glass on this c. 1680–90 pier-glass. Did this carpenter also provide for funerals, one wonders?

*61   Four ducal and one viscount's coronet in the Sackville
Vault at Withyham, Sussex. Stamped-iron funerary coronets
were left on the coffin in place of the silver-gilt originals.*

cambric.' The words 'lined with lead' open a new avenue. Until the end of the
eighteenth century the inner coffin was covered with a lead shell, but now we see
the introduction of the lead-lined coffin, i.e. sheet lead tacked to the inner sides of
the inner coffin. Taylor was also able to provide 'off the shelf' a lined and dressed
elm coffin with outer lead shell for any child of two feet to four feet 9 inches tall.

Not all coffins slavishly followed regulation patterns. Dr Clive Wainwright
suggests that the antiquary and collector William Beckford was probably cased
in a coffin designed by Henry E. Goodridge when he died in 1844.[21] The 1852
coffin of the Sixteenth Earl of Shrewsbury was designed by E.W. Pugin and made
by Hardman of Birmingham – 'the edges ... engrailed with gilt metal work; at its
foot the Shrewsbury arms were engraved in gilt metal'[22] – whilst in October 1887
Philip Webb sketches in his commonplace book the 'outside dimensions of coffin
& coffins for a six foot body for Lawrence Datchworth', suggesting an outer case
seven foot 6 inches long, three foot wide and two foot deep.[23]

Three coffins in the Bell vault at Milton, Kent, depict the development of case
decoration between the 1820s and the 1850s (*62*). Eleanor Bell (d.1827) has a
scarlet velvet upholstered elm case which, with its cherub grip-plates, might
have been equally at home in the 1720s were it not for the idiosyncratic
decoration of the lid. The turquoise upholstered case of John Bell (d. 1836) is
more *à la mode* with neo-Egyptian ormolou fittings and a typical early
nineteenth-century design in the upholstery nails: whereas Jane Bell (1855) has

an exceptionally elaborate 1½-inch waxed oak case with black-headed upholstery nails and neo-classical furniture.

Not all coffins were so beautifully made as Mrs Bell's. The following judgement appeared in the October 1858 minutes of the Dunmow Union Workhouse, Essex.

> Great complaint was made by the bearers and others of a Coffin supplied for William Taylor a pauper belonging to the parish of Great Bardfield by Mr Cole Contractor for Coffins for the Thaxted District. Samuel Hitching stated that he examined the Coffin carefully and that it had two canvas patches on where there were decayed places in the Wood – he also measured the thickness of the Board and they were only 5/8 of an inch at top and ½ an inch thick at the bottom – the lid was also warped that they could not screw it down properly – One of the bearers also stated that he was afraid it would fall in pieces before they got to the Church with it. Mr Cole appeared before the Board and acknowledged that the Coffin was not made according to his Contract whereupon he was strongly cautioned by the Chairman as to his future conduct.[24]

In marked contrast is an outer case provided in 1864 by Maria Taylor, trading in Coney Street, York, as 'Cabinet-maker, Upholsterer, Auctioneer, Appraiser and Undertaker', for the remains of the Seventh Earl of Carlisle.[25]

> Handsome Outer Coffin in Spanish Mahogany
> covered in fine Genoa Silk Velvet, Solid brass handles & time
> Silver breast plate to ditto engraved with Coronet and inscription

62   Three coffins in the Bell Vault at Milton St John, Kent, showing the transition from velvet-covered outer wooden cases in 1827 and 1836 to the introduction of a french-polished case in 1855.

115

63   Two of a series of six coffins from the third quarter of the
nineteenth century in the Sackville Vault, Withyham, Sussex,
based on an 1856 design by George Edmund Street.

64   The Manila Coffin of c. 1890 by Ingall, Parsons & Clive.
The painted zinc scroll on the side of the lid reads, 'Even so
saith the/ Spirit for they rest/ From their labours'.

The Coffin

In 1875 Francis Seymour Haden, FRCS, advocated by means of three letters to *The Times* a distintegrating coffin '... of some lighter permeable material, such as wicker or lattice-work, open at the top, and filled in with any fragrant herbaceous matters that happened to be most readily obtainable. A layer of ferns or mosses for a bed, a bundle of sweet herbs for a pillow, and as much as it would still contain after the body had been gently laid in it of any aromatic or flowering plant for a coverlet'.[26] From this, the Necropolis Company invented and patented the earth to earth wicker coffin. It met with some success, and on 19 June 1890 the Kensington Burial Board discussed the possibility of the Guardians of the Poor using such wicker baskets for pauper burials, but the Board of Guardians declined owing to their cost.[27] Meanwhile, the Earth to Earth Society was marketing a framed coffin covered in pulp; Dottridge Bros offered two versions of this in their 1902 catalogue, the 'Terra' and the 'Translation'.

Coffin designs were also changing in the 1870s. The earlier introduction of waxed and french-polished woods had already given greater scope to the imagination of the coffin-maker. In the De La Warr vault at Withyham, Sussex,

65   Coffins from the 1922 Dottridge catalogue. The framed and panelled Newman coffin is still available as are the solid cast-brass Gothic handles and the tapered brass depositum plate.

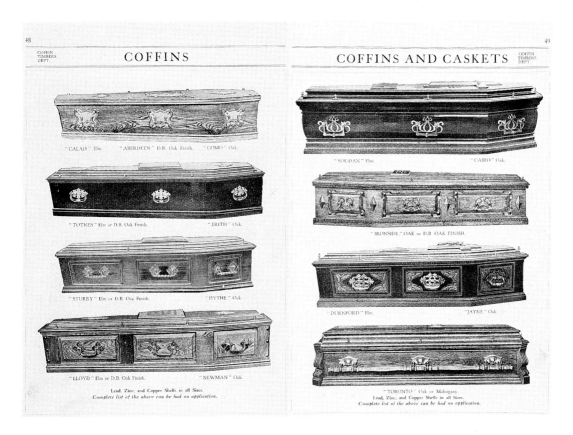

117

66 *Most late nineteenth-century funeral furnishers exhibited models of their trade in the shop window. This example was produced by Goswell & Son of Theale, Berkshire.*

is a series of polished oak coffins, rectangular in shape with tapering sides and flat lids, supplied between the 1870s and the 1890s, and based on an earlier design of 1856 by the architect George Edmund Street, as published in the Ecclesiological Society's *Instrumenta Ecclesiastica* (63). In the 1890s Ingall, Parsons & Clive of Birmingham were producing thirty-five designs, of which the 1½-inch Canadian elm 'Manilla', at £3 15s. was the most imaginative (64). Not to be outdone by their rival, Dottridge Brothers came up with some interesting designs too (65) – from the simple 'Calais' in waxed elm, the 'Cairo' with its art nouveau grips, and the stolid 'Newman' in framed and panelled oak. All four coffins shown on Plate 48 of their catalogue are available today. Unfortunately the smaller coffin-maker could not cope with the high-powered advertising of IPC and Dottridge Brothers, preferring to place miniature versions of their handiwork in the shop window for the benefit of passers-by (66), though they probably relied on the funeral furnishing warehouses for the supply of linings and coffin furniture.

5

Funerary Transport

> Suddenly a huge black object was dimly discernible entering the avenue and dragging its ponderous length towards the castle ... the snow ceased, the clouds rolled away, and the red brassy glare of the setting sun fell abruptly on the moving phenomenon, and disclosed to view a stately full-plumed hearse. There was something so terrific, yet so picturesque in its appearance, as it ploughed its way through waves of snow – its sable plumes and gilded skulls nodding and grinning in the now lurid glimmering of the fast-sinking sun – that all stood transfixed with alarm and amazement.

Lines spoken over a scene from a Hammer Horror film? No, rather an extract from a short story entitled 'Inheritance' from the *Quarterly Review* of 1844. Nevertheless, it captures the classic mental picture most have of the Victorian funeral. Nothing has provided greater scope or more footage for the film-maker than the mad journey of a hearse travelling at breakneck speed, pulled by wild-eyed nostril-flared horses through some area of the New Forest pretending to be the foothills of Transylvania, and driven by Igor the henchman, to Frankenstein's Disneyesque castle perched atop the slopes of a perilous mountain, a single candle burning in the window of a rain-lashed windswept turret. Thrilling and exciting as this may be, nothing could be further from the truth as regards English funerary transport.

The transportation of the dead has, generally speaking, been of the greatest interest to bereaved relatives. Consequently man has developed a system whereby the corpse can be reverently handled and decently transported to the place of disposal. Gradually, this 'progress of the dead' acquired its own ritual and pageantry, so much so that, when thinking of a funeral today, one is likely to conjure up more the procession itself than the attendant liturgy.

By their very nature funerals are stately and sedate affairs; greater attention

119

is paid to the appearance of the funeral car and the accoutrements of the attendants than to the high performance of the vehicle. There are exceptions to every rule, such as the Gosport funeral director apprehended in 1984 for driving a hearse at 102 m.p.h.[1] and the antics of the young chauffeur in Joe Orton's *Loot!*. Nathaniel Houlton's funeral at Bristol in the late Summer of 1767 is much closer to accepted norm: ' ... And the Manner of my Funeral I direct be exactly the same, or as near as possible, to that of my said late Wife, to wit, Two Coaches, A Chariot Hearse, two Mutes, and the same Under Bearers as at her's Attending, if they shall be then alive.'[2] From this we can deduce that Houlton was so impressed by the solemnity of his wife's funeral that he desired to have the same tradesmen undertaking his own arrangements. It was not at all rare for people to express a choice of undertaker; similar attitudes apply today.

Until the foundation of the private cemeteries in the 1820s and 1830s and the town cemeteries of the 1850s, the majority of the populace were buried in the graveyards surrounding the parish church, and transportation was a simple matter of either carrying the coffin at waist height, on the shoulders or by means of a hand-held bier. The private cemeteries' independence from parochial boundaries, and their typical location on the outskirts of the metropolitan conurbations, gave rise to a dramatic increase in horse-drawn vehicles and attendant carriages. For those burial grounds established by vestries and town councils, usually not quite so distant as the private concerns, the wheeled bier could be used – as it had been since the 1850s in those parishes with extensive burial grounds or in the larger villages and smaller towns where there was an improved quality in road surface. Occasionally one comes across wheeled biers resembling the glass-sided horse-drawn funeral cars. Again, some of the private cemeteries and public burial grounds had their own wheeled biers; this was necessary where inclines in landscape and narrow pathways made access to horses impossible. However, since the 1840s even the smallest undertaker endeavoured to emulate the larger concerns in providing horse-drawn transport and, outside the cemeteries, burial grounds and churchyards the wheeled bier was rarely seen. Thus, the glass-sided horse-drawn funeral car remained supreme until the introduction in the 1920s of motorized transport (though it is still possible to obtain horse-drawn vehicles should one so wish).

Bodies have also been carried by water, certainly in between the outlying Scottish islands and the Channel Isles, and as early as 1831/2 Henry Kendall was suggesting a water gate for Kensal Green Cemetery leading off the Grand Union Canal, with Benjamin Baud recommending a similar arrangement to the West of London & Westminster Cemetery Company at Brompton Cemetery in 1836/7, though nothing came of either proposal.

Railways also played their part in shunting the dead around the country and they continued to do so until 28 March 1988 when, due to lack of demand owing to improved road connections, motorized transport overtook British Rail's undertaking. One enterprising private cemetery, the London Necropolis Company at Brookwood, Surrey, had an arrangement between 1854 and 1941 with the London & South Western Railway to use their track from Waterloo to transport coffins and mourners – by first or third class – in specially designed carriages.

Until fairly recently, intercontinental transportation was by ship; this was usually reserved for the bodies of those who, having died abroad, wished to be buried in their native English soil – those who died at sea were usually buried at sea – and two coffins imported from India in the 1860s can be seen today in the catacombs beneath the Anglican Chapel at Kensal Green Cemetery, still in their original packing crates. Air transportation, or 'repatriation' as it is now known, is frequently used to bring back the bodies of those who die abroad or for those immigrants to this country who wish to be taken back to their land of birth. A rarer mode of air transportation is the rocket. The Portmeirion architect, Sir Clough Williams Ellis, had his cremated remains scattered over his idiosyncratic village by means of a number of specially packed fireworks. For those with a similar hankering for adventure, a British-based agent for an American company is currently taking names for a suitable pay-load of cremated remains – or 'cremains' to quote the sales publicity – to be launched into outer space.

Few gave as much attention to detail in organizing a funeral as did the philanthropist Edward Colston. Colston died at his Mortlake town house on 11 October 1721 at the age of eighty-five; his funeral instructions predate his death by nine years:

> As to what relate to my funeral, I would not have the least pomp used at it, nor any gold rings given; only that my corpse shall be carried to Bristol in a hearse and met at Lawford's Gate, and accompanied from thence to All Saints' Church by all the boys at my Hospital on St Augustine's Back, and by the six boys maintained by me in Queen Elizabeth's Hospital in the College Green. And also by the twenty-four poor men and women or so many of them are able in my Almshouse on St Michael's Hill, and only to the Church door of All Saints. Likewise by the six poor old sailors that are kept at my charge in the Merchants' Almshouse in the Marsh. And likewise by the forty boys in Temple parish, that are clothed and otherwise provided for me. To be drawn directly thither, so as it may be there in the close of the evening, or the first part of the night; and my further desire is, that at my interment the whole Burial Service of the Church, as it is now appointed, may be decently read and performed. And to signify that this is my desire, I have hereunto set my hand, this fifteenth day of July, 1712.[3]

So much for no pomp! But of inestimable surprise is a further instruction placed upon his executors:

> My sister, Ann Colston's corpse, is interred in Mortlake Church, under the rail in the south side of the communion table. But since it was her desire that her bones should lie in the same grave where I shall be buried; and forasmuch as my intentions are, that my corpse shall be carried to Bristol, and interred in All Saints' Church, in the grave that belonged to my ancestors; my desire is that my said sister's bones shall be taken up (if it be done by the authority of the minister, without the trouble of applying to the Bishop of Diocese) and put into and carried down in the same coffin with my body; or if that cannot be conveniently done, then in another small one, to be put in the same hearse, and buried in the same grave, with mine, in compliance with her request in that behalf.[4]

And this was done, after application to the Archbishop of Canterbury. A strange load indeed to be transported to Bristol.

Of greater social interest, from the point of funerary custom and transport, is Edward Colston's own estimate showing what he considered comprised a funeral without 'the least pomp':

	£	s	d
A Lead Coffin the inside, and the Elm Coffin run within, cear'd and lyn'd and ruffled with sup'fine Crape	6	0	0
A sup'fine Crape Shroud, Sheet, Pillow and Gloves	2	0	0
An Elm Case, Covered with the best Velvet, a double Silver'd Plate with Inscription, Coat of Arms and Flower; 3 Pair of Silver Chaced handles, and set off with 2 rows of best Silver'd Nails	14	0	0
A Brass Plate Engraved for the Lead Coffin	–	–	–
A Hearse and 6 Horses, 7 days at 35s per day	12	5	0
3 Mourning Coaches and 6 horsses, 8 days	36	15	0
Mourning Coaches and 6 horsses, to attend Corps to Brentford	–	–	–
8 Men in black to attend to Bristol, with Sadle horses, 7 days at 10s per day	28	0	0
2 Rooms hung in deep Mourning	6	0	0
8 Large Silver Candlesticks, round the body	0	16	0
4 dozen of Silver Sconces round the Rooms	2	8	0
25 pairs of Wax Candles for Ditto and Tapers, at 2s 8d	3	6	8
A Large Velvet Pall for the Journey	3	10	0
Velvet Covering for the hearse and horsses	3	10	0
17 Plumes of fine Ostrich feathers for ditto	4	0	0
A Lid with Plumes of ditto on the body for the Journey	2	0	0
A Rayle round the Body, with Plumes of ditto	1	10	0
An Atchievement Frame, etc	3	10	0
24 Silk Escutcheons for the Pall and Rayle, at 5s	6	0	0
9 dozen of Buckrum Escutcheons for Room, 30s	13	10	0
48 Buckrum Escutcheons Verged with Silver, 24 Shields, and 12 Chaps for the hearse and horsses, being 2 setts	10	10	0
12 Banners and 2 sets of Pencils for ditto	12	0	0
3 dozen Buck Escutcheons Verged for the Church	–	–	–
6 fine Mourning Cloaks for Gentn.	2	14	0
16 Mourning cloaks for Coachmen and horsemen	5	12	0
Best Shamy gloves	–	–	–
New Crape hatbands	–	–	–
26 Ord. Gloves and hatbands for Coachman and horsemen, Postilians and porters	4	4	6
4 Porters at Door in Gowns, Staves, etc.	2	0	0
12 Pages in black with Caps and Truncheons to attend the Hearse to Brentford	1	16	0
6 men in Black to attend the Coaches – ditto hatbands	0	18	0
A Room hung in Deep Mourning with Black Cloth on the road	4	4	0
6 Large Silver Sticks and 12 Silver Sconces for ditto	2	6	0
27 Wax lights and tapers for ditto, at 2s 8d	3	12	0
38 Favers for horsemen, Coachmen, Postilians, Porters and Pages	2	17	0
A sett of Silk Pencils for the Plumes about the Corps	4	4	0

6½ yards of Superfine Cloth at 18s per yard	6	1	0
6 yards of Prest bayes for the Type	0	12	0
a Pew hung with black Cloth, Nails, etc	–	–	–
A Hearse and pair of Horses that brought the lead			
Coffin, ferrying and Servants to help	1	10	0

In 1721, £213 for a funeral was an enormous amount of money, when a perfectly fitting funeral for a person of middle rank could be had for £10. Obviously Colston shopped around, hence his choice of the Brentford undertaker and his memorandum of forward expenditure, for a tradesman in nearby London could easily have supplied all that was necessary. The Brentford undertaker would certainly have been cheaper but the fact of the matter is that he would probably have had to sub-contract out to a London firm for the various accoutrements. The lion's share went to furnish the funeral whilst the cortège was in transit; so, together with the accepted burden of the heavy lead-lined coffin – and that of the additional passenger, his deceased sister – has to be added the bulk of the packing crates for the portable catafalque, hangings, candelabra, sconces and feathers. The innkeeper's bills do not survive but it would not be unreasonable to double Colston's manuscript estimate to account for seven days' overnight accommodation (and on-the-road luncheons) for the sixteen attendants, together with the stabling for twenty horses and shelter for the funeral car and the three mourning coaches; to this should be added the undertaker's attendance fee and the extra room taken at each inn along the route for the lying-in-state. May it be presumed that Ann Colston's coffin remained overnight on the funeral car?

The English can hardly be called a nomadic race and, until the agrarian and industrial revolutions of the early eighteenth century, people usually spent their entire lives in the towns and villages of their birth, with the occasional visit to the county town, and it was both expected and accepted that after death their bodies would be laid to rest in the graveyards encompassing their parish church. Such being the case, there was little distance to travel – usually not much more than a mile – and it was a simple matter to carry the body from the place of death to the place of burial. Nevertheless, transportation was slightly more complicated if a body had to be brought from a dwelling in an outlying part of the parish – for the nearest church building would not necessarily be the designated parish church: careful consideration had to be given to the route, taking care that parish boundaries were not trespassed. More often than not small streams were unbridged and had to be forded by bearers and mourners alike, whilst worked fields presented their own hazards, especially where headlands had been cut back in an attempt to utilize the land to its utmost crop-growing capacity. And pity the bearers who had to struggle across rough terrain in torrential rain. It was not all sweetness and light in the Merrie England of *c.* 1450.

Before a body could be transported it had to be made 'decent'. This usually entailed washing, straightening of the limbs, the emptying of the bowels and the plugging of the orifices to minimize seepage. Embalming, or 'hygienic treatment' as it is euphemistically called today, was usually reserved for the corpses of royalty and nobility. A cheap hygienic barrier could be achieved by sewing the corpse up in cerecloth, though the more usual method was to employ a flannel shroud or, if the purse allowed, one of linen. In later centuries, as has been shown, particular regulations relating to shroud material were introduced in an attempt to rescue the declining woollen industry. The laying-out and dressing of corpses was usually the responsibility of the women of the household – the modern system whereby preparation takes place on the funeral directors' premises is a recent introduction – although almost every community had one 'lady' who could be relied upon to perform this task for a fee, the precursors of those two redoubtable ladies exposed by Dickens in the persons of Mrs Gamp and Mrs Prig.

Almost without exception each parish had its own burial guild and it was they who provided the necessary transport and coffin to get the body from the house to the church. The number of guild members attendant at a funeral depended on the size of its membership and the rank of the deceased, though it seems improbable that anything less than four would have been practicable. The family and friends having gathered at the house of the deceased, the guild representatives would congregate outside awaiting the arrival of the priest and parish clerk, whilst two or more of their brethren went into the dwelling with the parish coffin to encase the corpse – individual coffins being rare prior to the seventeenth century. This would be the signal for those inside the house to come out and form into an orderly procession. The priest, assured that all was ready, would signal to the parish clerk to lead the cortège off to the church. First would go the clerk ringing a small handbell, then the priest followed by the coffin, with the relatives and friends bringing up the rear. Coffins were rarely shouldered – it was impracticable to do this where uneven road surfaces and fair distances were concerned – rather they were carried at waist height on short poles not much more than four feet in length. No late medieval parish coffins survive but logic, together with close examination of contemporary and later illustrations,[5] suggests that these poles were fixed to the base of the coffin across its width.

On arrival at the church the body was taken straight in and placed at the entrance to the chancel, feet facing east, on two low stools provided either by the burial guild or from the general furniture of the church; coffin stools continue to be used in some areas, not necessarily rural ones only, and numerous oak sets dating from the late seventeenth century survive (*67*). These stools were not much more than eighteen inches high and so the coffin could be set down without additional lifting, thereby contributing to the continuing decorum of the ritual. Once in position, the hearse was brought forward and placed around it. Catafalques did not make their appearance until the early eighteenth century.

The last responsibility of the burial guild was to transport the corpse from the church to the grave itself. At the appropriate moment it was lifted up from the coffin stools, turned a full 180 degrees and, with the procession re-formed in a like manner to its entrance, they went into the churchyard. The precise moment in the burial service when the body was placed in the grave is dealt with in another chapter; suffice it to say that the coffin was opened, the shrouded corpse taken out and passed to either the sexton and his mate or two members of the guild already standing in the grave waiting to receive it (*26*). Contemporary illustrations depict the body in a rigid position: could it be that a plank was placed beneath the corpse to facilitate its transfer from the coffin to the grave?

67   Pair of oaken coffin stools from the late seventeenth century.
Many churches used pairs of tall stools for coffin supports.
Numerous sets remain in use for the same purpose.

With the funeral over, the only task left to the burial guild was to transport the coffin back to its place of storage in the parish church where, reunited with the hearse, it would wait until the next member of the community died.

With the dissolution of the religious guilds and fraternities in the mid sixteenth century the responsibility for providing the communal coffin lay full-square on the shoulders of the parish. J.C. Cox, in his book on churchwardens' accounts, records the parish of St Alphage, London Wall, spending five shillings on having such an item made in 1569.[6] In some areas, encoffined burial was regarded as a statement signifying wealth or social status and therefore not for the poor. The town council at Rye, Sussex, decreed in 1580 that 'no person who shall die within the Port of Rye under the degree of Mayor Jurat or common councilman, or of their wives, except such person as the Mayor shall give licence for and being paid to the Mayor for the use of the poor, shall be chested or coffined to their burial, and if any carpenter or joiner make any chest or coffin for any person to be buried (other than for the persons aforesaid excepted) he shall be fined ten shillings for every coffin so made by him'.[7] Neither were all corpses neatly shrouded, such as at Poyning, Surrey, in 1608 when 'John Skerry, a poore man that died in The Place Stables and being brought half naked with his face bare, the parson would not bury him soe, but first he gave a sheete and caused him to be sacked therein, and they buried him more Christian-like, being much grieved to see him brought soe unto the grave.'[8] Whilst accepting that 'shroud only' was the usual request, some parishes were quite used to entertaining coffins, especially when it came to intramural burial. But what a surprise awaited those who had transported the remains of Margaret Barnard to her grave in the nave of the parish church at Lindsell, Essex! 'Margaret Barnard widdowe and verie aged was buried the 14th daye of Julye 1608 and which is worthie note she was coffynn and all, layd within her housbands coffynn & in ye same grave in the middest of the midle aley in ye church, the bodie of her housband Richard Barnard beinge consumed to dust his bones laye all in order proportioning his bodye, hee beinge buryed there 19 years before.'[9]

Nothing changed regarding funerary transport until the third quarter of the sixteenth century; street processions continued to be marshalled in the customary manner, coffins being used regardless of the social status of the deceased – the poor being treated with equal solemnity and respect as the rich. But with the Reformation and the consequent suppression of the religious guilds and fraternities, the changes introduced in the liturgy also affected the ritual, especially those aspects involving the participation of the laity. These changes took place within a very short space of time, in fact between 1552 and 1559. Some explanation is needed here. The 1549 *Booke of the Common Prayer*, known as the First Prayer Book of Edward VI, was little more than a modified translation of the Roman liturgy and hardly affected the funeral ritual. On the other hand, the 1552 *Boke of Common Prayer*, the Second Prayer Book of Edward VI, had a far briefer liturgy for the 'Buriall of the Dead', omitting the 'Celebracion of the holy communion', and although it was permitted within the rubric for the body to be taken into the church, the liturgy was better suited for reading at the graveside. This was a tremendous change and Cranmer justified his revisions thus:

> ... the most weightie cause of the abolismet of certaynn Ceremonies was, that thei were so farre abused, partly by the supersticious blyndnes of the rude and unlearned, and partly by the unsaciable auerice of such as sought more their own lucre, then the glory of God; that the abuses could not well be taken away, the thing remaynng stil. But now as cōcerning those persones, which peraduenture wylbe offended, for that some of thold ceremonie are reteyned styl: if they cōsider, that withour some Ceremonies it is not possible to kepe any ordre or quiete discipline in the churche, they shal easely percyue just cause to reforme their judgemēts.[10]

This 1552 service for the burial of the dead was ratified by the 1558 Act of Uniformity and appeared unaltered in 1559 in the *Prayer-Book of Queen Elizabeth*. Any who might be tempted to revert to the 1549 or 1552 liturgies were given the following warning in the final paragraph of the Act: 'And be it further enacted by the aucthoritie aforesaid, that al lawes, statues and ordinaunces, wherein or whereby any other Seruice administration or Sacramentes or Common Prayer, is limited, established, or set forth to be vsed within this Realme, or any other the Quenes dominions or Countreys, shall from hensforth be vtterly voyde and of none effect.'[11]

Few incumbents now saw the need to take the coffin into the church and the majority of what remained of the burial service was being read either beneath the lich-gate or at the graveside itself. Consequently, changes had to be made regarding the attendant ritual, for the bearers could not be expected to stand holding the coffin on its supportive poles for the duration of the service. So what was to be done? Some churches provided stone plinths within the lich-gate upon which the coffin could be placed, such as at St Euny's, Redruth, Cornwall (later extended north and south so as to accommodate three coffins, owing to the frequency of mining disasters in the area), whilst others had simpler ones of wood, as at Chiddingford in Surrey. However, it seems that most parishes elected to use the 'new fāgled' bier: a slatted wooden stretcher with integral handles and legs. This contraption had five advantages and one major disadvantage. In its favour, it could be carried by either two or four bearers – two where children's corpses were concerned – it could be set down neatly at the church stile, lich-gate or at the graveside, it obviated the necessity of the church's providing coffin stools should the coffin be taken into the building and it allowed for the transportation of bodies *sans* coffin. The disadvantage was that the legs were an obstacle when traversing uneven ground, and to cope with this some biers had hinged legs allowing them to be hooked back to the undercarriage when not in use.

One of the earliest representations of a bier appears on the Foljambe monument of *c*.1580 at Chesterfield, Derbyshire (*29*). Below a tripartite panel with reliefs of Death flanked by Childhood and Old Age, is a fully shrouded corpse resting on a very simple bier, the whole supported by a plinth bearing emblems of Death and Decay: a skull, bones, a spade and a hoe. A modern parallel would be a coffin within a flower-decked motorized hearse. An appreciable number of wooden biers survive in the more remote country churches, the earliest being that of 1611 at South Wootton, Norfolk (*Col. 17*) – a county particularly rich in such items – presented by Henry Kidson on the occasion of his fortieth year as rector of the parish. It is a somewhat cumbersome item and would have been extremely heavy to carry through the streets; yet from its construction it appears that it would have been used for shrouded bodies only, the top section – the 'hearse' – being draped with a hearse cloth so as to give some privacy and protection to the load within. Further seventeenth-century wooden biers can be seen in other Norfolk churches at Gissing, Ickburgh, Little Saxham, Stradsett, West Bilney and West Dereham (dated 1683), whilst a particularly good example of the Chesterfield type, dated 1688 and carved with the initials of the churchwardens, sits in the north aisle at South Creake, Norfolk (*68*). This has recently been conserved, and is now as perfect an item as one could wish to see.

Much confusion has arisen regarding the correct use of palls and hearse cloths. F. Tate tells us that 'the coffin or bier is covered with a sheet over which lieth a black cloth ... and so he is carried towards the grave.'[12] This black cloth is a pall, not a hearse cloth. The confusion in terminology arose in the seventeenth century and has remained with us ever since. Once the coffin or shrouded corpse had been placed on the bier a white cloth – either of wool or linen, depending on the quality of the funeral – was laid over the same; on top of this was placed a black cloth, the pall, somewhat smaller in dimension than the white sheet. By the close of the seventeenth century these two items had become amalgamated, producing the white-hemmed pall, which was to remain in fashion until the last quarter of the nineteenth century. In a few instances the palls were lined white, the hem falling some ten or twelve inches below the line of the black cloth, and sometimes used inverted over the coffins of spinsters, with a reduced version available for

68   *The bier was the cheapest form of conveyance and doubled*
up as a catafalque for the funeral service. This example, dated
1663, is at South Creake, Norfolk.

children's coffins. The hearse cloth *per se* was that piece of black material placed over the wooden hearse – or frame – surrounding the coffin whilst in church or the wooden/metal hutch affixed to the top of a bier, such as would have been used in conjunction with that at South Wootton, Norfolk.

Some churches had their own palls – more often than not leftovers from the disestablished guilds (the one existing at Dunstable Priory once belonged to the Guild of St John) – and it was not unknown for private families to maintain their own pall, such as the embroidered purple velvet example at St Giles, Colchester, Essex,[13] commissioned by the Lucas family in 1628. Again, as coffin and bier were available on hire from the parish church, so too were palls, or 'hearse cloths' as they were increasingly called from the early seventeenth century. Cox tells us that the parish of St Botolph Without, Bishopsgate, had three such 'hearse cloths' available for hire: the best at one shilling, another at eightpence and a third, probably a worn-out creature that had seen better days, at fourpence. Not everybody wished to be carried to the grave beneath such fabrics. John Morgan, the vicar at Matching, Essex, drafted specific instructions in 1732 asking to be 'buried in Linnen and as private as maybe at four o'th'Clock in the afternoon without Paul or Paul Bearers.'[14]

Undertakers did not appear in England until the middle of the seventeenth century, so who was it that carried the bier after the disappearance of the religious guilds? In short, we do not know. Obviously the bier had to be got from the church to the house and it would not be unreasonable to expect this to be done by the sexton and his mate. Again, general opinion has it that the bier was carried from the house to the church and from the church to the graveside by relatives or friends of the deceased. Tate comes into his own on this particular matter: ' ... the corpse is taken up and carried either by poor people chosen for the purpose, or by the servants of him that is dead'. Some contemporary accounts survive where the deceased makes specific reference to those who should be bearers.

The method of shouldering seems to have been widespread in the early seventeenth century. In fact there have never been any hard and fast rules relating to the method of conveyance, as can be read in Edwin Chadwick's repetition of Lord Justice Stowell's judgement in the case of *Gilbert* v. *Buzzard & Boyer (Undertakers)*: 'In what way the mortal remains are to be conveyed to the grave ... I do not find any positive rule of law, or religion, that prescribes. The authority under which the received practice exists, is to be found in our manners, rather than our laws.'[15] So we have to turn our attention to contemporary broadsides, trade cards and funeral invitation tickets to ascertain the facts. On the title page of a 1641 polemical tract on the Great Plague[16] is an illustration of a London funeral on its way through the streets to a walled churchyard, showing a coffin covered by a short pall – some nine foot long and five foot wide – supported on the shoulders of four bearers and closely followed by six male mourners walking in pairs, six female mourners in pairs and then a host of other friends and relations; the six male mourners are shown holding sprigs or rosemary, a herb not only symbolic of 'remembrance' but also a fairly powerful – and sometimes necessary – barrier against the smells associated with decomposition.

John Dunstall, a minor artist working in London during the plague years has left us with a series of harrowing illustrations depicting the burial of the dead, his fifth frame (*69*) showing two methods of transporting children's coffins (on the shoulder and on the head) and five ways of getting an encoffined adult to the grave (strapped to the back; carried on the shoulder by two men; carried on the shoulders by four men; carried on a shouldered stretcher by two men and on a shouldered bier by four men); in the lower left-hand corner can be seen the parish clerk (?) leading the way for the front two shouldered coffins, holding a staff and a small handbell, the latter being a remnant of the late-medieval ritual. In the main, plague corpses went to the grave in a communal cart:

> The cart had in it some sixteen or seventeen bodies; some were wrapped up in linen sheets, some in rugs, some little other than naked, or so loose that what covering they had fell from them, in the shooting out of the cart, and they fell quite naked among the rest; but the matter was not much to them, or the indecency much to anyone else, seeing they were all dead, and were huddled together in the Common Grave of Mankind, as we may call it, for here was no difference made, but poor and rich went together. There was no other way of burials, neither was it possible there should, for coffins were not to be had for the prodigious numbers that fell in such a calamity as this.[17]

*69   Transporting the dead, from a pictorial broadside of Plague
Scenes, 1665. Decorum has fled and speed has taken its place.
Getting the corpse to the grave quickly was of paramount
importance at this time.*

An invitation ticket dated 7 October 1677 in the Bodleian Library, Oxford, for the burial of Thomas Foley depicts a palled coffin carried on the shoulders of four men, whereas one issued for the burial of Sir Edward Sebright, Bart., at Besford, Worcestershire, on 13 January 1702 has the palled coffin supported on the shoulders of six bearers.[18] Furthermore, an engraving by G. Beckham on an invitation to a funeral in 1722 at St Botolph, Aldgate, shows six attendant pall-bearers supporting the hem of what appears to be a self-levitating coffin – artist's licence has chosen to omit the bearers beneath the pall; the same is repeated in an almost identical engraving by J. Sturt on a ticket issued by John Carter, Undertaker in Whitechapel, in 1743.[19]

Illustrations of horse-drawn funeral cars, or chariots, began to make their appearance on funeral invitation tickets in the mid eighteenth century. Whether they were used for those dying within the parish is debatable. Was the corpse of Mrs Elizabeth Cordiner taken from Aston's Quay to the church of St Andrew-by-the-Wardrobe, a distance of not more than 500 yards, by horse-drawn chariot? Almost certainly not. Yet here is shown a splendid open vehicle pulled by six horses sporting ostrich-feather plumes and emblazoned velvets, the chariot itself trying its hardest to be little more than a large wheeled bier with pelmeted canopy, embroidered with heraldic devices imitative of the funerals of the nobility. As feathers were by this time ornamenting the top of the palled coffin of the street procession, so we see them here – the undertaker not wanting to skimp on any part of his available panoply – not only atop the corner of the chariot but also in the centre. Unfortunately the engraver of this invitation card was not well

130

versed in funerary ritual, as he cut the block portraying the coffin the wrong way round within the chariot – such items were inserted feet first rather than head first. Whilst the two mutes leading off the procession are absolutely correct there is a minor misunderstanding by the artist as regards the postillion, who is shown wielding a driving whip in emulation of the coachman. One would probably be correct in assuming that either the block-cutter is at fault or the artist has incorrectly copied another invitation ticket. For a clearer view of what is properly intended one has to look at a funeral ticket issued by a London burial society in 1761 for the interment of Edward Williams, for here the postillion is shown holding a flambeaus – illuminating the way through the night for the driver. This becomes evident once one knows that this particular burial society performed their funerals in the evening, though it is doubtful that they would have paraded the helm and bannerols at every funeral as the engraving would have one believe (*70*). The chariot has now become a closed funeral car, the superstructure being closely fitted with black cloth, upon which are stitched – where appropriate – painted canvas escutcheons displaying the deceased's coat-of-arms (though it was not unknown for the trade to decorate these cars – and the horse velvets –

70   A nocturnal funeral procession from the funeral ticket of Sir Edward Sebright, 1702. On the right, the procession towards the church and, on the left, the burial. Note the night stars.

with spurious escutcheons of their own invention). In addition, not to be outdone by the shouldered street processions, ostrich-feather plumes are now to be seen not only at the corners and the centre of the car but also along the sides. It is from this particular time, the third quarter of the eighteenth century, that the English funeral gradually increased in size, that is as far as the trade itself could get away with. There were, as Lord Justice Stowell observed, no set of agreed rules relating to the size or style of the procession attendant on the journey of the dead to the grave, and undertakers would add and subtract depending on the social status and, by this time, the purse of the deceased. Caution was beginning to be thrown to the winds and it was quite possible to arrange a funeral usually reserved in its complexity to those of a higher social status and money, rather than breeding. Be that as it may, the type of car shown in the invitation ticket for Edward Williams was the more popular and remained so for the grander funerals until the third quarter of the nineteenth century.

The 'hearse', as the funeral car was now being called, was the largest item of funerary equipment owned by the undertaker. Only one horse-drawn hearse of the late eighteenth century survives, dated 1783, belonging to the parish of Bolton, East Lothian. Stylistically, this is a transitional item linking the funeral chariot shown on the Cordiner invitation card and that depicted in the lower margin of the Williams 'ticket'. The decoration of wreath-encircled skulls and hour-glasses is really too recherché and instantly recalls to mind the decoration of the 1611 bier at South Wootton, Norfolk; indeed, the Bolton hearse would not have looked out of place on the streets of late seventeenth-century England. Bolton had purchased its first hearse in 1723 and it proved to be a profitable enterprise, being hired out within the county of East Lothian whenever required. By 1783 it was looking a little tired and it was decided that 'a new fashionable hearse' should be acquired and, to facilitate this, a loan was taken out. The total cost of the new hearse was £37 14s. 9d. sterling; however, 'new' it was not, for, though the superstructure was certainly made from scratch, it was mounted on an extended undercarriage of the mid seventeenth century, thereby making it the oldest surviving wheeled vehicle in Scotland. And it was profitable for the parish too, realizing £8 hire fees in the following year.[20]

The pomp displayed at funerals during the eighteenth century, certainly within the City of London, was held in low esteem by the intelligentsia. John Gay aptly described the loathing as early as the 1720s:

> Why is the Herse with 'Scutcheons blazon'd round,
> And with the nodding Plume of Ostrich crown'd?
> No, the Dead know it not, nor profit gain:
> It only serves to prove the Living vain.
> How short is Life! how frail is human Trust!
> Is all this Pomp for laying Dust to Dust?[21]

Nevertheless, such vain pageantry was 'customary' and the undertaker pulled out all the stops to provide everything necessary for a 'fitting' funeral, with London blazing the trail and the provinces bringing up the rear. James Clark had his business in Paternoster Row near St Paul's Cathedral, and his elaborate trade card of the 1740s proudly announces: 'James Clark in Pater-nofter Row, Undertakes and Furnishes Funerals, to any part of Great Britain, with yᵉ beft Goods viz Coffin, Burying Suit, Pall, Hangings, Scarves, Favours, Gloves, Escutcheons, Feathers, Coaches, Hearse, Wax-lights, Tickets and all other Necesfaries.'[22] A trade card of the 1760s, issued by a Shropshire undertaker, bears an alarming similarity to John Clark's: 'Richard Chandler, Armes-painter and Undertaker, at St Lukes Head, in Hill-Lane in SHREWSBURY. Compleatly Furnishes Funeralls with Coffin burying fuit Pall Hangings, Silver'd Sconces & Candlesticks, Cloakes, Hatbands, Scarves, Favours, Funerall Escocheons, Coaches, Hearse, Wax Lights, Flambeaux Links, Torches, Ticketts &c. and performed after yᵉ same manner, as by yᵉ Undertakers at LONDON, at Reafonable Rates.'[23]

Occasionally one meets with exceptions to the rule and Benjamin Dod's 1714 funeral must have created quite a spectacle: 'I appoint the Room, where my Corps shall lie, to be hung with Black, and four and twenty Wax Candles to be burning; on my Coffin to be affixed a Cross, and this inscription, *Jesus, Hominum Salvator*. I also appoint my Corps to be carried in a Herse drawn by Six white Horses, with white Feathers, and followed by Six Coaches, with Six Horses to each Coach, to carry the four and twenty persons (I desire to be at my burial).'[24] Mr Dod, a Roman Catholic, was stipulating white as the colour associated with resurrection. So utterly pompous and ludicrous were these eighteenth-century funeral processions that their fame spread abroad and there exists a contemporary French engraving entitled *Convoi Funèbre des Anglois*, which depicts an evening funeral rounding the corner of a highly fashionable London street towards the west door of the parish church; even a dog has managed to get a look-in. Indeed these street processions were quite an amusement to the foreign traveller and one of the finest accounts of contemporary English funeral customs was noted down by a Swiss visitor, M. Misson, in 1719;[25] indeed, more can be learnt from Misson about the eighteenth-century English funeral than from any other source.

Obviously undertakers' trade cards are going to illustrate the more elaborate end of their craft, exhibiting sumptuous processions attended by throngs of people and grandiose vehicles of transportation. Yet nothing could be further from the truth in the day-to-day round of business. Happy the upholder – and joyous his banker – able continually to perform funerals of the type they chose to advertise! In the main, funerals were modestly furnished, attended by not more than a dozen or so close relatives and friends, taking place within three or four days after death. Here W. Heath comes to our aid in his witty engraving *The Funeral of Madame Genevas* (1752). No elaborate funeral car, no great triumphal chariot with escutcheons and plumes of rich ostrich-feathers; rather, a bare-board coffin, pathetically draped with a mean and paltry rag which he would have us believe is a pall, and carried on the shoulders of four gin-mashers towards the gateway of St Giles-in-the-Fields.

In the 1780s and 1790s the street procession was beginning to wane, for, as they wound their way along the main thoroughfares (more as an advertisement for the undertaker than the convenience of the mourners), no one could ignore the increase in commercial traffic and the general bustle of the town and city streets. Even the most humble undertaker succumbed to the introduction of the enclosed hearse in an attempt to maintain dignity, though some of the lower-class funerals continued to be shouldered through the streets. Slowly, the horse-drawn hearse gained the upper hand, so that by the 1820s and 1830s it had become a familiar sight within towns. The revolution in funerary transport had been achieved.

The major influence contributing to the introduction of horse-drawn transport lay with the establishment of the private cemetery companies (The Rosary, Norwich – for Dissenters – 1819; Chorlton Row, Manchester, 1821; Every Street, Ancoats, Manchester, 1824; Low Hill, Liverpool, 1825; St James's, Liverpool, 1829; Kensal Green, London, 1833), profit-making concerns which had somehow to shoulder the responsibility of coping with the scandalous overcrowding of the city churchyards. Interdenominational, unaffiliated to the established Church – though boasting 'consecrated' areas for conformists – and often on the outskirts of the town, these cemeteries had a slow beginning. By the 1840s, however, they were doing brisk business, the fortunes of Kensal Green having been assured in 1843 when the body of Augustus Frederick, Duke of Sussex, was deposited in a private vault in the lawns before the Anglican Chapel – a site selected some years earlier after he had witnessed the confusion at William IV's funeral at St George's Chapel, Windsor, in 1837. Kensal Green received further royal patronage in 1848 with the burial of Princess Sophia – in a vault adjacent to her brother – and in 1904 with the construction of a granite mausoleum for George, Duke of Cambridge and his family. The emerging popularity of these private cemeteries forced the undertakers to review the organization of funerary transport, for it would have been unreasonable to have expected bearers to shoulder a coffin from, say, Belgravia to Norwood. In the early engravings of such cemeteries the enclosed hearse remained the accepted form, the glass-sided version not making an appearance until the 1860s and 1870s.

Yet something more drastic was soon to be introduced. Acknowledging the success of the private cemetery companies and mindful of pressure placed on central government to 'do something' about the overcrowded conditions of the inner-city churchyards and the more dubious 'speculative' burial-grounds, the Metropolitan Interments Act of 1850 provided that a Board of Health be vested with the power to provide cemeteries and forbid further burials in churchyards; between 1852 and 1862 five hundred Orders in Council secured the closure of 4,000 churchyards and burial-grounds in the metropolitan areas. And this was not before time, bearing in mind the comments made by the Revd Stone, Vicar of Christchurch, Spitalfields, in 1843:

> The eastern part of my parish ground ... abuts upon Brick-lane, one of our most crowded and noisy thoroughfares, and at one corner stands a public-house, which, of course, is not without its attraction to all orders of street minstrels. In performing the burial service, I have left the church, while the organ has been playing a beautiful and impressive requiem movement, and proceeded to the grave, where it was purely accidental if I did not hear [a] very inappropriate tune ... Indeed, as my church extends along one side of another crowded street, I have had the most inappropriate musical accompaniments, even during that part of the burial service which is performed *within* the

church. My burial ground is partially exposed to the street at the west end also; and there, as at the east, it is liable to be invaded by sounds and sights of the most incongruous description. Boys clamber up the outside of the wall, hang upon the railing, and, as if tempted by the effect of contrast, take a wanton delight in the noisy utterance of the most familiar, disrespectful, and offensive expressions. To this wilful disturbance is added the usual uproar of a crowded thoroughfare, the whole forming such a scene of noisy confusion as sometimes to make me inaudible. Amidst such a reckless din of secular traffic, I feel as if I were prostituting the spirituality of prayer, and profaning even the symbolic sanctity of my surplice. The ground is hardly less desecrated by the scenes within it; ... I generally have to force my way to a grave through a crowd of gossips, and as often to pause in the service, to intimate that the murmurs of some or the loud talk of others will not allow me to proceed. I hardly ever witness in any of these crowds any indication of religious sentiment. If, in such a case, the corpse is brought into my church, this sacred and beautiful structure is desecrated and disfigured by the hurried intrusion of a squalid and irreverent mob, and clergyman, corpse, and mourners are jostled and mixed up with the confused mass, by the uncontrollable pressure from without. I will not, indeed, venture to say that, on these occasions, the mourners always feel and dislike this uproar, for I believe that among the working classes they often congratulate themselves upon it.[26]

If nothing else, the private cemeteries could limit access.

With their extensive carriage-ways and leafy broadwalks the private cemeteries afforded a splendid and dramatic setting for the pompous spectacle of the nineteenth-century funeral. At Kensal Green it was a full half-mile from the Harrow Road gateway to the Anglican chapel, and, once on the company's land, the undertaker had ample opportunity to exercise the complete panoply of his trade without fear of interference. The mutes would lead the way, followed by the enclosed hearse, whose driver, at the flick of a wrist, could instruct the leading horses to nod and prance their way to the chapel. The bearers would flank the hearse, and mourning coaches brought up the rear. A wheeled bier was usually provided by the cemetery where access to the grave was restricted: the coffin would be brought out of the chapel at the end of the service and be loaded on to the bier for the final leg of the journey, the cemetery superintendant and officiating minister leading the way with the mourners walking behind the bier. In some parts of the country this tradition is maintained, though it is now customary for the motorized hearse to get as close as possible to the grave and then for the bearers to either shoulder or carry the coffin the last part of the way. Sometimes the bier was kept in a purpose-built hearse-house – stone or brick (with a tile or slate roof) being the favoured materials, often with the window-frames and doors painted green – though many have now fallen into disrepair or taken on a new lease of life as a tool-shed. The one at Bury Green Cemetery, Cheshunt, resembles a pseudo-Gothic gazebo, though it could easily be mistaken for a mausoleum, whilst a picturesque hearse-house at Beckington, Somerset, would seem more at home accommodating Cinderella's coach than a conveyance for the dead.

Arguably the most curious conveyance for the dead, associated with the public and private cemeteries, was Shillibeer's Funeral Omnibus (*Frontis.*). It was not terribly popular with either the clergy or the trade. J.C. Loudon, the 'father' of the landscaped nineteenth-century cemetery and commentator on funerary etiquette, was rather fond of Shillibeer's 1841 patent, writing in 1843:

> The expense of Funerals has last year been considerably lessened about the metropolis by the introduction of one-horse hearses, which convey the coffin and six mourners to the place of interment. These appear to have been first suggested in 1837, by Mr J.R. Croft, in an article in the *Mechanics Magazine*, vol.xxvii, p.146, and the idea has subsequently, in 1842, been improved on and carried into execution by Mr Shilibeer, to whom the British public are indebted for the first introduction of the omnibus. Mr Shilibeer's funeral carriage embraces in itself a hearse and a mourning coach, is very neat, and takes little from the pomp, and nothing from the decency of the ordinary funeral obsequies, while it greatly reduces the expense; the hire of a hearse with a single horse costing only £1 1s, and with two horses, £1 11s 6d. These carriages have one division for the coffin, and another for six mourners; and when the coffin has been taken out for interment, before the mourners re-enter to return home, the front part of the carriage and the fore wheels are contracted and drawn close up to the hinder or coach part of the carriage by means of a screw, so that the part for containing the coffin disappears, and the whole, when returning from the place of interment, has the appearance of a mourning coach. The invention is ingenious and most useful.[27]

During the 1870s the glass-sided hearse made its appearance. It was lighter and far less sombre than the enclosed variety and it became an overnight success: the mourners – and the passers-by along the route – could now see the coffin and, therefore, the undertaker's handiwork. And, should one have looked closer, a metal trade plate giving the name of the undertaker could be seen close to the centre of the 'window', affixed to the deck or the decorative inner rail. There was some prestige in this, not only for the undertaker but also for the smug comfort of the mourner who had chosen to go to one of the 'better' – that is to say, more expensive – undertakers. Indeed, this system of discreet advertising is still used today. One of the largest firms of funeral suppliers in the nineteenth century, Messrs Dottridge Brothers of Tottenham, was amongst the first to patent a glass-sided hearse. Their 1878 catalogue eulogized its beauty, with its open 'ornamental roof supported by four elegant twisted columns, relieved in colour. The framework is of polished oak, and at each end is an appropriately carved pillar. At the sides are ornamental railings, and from the violet roof, relieved with gold, curtains are gracefully draped, which are especially intended for wet weather. The whole effect is exceedingly pleasing'.[28] They soon became the rage. However, there was one drawback: whereas the enclosed hearse, *sans* feathers, was used as a collection vehicle, the glass-sided hearse did not lend itself to this duty very well.

Dottridge Brothers did not have a monopoly on the glass-sided coach; rather they were influential in its introduction. This type of hearse remained a reliable stock in trade for the next fifty years and it was still being advertised, together with a 'spare parts' service, in their 1923 catalogue (*71*).[29]

As most private and parochial cemeteries were some distance away from residential areas, consideration had to be given to the speed at which funerals

TRANSPORT DEPT.

SALOON HEARSE.

No. 16. LIGHT BIER.

No. 8a. BIER.

THE WASHINGTON CAR.

*71   Dottridge's funeral vehicles of 1922. The Daimler saloon
hearse takes precedence over the horse-drawn Washington Car.
Two hand-steered wheeled biers were also available.*

should now travel. No longer were hearses being 'paged' (i.e. preceeded by the funeral furnisher on foot) all the way from the house of the deceased to the place of burial, and by the 1880s it was more usual for the paging to stop at the nearest main road or, in the instance of the funeral of a local rogue, some way along the main road. At a given nod from the undertaker the mutes would unhook the horse velvets, fold them and pass them up to the driver who would put them in the box under his seat. Mutes and bearers then got up next to the drivers of the hearse and mourning coaches, and the cortège would travel along at a sedate pace. As the cemetery gates came into view the mutes and bearers would regain their position, having first reattached the horse velvets, and the procession would slow down to walking pace as they pulled into the main avenue – a click on the reins and the front two horses nodded and pranced their way to the chapel. And this is quite logical: the velvets would only have flapped in the breeze, slowed down the horses' progress and probably have scared other steeds had they been left on for the duration of the journey – in torrential rain they would have become saturated and hence a nuisance to the animals, as well as an unwanted additional weight, let alone the damage that the pile itself would have incurred. And prancing was certainly not allowed along the main roads, for the animals would have become exhausted before the cemetery gates had come into view. Belgian blacks were sturdy and reliable but even they had their limitations (72).

In the shires, not for them the newfangled gewgaws and whirligigs of the town; funerals continued to be had from the local builder/joiner – in most villages and small country towns the same applies today – with requirements over and above their capabilities being furnished by the undertaking establishments in the nearest large town. The wheeled bier – another near monopoly in the hands of Messrs Dottridge Brothers (71) – would be the sole conveyance, taking coffin from house to church to graveside. It was used for rich and poor alike, it knew no preference, taking Gladstone's body from his house in Hawarden to Broughton Hall Station in 1898 and Fr Stanton's coffin through the streets of London in 1924 from St Alban's, Holborn, to the London Necropolis Railway Station at Waterloo.

The Metropolitan Interments Act of 1850 also allowed for the conveyance of coffins by rail. Many mainline stations had their own coffin trolleys, being little more than enclosed wheeled biers, painted in the appropriate livery. Only the London Necropolis & National Mausoleum Company, the proprietors of Brookwood Cemetery, Surrey, entered into an arrangement with a railway board for special train services. Negotiations began in 1852 with the London & South Western Railway. The Secretary of the railway board was enthusiastic, justifying his argument in a writen report: ' ... it is obvious the cemetery is likely to produce a vast amount of traffic from persons who will for years come to visit the spot, and frequent the Churchyard [sic]; and I can conceive of no duty more obvious for the Director than to make the best bargain they can with the Cemetery Company without consulting their proprietors.'[30] The scheme was finally established in 1854, the first London terminus being at York Street, Waterloo, until 1899 when a new agreement was entered into for a small branch-line terminus, complete with offices, waiting-rooms (first and third class) and *chapelle ardente*, off Westminster Bridge Road. This opened in 1902 and remained the London

138

72   *Wellington's funeral car, designed by Richard Redgrave RA
in 1852. Weighing in at eleven tons, it took twelve sable horses
4½ hours to pull it from St James's Park to St Paul's Cathedral.*

139

terminus until 1941. At Brookwood Cemetery itself a single branch-line led off from Brookwood Station, passing through double wooden gates and down through an avenue of Wellingtonias, to the north station (Roman Catholics and Nonconformists) via the masonry works siding and across the Pirbright Road to the south station (Anglican).

In 1901 the remains of Queen Victoria were taken from Gosport to

73   *The first-recorded motor hearse. The coach was built by the Sheffield funeral furnisher Reuben Thompson on to a 12hp Wolseley chassis, making its début in April 1900.*

Waterloo on the Royal Train and thence from Paddington to Windsor. Since then it has been the custom for the body of a deceased monarch to be transported by rail: Edward VII was taken from Paddington to Windsor in 1910; George V from Wolferton (the station serving Sandringham) to King's Cross and thence from Paddington to Windsor in 1936; and George VI on the same journey in 1952. The hatchments from the front of these trains are now to be seen in the tower space at Sandringham.

It was certainly not unusual for bodies to be transported by water: Queen Elizabeth I was taken from Greenwich Palace to Westminster in April 1603 by barge; and what more fitting obsequy for Lord Nelson than a similar progress up the Thames in his own barge, also from Greenwich to Westminster, in 1806? The naval connections were maintained in the construction of the funeral chariot, with ' ... an elevated canopy with plumes, supported by columns resembling palm

74 *The funeral of a London shopkeeper, 1901. Writing to the
photographer Benjamin Stone, D. McKenzie said, 'The pictures
you have been able to secure will, I am sure, be of interest to
future historians of the morals and manners of the nineteenth
century.'*

trees, and having in its front and back a carved representation of the head and
stern of HMS the Victory' (*Col. 18*)[31]. One of the most moving instances of barge
transport was that arranged for Sir Winston Churchill in 1965 when, as his body
was taken down the Thames from Tower Pier, the dockers lowered the jibs of
their derrick cranes in silent salute as he sailed by.

Reuben Thompson of Sheffield is credited with the production of the first motor
hearse, driving his Wolseley twelve horsepower conversion on to the streets in
April 1900 (*73*). However, the first 'silent' motor hearse capable of being driven at
walking pace was produced by Pargetter of Coventry on a 16/20hp Coventry Lotis
chassis in about 1910; it was an impressive vehicle, reminiscent of the earlier
Shilibeer's funeral omnibus. Whilst Sturmey Motors showed a professional
interest in motor hearses it was Daimler which led the market in the 1920s,
manufacturing not only hearses but also limousines. Almost immediately, the
ever innovative wholesale funeral furnishers, Dottridge Brothers, snapped up a
fleet of Daimler hearses and limousines, advertising them for hire in their 1923
catalogue (*71*). Daimler continue to supply the trade, the coachwork being
contracted out, though not for much longer, as the much revered Daimler DS420

is to cease production some time during 1991.

The trade was slow to accept the introduction of the motor hearse; they were expensive and demanded a considerable cash outlay: therefore both motorized and horse-drawn hearses were to be seen on the streets in the 1920s and 1930s, the former gaining supremacy shortly before the outbreak of World War II. Daimler continued to lead the way, and it was only the more prestigious manufacturer, Rolls-Royce, which stood any chance of ousting them. Certainly Rolls-Royce was more expensive but the outlay on such a fleet had its dividend for the funeral director, for he or she with the better rig stood to attract more custom.

Today, most motorized transport is liveried black though some funeral directors prefer black/grey, thereby enabling them to hire out limousines at weekends for weddings. One large chain of funeral directors, PHK International PLC, is introducing dark blue livery, though it has not proved very popular in the South-east, whilst Glenfrome of Bristol and Crowndeed of Horam can offer white hearses and limousines.

Not many people agonize over the details concerning their final journey to the grave, though a certain Mr Drax of Holnest, Dorset, was adamant that all was to be performed to his satisfaction at the last. He held regular rehearsals during the 1880s, being carried down the drive of Holnest Park in a coffin borne on the shoulders of his gardeners, sometimes halting the procession to say, 'Hi, down your eyes, keep step! You are shaking the corpse.'[32]

For all the undertakers' ingenuity and innovation, nothing could compare with the pathetic spectacle and poignant drama of the simple country funeral, eloquently portrayed in Frank Holl's magnificent painting of 1877, *Her First Born (Col. 30)*. No simpler method of funerary transportation was to be had, yet it draws out from us so much sympathy and compassion towards the anguish of the young parents and the sorrowing grandfather. Better this than the sham theatricalities staged by the city undertakers of that time *(74)*.

15   An outer wooden case of 1869 in the Sackville Vault at Withyham, Sussex, covered with black Utrecht velvet, and the lid secured with one-inch-square cast brass bolts.

16   Design for the outer case made in 1806 by Mr Chittenden of the crown undertakers, France & Banting, for Horatio Nelson, with fittings by Holmes & Bidwell and R. Ackerman.

17   *The covered bier at South Wootton, Norfolk, presented in 1611 by Revd Henry Kidson on the occasion of his fortieth year as rector of the parish.*

18   The Magnificent Funeral Car. *'Built for the sole purpose of Conveying the Remains of Vice Admiral Lord Viscount Nelson to S.t Paul's Cathedral, for Interment, on Thursday the 9th. of Jan.y 1806*

19   The Burial of Charles I, from a fresco by C.W. Cope in the Palace of Westminster. The coffin is about to enter St George's Chapel, Windsor, as the Constable of the castle prohibits Bishop Juxton from reading the funeral service.

20   An Undertaker's Visit! Whilst some undertakers were blamed for posting a watch outside the homes of the terminally ill, few would have gone as far as the man shown in this 1806 caricature by Newton.

21   A Herald's tabard, displaying the royal arms as used between 1714–1801.
Tabards as grand as this eighteenth-century example would have been
commonplace at funerals of the nobility organized by the College of Arms.

22   At the funerals of archbishops and bishops organized
by the College of Arms, the
military achievements were
replaced by ecclesiastical ones.
This mitre and pastoral staff
were supplied for the funeral of
Bishop Fell of Oxford in 1686.

23 *Cheyne Walk in 1776. James Millar's elegant watercolour pays full attention to the day-to-day life of eighteenth-century Chelsea: witness, for example, the joiner hanging a hatchment on the house to the left.*

24 *On the occasion of the obsequies of George, Baron Howard of Henderskelfe in 1984, a catafalque was erected beneath the dome of Hawksmoor's mausoleum at Castle Howard.*

25   *Nelson's 1806 lying-in-state at Greenwich was organized by the College of Arms and arranged by the crown undertakers, France & Banting. It was a sumptuous affair.*

26   *The chancel floor at Thaxted, Essex, provides an opportunity to study at first hand the types of markers used in association with intramural burial from the sixteenth through to the mid nineteenth centuries.*

27 Between the late seventeenth and early nineteenth centuries, city and town churches were heavily used by the middle class for intramural burial. The 1983/84 excavations at St Augustine-the-Less, Bristol, exposed 107 such private vaults.

28 The c.1737 Lethieullier Vault at St Mary's, Little Ilford, Essex. Contrast the rough mortar of the roof and the neat pointing meted out to the floor, walls and access steps.

29   Commissioned in 1731 from Nicholas Hawksmoor (d.1736) by the Third Earl of Carlisle (d.1738), neither architect nor patron lived to see the mausoleum at Castle Howard completed. Its romantic setting so enthused Horace Walpole that he described it as 'a mausoleum that would tempt one to be buried alive'.

30   No simpler funeral than this was to be had – and never was grief so poignantly portrayed as in this sorrowful painting of 1877 by Frank Holl, Her First Born, Horsham Churchyard.

6

The Common Funeral

It is said that if one wishes to find out about one's own country's customs, recourse should be made to what foreigners have written on the subject. Nowhere is this anthropological approach more pertinent than for the funeral. The Swiss traveller Misson recorded more about English funeral customs during his early eighteenth-century peregrination in the country than did any contemporary indigenous commentator:

As soon as any Person is dead, they are oblig'd to give Notice thereof to the Minister of the Parish, and to those who are appointed to visit dead Bodies. This Custom of visiting dead Bodies was establish'd after the dreadful Plague that ravag'd London in 1665, to the Intent that it might be immediately known if there was any Contagious Distemper, and proper Methods taken to put a Stop to it. They are generally two Women that do this. The Clerk of the Parish receives their Certificate, and out of these is form'd an Abridgment that is publish'd every Week. By this Paper you may see how many Persons of both Sexes dy'd within that Week, of what Distemper, or by what Accident.

There is an Act of Parliament which ordains, That the Dead shall be bury'd in a Woollen Stuff, which is a Kind of thin Bays, which they call Flannel; nor is it lawful to use the least Needleful of Thread or Silk. (The Intention of this Act is for the Encouragement of the Woollen Manufacture.) This Shift is always White; but there are different Sorts of it as to Fineness, and consequently of different Prices. To make these Dresses is a particular Trade, and there are many that sell nothing else; so that these Habits for the Dead are always to be had ready made, of what Size or Price you please, for People of every Age and Sex. After they have wash'd the Body thoroughly clean, and shav'd it, if it be a Man, and his Beard be grown during his Sickness, they put it on a Flannel Shirt, which has commonly a Sleeve purfled about the Wrists, and the Slit of the Shirt down the Breast done in the same Manner. When these Ornaments

143

are not of Woollen Lace, they are at least edg'd, and sometimes embroider'd with black Thread. The Shirt shou'd be at least half a Foot longer than the Body, that the Feet of the Deceas'd may be wrapped in it as in a Bag. When they have thus folded the End of the Shirt close to the Feet, they tye the Part that is folded down with a Piece of Woolen Thread, as we do our Stockings; so that the End of the Shirt is done into a Kind of Tuft.

Upon the Head they put a Cap, which they fasten with a very broad Chin Cloth, with Gloves on the Hands, and a Cravat round the Neck, all of Woollen. That the Body may ly the softer, some put a layer of Bran, about four inches thick, at the Bottom of the Coffin. Instead of a Cap, the Women have a Kind of Head Dress, with a Forehead Cloth. The Body being thus equipp'd and laid in the Coffin (which Coffin is sometimes very magnificent), it is visited a second time, to see that it is bury'd in Flannel, and that nothing about it is sowed with Thread. They let it lye three or four Days in this Condition; which Time they allow, as well to give the dead Person an Opportunity of Coming to Life again, if his Soul has not quite left his Body; as to prepare Mourning, and the Ceremonies of the Funeral.

They send the Beadle with a List of such Friends and Relations as they have a Mind to invite; and sometimes they have printed Tickets, which they leave at their Houses. A little before the Company is set in Order for the March, they lay the Body into the Coffin upon two Stools, in a Room where all that please may go and see it; they then take off the Top of the Coffin, and remove from off the Face the little square Piece of Flannel, made on Purpose to cover it, and not fastened to any Thing; Upon this Occasion the rich Equipage of the Dead does Honour to the Living. The Relations and chief Mourners are in a Chamber apart, with their more intimate Friends; and the rest of the Guests are dispersed in several Rooms about the House.

When they are ready to set out, they nail up the Coffin, and a Servant presents the Company with Sprigs of Rosemary; every one takes a Sprig and carries it in his Hand 'till the Body is put into the Grave, at which Time they all throw their Sprigs in after it. Before they set out, and after they return, it is usual to present the guests with something to drink, either red or white Wine, boil'd with Sugar and Cinnamon, or some such Liquor.

The Parish has always three or four Mortuary Cloths of different Prices, to furnish those who are at the Charge of the interment. These Cloths, which they call Palls, are some of black Velvet, others of Cloth with an edge of white Linnen or Silk, a foot broad, or thereabouts; For a Bachellor or Maid, or for a Woman that dies in Child Birth, the Pall is white. This is spread over the Coffin, and is so broad that the Six or Eight men that carry the Body are quite hid beneath it to their Waste, and the Corners and Sides of it hang down low enough to be borne by those who, according to Custom, are invited for that purpose. They generally give Black or White Gloves and black Crape Hatbands to those that carry the Pall; sometimes also white Silk Scarves.

Every Thing being ready to move (it must be remember'd that I always speak of middling People, among whom the Customs of a Nation are most truly to be learn'd), one or more Beadles march first, each carrying a long Staff, at the End of which is a great Apple or Knob of Silver. The Minister of the Parish, generally accompany'd by some other Minister, and attended by the Clerk, walks next; and the Body carry'd as I said before, comes just after him (75). The Relations in close Mourning, and all the Guests two and two, make up the rest of the Procession. The Common Practice is to carry the corpse thus into the Body of the

144

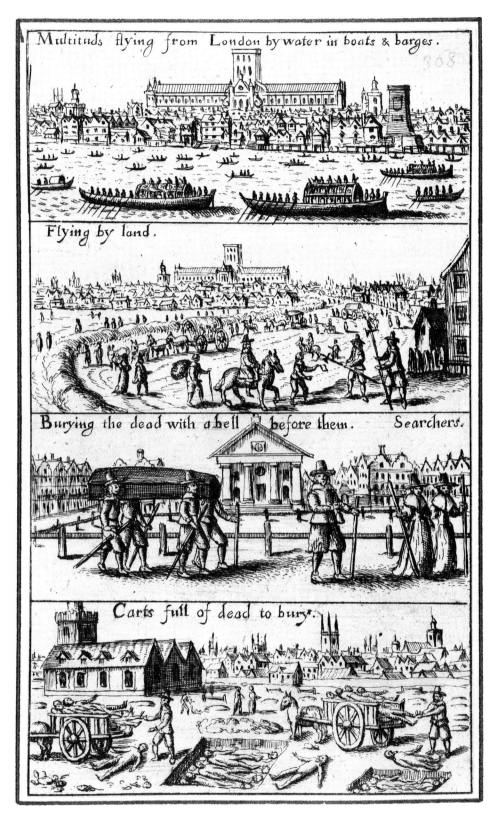

75 Burying the dead with a bell before them. Engraving of Plague Scenes of c. 1655 attributed to John Dunstall. The sexton, with staff and bell, announces the approach of the cortège.

Church, where they set it down upon two Tressels, while either a Funeral Sermon is preach'd, containing an Eulogium upon the deceased, or certain Prayers said, adapted to the Occasion. If the body is not bury'd in the Church, they carry it to the Church Yard belonging to the same, where it is interr'd in the Presence of the Guests, who are round the Grave, and they do not leave it 'till the Earth is thrown in upon it. Then they return Home in the same order that they came, and each drinks two or three Glasses more before he goes Home.[1]

To see how this ritual developed, and to enable us to understand the aims and objectives of each stage, we have to go back 150 years before Misson penned his account.

Take any small rural community in England during, say, the middle of the sixteenth century. It is early autumn; the last few stragglers hurry along the main street to join their friends at the lich-gate as the single bell sounds out its hollow knell. Some tilling the fields on the outskirts of the village stop work for a while, just long enough to offer up a silent prayer for the soul of the departed, perhaps making the sign of the cross as they had been taught to do in childhood, for old habits died hard in such remote areas. Others continue working, the distant bell reminding them of their mortality and eventual end. Meanwhile, the cowled cortège wends its way through the village, its approach heralded by the clerk ringing a handbell (*76*). On arrival at the lich-gate the procession re-forms,

76   Sexton's handbell, inscribed 'MEMENTO + MORE + 1638.' This is the type of bell carried by the sextons shown in plates 69 and 75.

146

the short respite being a welcome interlude for those carrying the bier; the pall is readjusted over the shrouded corpse and the priest leads off towards the grave or church. The funeral proper has begun. 'I am the resurreciō and the life (sayeth the Lord): he that beleueth in me, yea though he were dead, yet shall he liue. And whosoeuer lyueth and beleueth in me: shall not dye for euer.'[2] Comforting words – words that have been in use for at least three quarters of a millennium as the opening sentence of the Order for the Burial of the Dead, except for those that died unbaptized, unrepentant, excommunicated or who had laid violent hands on themselves.

In the early Church death was regarded as a release from the trials and tribulations of a wicked and sinful world to a larger, fuller life in heaven. The anniversary of a death – the 'year's mind' as it was later called – was, therefore, greater reason for celebration than a birthday, as the latter merely established the increase in years spent away from God's nearer presence: death was the last stage of the weary pilgrimage, heaven the goal, Christ the prize. There was good reason, then, for the funeral to be a joyful event, though it would be erroneous to say that it lacked solemnity, for the soul of the good and faithful servant had detached itself from the body for a glorious reunion with God. An especial grace was imparted to the family of the deceased were they to invite the poor and needy to share in the funeral feast which followed the burial. This feast was itself an anticipation of the Common Meal to be enjoyed by all in the New Jerusalem when Christ, the Sacrificial Lamb, will invite all to sit at the same board and partake. Such being the case, how could death be regarded with terror, when life was merely being changed, rather than taken away? It is probably for this reason that white, the liturgical colour associated with resurrection and rebirth, was adopted by the early Church for mourning.

It would be a misunderstanding to presume that such celebrations were devoid of sorrow. Human emotion will find an outlet no matter the event, and the loss of a parent, spouse or child would have given as much rise to grief then as now, though it should not be forgotten that tears shed are more for the living than the dead. Was it not, then, that the funeral was seen both as a celebration to mark the soul's triumphant translation into Paradise and as a means of comfort and reassurance for the bereaved?

By contrast, the doctrine dominant in the Western Church from the fifth to the sixteenth centuries was set by St Augustine of Hippo, who expounded the theory of purgatory, whereby the faithful might be called after death to pass through a purifying fire, the *ignis purgatorius*, before finally receiving the Crown of Life. Augustine's theory received papal ratification and was raised to the rank of dogma by Gregory the Great. From the outset of her conversion, England was darkened by the gloom which this unhappy surmise cast over the state of the dead. Be that as it may, the new converts accepted this and within this belief the liturgy connected with death and burial took shape. It is hardly surprising that the attitude of peace, hope and triumph which had characterized the earlier approach to the funeral was exchanged for one of doom and gloomy apprehension.

It is of paramount importance to remember that the Church's concern with the welfare and salvation of the soul began at baptism and that Holy Mother Church

147

jealously guarded her educative and protective role right through until death. With this in mind it is easy to understand that the protracted ritual leading to the burial of the dead began with the Order for the Visitation of the Sick.

In the Sarum Manual (the modification of the Roman rite which dominated the Church in England from the fourteenth century to 1549) the parish priest is supplied with offices both for the Visitation and for Unction. When he was called to visit the sick the priest went with the servers to the house, saying on the way the seven penitential psalms, with the antiphon, 'Remember not, Lord, our offences.' When he reached the house he invoked peace upon it and, on coming into the sick person's presence, sprinkled him with holy water whilst saying the *Kyrie*, the Lord's Prayer and suffrages – similar to the format existing in the 1662 Book of Common Prayer – together with a number of collects. The priest then examined the sick person as to his faith, using either a summary of the *Quicunque* or, in the case of the illiterate, a far simpler form based on the Apostle's Creed; finally, he then exhorted him to charity and patience, heard his confession and gave him absolution, closing with prayers and a blessing.

The Sacrament of Unction followed. The Office began with a psalm accompanied by the antiphon, 'O Saviour of the world.' When it came to the anointing, the priest, smearing the thumb of his right hand with the oil, applied it to the organs of the senses, the feet and loins, saying at each application, 'By this unction, of His own most tender mercy, may the Lord forgive thee whatever sins thou hast committed by the sense of touching' – seeing, hearing etc., as the case might be. After unction the Blessed Sacrament was exposed and, on having signified his belief in the true body and blood to be present in one kind, he received. If, however, he was too ill to consume the host, the priest was able to say, 'Brother, in this case it suffices for thee to have a true faith and good will; believe only, and thou hast eaten.' Finally, when the person was *in extremis*, the priest visited the house again and, using the 'Commendation of a Soul in the Article of Death', began with a specially adapted litany, followed by the *Proficiscere anima Christiana* and a few short sentences, the Church's *bon voyage* for the release of the dying spirit. There were no startling changes brought about with the revision of the Prayer Book at the Reformation; the 1549 Office for the Visitation of the Sick ran very much along the old lines. The greatest change was the removal of the act of anointing from the 1552 and subsequent prayer books, though this could have been foretold from the reduction of the act in the 1549 Prayer Book when only the forehead and breast were marked.

In the Sarum Manual the rites which follow death begin with a *Commendatio animarum*, prayers and psalms for the departed. The corpse was then washed, wrapped or sewn into its winding-sheet. By this time news of the death would have already spread through the community, more so in areas where it was customary for the church bell to be tolled during the Article of Death.[3] Although the precise details are not known, one assumes that either the priest, parish clerk or sexton informed the burial guild of the impending death so as to put them on the alert.

Once the house offices were over, the body was carried in procession to the church, proceeded by the crucifer and acolytes, the parish clerk or sexton following behind and ringing a handbell at intervals to invoke all those that

77   The Office of the Dead. *From the London Hours of René of Anjou, early fifteenth century. A simple wooden hearse, with thirteen wax tapers, surrounds the palled coffin.*

heard it to pray for the repose of the soul of the departed. Behind him came the priest and his ministers – if any – robed in albs and singing psalms. Next came the bier, followed by the chief mourners in black cloaks and hoods, and then the other relatives and friends of the deceased, all holding tapers. With the Reformation the form of the procession changed; gone were the crucifer and acolytes, and the priest now met the body at the 'church stile' or lich-gate.

On its arrival in the church the bier was placed at the entrance to the chancel, feet addressed to the east, and covered with the pall. Around the bier was placed a hearse (77) upon which went the votive candles or, if the church did not own such items, simple brass altar candlesticks were stood on the floor at the corners of the bier. With the mourners standing in the body of the church and the priest in his stall, the *Officium pro Defunctus* – the Office of the Dead – began. In the Sarum rite, Vespers of the Dead were sung in the early evening proceeding the funeral,[4] and were more commonly known as the *Placebo*, deriving its name from the opening antiphon, *Placebo Domino in regione vivorum*. This over, the body rested in church overnight. Then, early next morning when the penitential matins and lauds were being sung, the priest, vested in alb and stole, went into the churchyard, made the sign of the cross over the ground appointed for the grave, sprinkled it with holy water, and then marked out its length and breadth by digging out the shape of a cross on the ground with the spade whilst saying words from verses 19 and 20 of Psalm 107: 'Open ye to me the gates of justice; I will go into them, and give praise to the Lord. This is the gate of the Lord; the just shall enter into it.' This done, he returned to the church to sing the requiem mass. This was all done away with at the Reformation on the publication in 1551 of the Second Prayer Book of Edward VI.

At one time there were three masses: two early ones – one of the Holy Trinity and the other of the Blessed Virgin Mary – and a third, the exequial high mass of requiem, after the mourners had partaken of breakfast. The Sarum rite limited this to one mass of requiem. After the post-Communion prayer the priest took off the chasuble and put on a cope and, with the deacon by his side, approached the body and walked round it anticlockwise, first sprinkling it with holy water and then censing it. That done, the altar party and mourners re-formed into procession and went out into the churchyard singing the antiphon *In paradisum*: 'May the angels lead thee to paradise, may the martyrs receive thee at thy coming and bring thee into the holy city Jerusalem. May the choir of angels receive thee, and with Lazarus, who once was poor, mayst thou now have eternal rest.'

On coming to the grave, which would have been dug whilst the requiem mass was being said, the body was incensed and sprinkled a second time. Having been put into the shallow grave by either the sexton or some members of the burial guild, the priest then placed on to the breast of the shrouded corpse a parchment scroll upon which was written the Absolution. Sometimes a simple stamped lead cross would suffice. Now safely in the grave, the body was sprinkled and censed for the third and final time and, after the recitation of Psalm 131 and further prayers for the soul's repose, the priest began the primary infilling, spading the first few crumbs of soil on to the corpse in the form of a cross. This done, the burial party returned to the church singing the seven penitential psalms, leaving the sexton behind to complete his work. Again, all of this was abandoned with the post-Reformation prayer books.

One would have thought that this elaborate and protracted ritual would have secured absolute rest for any soul. Not so. There were then masses to be said every day for a month, known as the Trental, with especial solemnity on the third, seventh and thirtieth days, when the chief mourners were expected to attend. This was all well and good in a small village community where deaths were infrequent; one wonders how the busy priest of a town or city church would have coped. Yet as each mass was accompanied by a fee, he was probably not so distressed as one might imagine. However, this drawn-out liturgy began to wane during the early years of the fifteenth century and had almost ceased by the time of the Reformation.

For those regarded as better off, doles of money, food and mourning clothes were made to the poor, not only on the day of the funeral but also on the third, seventh and thirtieth days after death. With the waning of the Trental this practice also died out, its place being taken by a single feast for the chief mourners after the funeral. This custom continues to survive, though generally the fare is now limited to ham sandwiches, quiche and a cup of tea.[5]

The Church did not enjoy a good press at the beginning of the sixteenth century; public opinion was hostile and it was generally felt that some liturgical reform was well overdue. Henry VIII, though at variance with the Pope, had no intention of committing himself to any swingeing liturgical changes and went no further than allowing the issue, in 1542, of a revised edition of the Sarum Breviary and the commissioning of a Committee of Convocation under the chairmanship of Archbishop Thomas Cranmer to consider further reform of the service books. Cranmer was much impressed by Martin Luther; Henry VIII was not. Being an astute fellow, Cranmer kept his draft prayer book on the back burner until such time as it would be appropriate for him to produce it. He did not have to wait long; Henry VIII's successor, the boy king Edward VI, was completely in the hands of the reformers. Cranmer saw his chance and leapt in. This was a great coup and, hardly surprisingly, almost the entire Court agreed that his was an excellent formula and just what they had all been looking for. Consequently, an Act was passed in January 1549 ordering that the new prayer book be brought into use by the Feast of Pentecost of that year. We have already seen the liturgical differences between this and the Sarum Manual. However, it soon became clear that Cranmer's 1549 success was but a prelude to a more radical overhaul of the liturgy, with the publication of the Second Prayer Book of Edward VI in 1552.

Not all funeral customs were swept away on the introduction of the 1549 Prayer book, as Henry Machyn relates in his diary entry for 22 September 1551:

> The xxij day of September was the monyth ['s mind of the] ij dukkes of Suffoke in Chambryge-shyre, with [ij] standards, ij baners grett of armes and large, and banars rolles of dyver armes, with ij elmets, ij [swords, ij] targetts crownyd, ij cotes of armes, ij crests, and [ten dozen] of schochyons crounyd; and yt was grett pete of [their] dethe, and yt had plesyd God, of so nobull a stok they wher, for ther ys no more left of them.[6]

The Machyn Diary, covering the year 1550–63, is the most important surviving document on the post-Reformation common funeral. To find out who Machyn was, we need to refer to John Gough Nichols, his commentator: 'Machyn himself has been taken by some for a herald, or at least a painter employed by the heralds. In the absence of any direct proof of his occupation, I rather think that his business was in that department of the trade of a merchant-taylor which we now call an undertaker or furnisher of funerals ... the circumstances of [the diary's] closing at a time when the plague was prevalent in London, renders it not impossible that the author was a victim of that deadly scourge.'[7] Nichols continues, 'On religious matters his information is valuable, so far as it represents the sentiments and behaviour of the common people at this vacillating period of our ecclesiastical history. It is evident ... that his own sympathies were inclined to the old form of worship; which, indeed, with its pompous ceremonial, was the best encourager of the craft by which he gained his livelihood. He hailed with delight its re-establishment and the accession of Mary, and rejoices to chronicle all the ceremonies and processions which then enlivened the churches and streets of the city.'[8]

With the accession of Queen Mary in 1553 some of the pre-Reformation ritual returned. Again, Machyn helps us here:

> The sam day [1 July 1555] was bered good master Thomas ... altherman, sum tyme sheryff of London, and a [hearse] with ij whyt cranchys and xij longe torchys [a hearse] stayff torchys and iiij grett tapurs, and xij gownes gyffen unto xij pore men of blake peneston, and the compene of the Clarkes and mony prestes and ... armes of the body and the tapurs, and ther wer ... blake gownes. and after durge speysse-bred and wine; and the moorw masse of requeem, and ther dyd pryche a frer of Grenwyche, and a grett dolle.[9]

Cinnamon-spiced bread and 'hippocras', a mulled wine, were the common fare for such occasions. Even at the funerals of the poor it was customary for food and drink to be given to the assembled company, though before the funeral rather than afterwards. Whatever the arrangements, food played an important part in the civil observances of all funerals, and Machyn frequently closed his accounts of the ecclesiastical ceremonies of the rich and well-to-do with the words, '... and after all done a gret dener'.

That Machyn abhorred the revised liturgy being introduced by Queen Elizabeth I towards the close of 1558 can be judged from his account of a middle-class earth burial at which he officiated on 7 April in the following year:

> The vij day of Aprell [1559] was browth unto [Saint Thomas] of Acurs in Chepe from lytyll sant Barthellmuw Loethbere masteres ... and ther was a gret compene of pepull, ij and ij together, and nodur prest nor clarke, the nuw prychers in ther gownes lyke ley-[men], nodur syngyng nor sayhyng tyll they cam [to the grave,] and a-for she was pute into the grayff a [collect] in Englys, and then put in-to the grayff, and after [took some] heythe and caste yt on the corse, and red a thynge ... for the sam, and contenent cast the heth in-to the [grave], and contenent red the pystll of sant Poll to the Stesselonyans the (blank) chapter, and after thay song *pater-noster* in Englys, boyth prychers and odur, and [women] of a new fassyon, and after on of them whent in-to the pulpytt and mad a sermon.[10]

Little did Machyn know that he was witnessing the revived liturgy of 1552 which, within eleven weeks, was to be published as part of the new Prayer Book of Queen Elizabeth I.

If we were slavishly to follow Machyn as our guide, he would have us believe that the Elizabethan Office for the Burial of the Dead was without beauty; admittedly the requiem mass was gone, together with the protracted rites temporarily reintroduced by Queen Mary, but the revived service had a special beauty in its language and a no-nonsense attitude towards the occasion: it was a format to accompany the burial of the Christian dead, and that is precisely what it did, with no frills attached. Again, it would be wrong to say that funerals were without incident. Writing on William Herbert, Earl of Pembroke, John Aubrey related a touching story: 'This William (the founder of the Family) had a little reddish picked nose Cur-dog: none of the Prettiest: which loved him, and the Earl loved the dog. When the Earl died [1570], the dog would not goe from his Master's dead body, but pined away, and dyed under the hearse; the picture of which Dog is under his picture in the Gallery at Wilton.'[11]

Within a comparatively short period, 1549 to 1559, England had experienced four prayer books. To the common man it must have been confusing, possibly fatal during Queen Mary's time, to have picked up the wrong book. One is left wondering how these changes affected the funeral in the more distant parts of the realm. For example, are we really to understand that all of the old countrywide customs were swept away with the introduction of the Second Prayer Book of Edward VI in 1551 only to be brought back in 1553 on the accession of Queen Mary? Probably not. The chance to adopt real change came with the introduction of Queen Elizabeth's Prayer Book, which enjoyed a span of at least ninety years. No amount of published alternatives will immediately change the mind or the habits of a lifetime and there were many in the mid-sixteenth century who refused to conform and continued in their old ways, retaining the beliefs which they had been taught at their mother's knee. Conversely, there were those who thought that the changes were not radical enough and, as with most radicals, they were more successfully vociferous in their condemnation than were the seemingly passive supporters of the status quo. In the end it was the radicals, better known as the Puritans, who won the day. It was left to the clergy to expound the value of the new services to the people. This was no easy task at a time when churchgoing was practically compulsory by law and the clergy were held in contempt by a large section of society. Indeed, even Elizabeth I had difficulty coming to terms with clergy marriages, once making her views known during an encounter with Mrs Cranmer who, poor lady, sometimes had recourse to travel in a linen basket for fear of the verbal abuse of the people.

Machyn himself especially disliked the preacher Veron, rector of St Martin's, Ludgate, a French Protestant, who had been ordained by Bishop Ridley, and was 'a leader in the change from the old ecclesiastical music for the services to the psalms in metre, versified by Sternhold and Hopkins'.[12] P.H. Ditchfield relates a terrible state of affairs that took place in 1566 when some members of the Parish Clerks' Company caused the disgrace and suspension of Robert Crowley, vicar of St Giles', Cripplegate. He loathed surplices as 'rags of Popery' and could not bear to see the clerks marching in orderly procession singing and chanting. A funeral took place at his church on 1 April 1566. A few days before, the Archbishop of Canterbury had issued his advertisements ordering the use of the surplice. The friends of the deceased had engaged the services of the parish clerks, who, believing that the order applied to them as well as the clergy, appeared at the door of the church attired according to their ancient usage. A scene occurred. The angry Crowley met them at the door and bade them take off those 'porter's coats'. The deputy of the ward supported the vicar and threatened to lay them up by the feet if they dared to enter the church in such obnoxious robes. There was a mighty disturbance. 'Those who took their part according to the queen's prosedyngs were fain to give over and tarry without the church door.' The Lord Mayor's attention was called to this disgraceful scene. He complained to the archbishop. The deputy of the ward was bound over to keep the peace, and Crowley was ordered to stay in his house, and for not wearing a surplice was deprived of his living, to which he was again appointed twelve years later. The clerks triumphed, but their services at funerals soon ceased. Puritan opinions spread; no longer did the clerks lead the singing and processions at funeral pageants, and a few boys from Christ's Hospital or schoolchildren took their place in degenerate ways.[13]

One important duty which the parish clerks of London – and also of some provincial towns – fulfilled was the publishing of bills of mortality for the City, though the earliest surviving bills date back to the reign of Henry VIII, when the clerks were required to give information in connection with deaths from the plague as well as from other causes. From these can be gleaned a wealth of information. The return of casualties of the plague are sometimes very large, accounting for 17,404 of the 20,372 deaths in 1562 for example. Obviously, such an enormous number of deaths soon filled up the City churchyards, so the parish clerks were in addition charged to report on the availability of burial space. It was the clerks who also had the unenviable task of locating those houses in the parish where plague was present. At its height, weekly bills were issued during the plague of 1665. From this can be ascertained the severity of the pestilence; during one week in April, fifty-seven people died, whilst by September the number of reported deaths had reached 6,544.

The methods of making out these returns were very curious, and did not lend themselves to infallible accuracy. In each parish there were certain persons known as 'searchers', ancient women who were informed by the sexton of a death, and whose duty it was to visit the deceased and report the cause of death to the parish clerk. They had no medical knowledge whatsoever, and therefore their diagnosis could only have been conjectural. The clerk made out his bill for the week, took it to the hall of the company, and deposited it in a box on the staircase. All the returns were then tabulated, arranged and printed, and when copies had been sent to the authorities, others were placed in the hands of the clerks for general sale.

The system was a good one, but its execution was defective. Negligent clerks did not send their returns in spite of admonition, caution, fines, or brotherly persuasion. The searchers' information was often unreliable. Complications arose on account of the Act of the Commonwealth Parliament, which required the registration of births instead of baptisms, or civil marriages, and banns published in the market place – also on account of the vast mortality caused by the Great Plague, the burials in the large common pits and public burial-grounds, and the opposition of the Quakers to inspection and registration. All these causes contributed to the issuing of unreliable returns, though the company did their best to grapple with all these difficulties. But whatever the hardships might have been, the bills of mortality provided information not recorded in parochial burial registers: the cause of death. The Worshipful Company of Parish Clerks continued issuing bills of mortality until 1859, by which time the Public Registration Act had rendered unnecessary a task which they had carried on for three centuries to the best of their ability.

By the end of the sixteenth century murmurs were being made as to the need for reform of the secular ritual of the funeral; the form of service having itself been changed, it was now time to direct attention to the practices of the trade and their continuance of what was, in the main, a pre-Reformation panoply. Clare Gittings cites the instructions of Sir John Millicent of Barham, Cambridgeshire, whose 1577 will directed that his 'burial be done without any manner or pomp, and without the wearing of black gown or coats, or the jangling of bells, or any other ceremonies to be had thereof, for they are but vain, chargeable and superstitious'.[14] Yet old habits die hard, and precious few tradesmen charged with the furnishing of funerals were going to be willing to abandon all sources of profit obtainable from the provision of 'black gown or coat', pall or torches, and neither did they want to recognize that persons in some quarters were advocating reform. Certainly not Henry Machyn, whose sole profit came from the 'manner of pomp' he provided.

The Church had little to say at this time regarding the secular observances of the street procession, preferring to keep its own counsel. Dom Gregory Dix sheds some light on this silence: 'Mourning customs are always one of the most persistent elements of older practice through all changes of religion, chiefly because they depend on private observance by grief-stricken individuals much more than on official religious regulation; and no ecclesiastic is going to go out of his way to rebuke harmless conventions which may do little to assuage sorrow at such a time.'[15] Indeed, nor were the people and, though the financial constraints imposed on the exchequer during the reigns of James I and Charles I permeated down through society, few exercised restraint when it came to furnishing funerals, as surviving contemporary documents prove. And not all funerals at this time were performed in complete silence. In 1629 John Whitson of Bristol 'was buried very honourably; besides all his Relations in mourning, he had as many poor old men and women as he was yeares old in mourning gownes and hoodes, the Mayor and Aldermen in Mourning; all the Trained Band (he was their Colonel) attended the Funerall and their Pikes had black Ribons and Drummes were covered with Black cloath.'[16]

With the accession of James I in 1603 the Puritans recognized an ally in respect of certain alterations they wished to have made to Queen Elizabeth's Prayer Book, together with other reforms affecting Church government and the liturgy in general. As J.H.R. Moorman relates, 'the Puritan party was active, self-confident and aggressive. On the ecclesiastical side it represented those who wished to advance from the restrained conservatism of the Elizabethan

Settlement to much greater liberty in both worship and in church government. It disliked both the Prayer Book and episcopacy because each put a curb on the liberty of the individual'.[17] Yet all they gained were a few minor additions to the Prayer Book and the agreement to a new translation of the Bible, the 1611 'Authorized Version'. The Order for the Burial of the Dead remained in its unaltered state. However, a much greater Puritan influence was seen during the time of Charles I, culminating towards the cessation of his reign in the reception by Parliament in December 1611 of the Root and Branch Petition, a document demanding the abolition, 'root and branch', of all government by archbishops, bishops, deans and archdeacons on the grounds that such government led only to an increase of Romish superstition and ceremonial.

As soon as the Civil War began in 1642, Parliament abolished the episcopacy and introduced the Solemn League and Covenant for the 'extirpation of popery, prelacy (that is Church government by archbishops, bishops, their chancellors and commissaries, deans, deans and chapters, archdeacons, and all other ecclesiastical officers depending on that hierarchy), superstition, heresy, schism, profaneness, and whatsoever shall be found contrary to sound doctrine and the power of godliness,'[18] in February 1644. The fall of the episcopacy meant also the fall of the Book of Common Prayer, this being replaced in 1644 by the Directory of Public Worship. The funeral suffered dreadfully, almost died a death in fact, for, according to the new rubric all customs of praying, reading and singing, both *en route* to and at the grave, were said to have been grossly abused. The following simple direction was therefore given, that 'When any person departeth this life, let the dead body, upon the day of burial, be decently attended from the house to the place appointed for public burial, and there immediately interred, without any ceremony.'[19] The ministrations of the Church to the dead and the bereaved were done away at a stroke and the corpse – albeit 'decently attended' – went to the grave as if it were a dead dog on its way to a local authority refuse dump. Gone were the services of the parish clerk proceeding the cortège with handbell, his place being taken in some City parishes by the beadle, fully attired and with his silver-topped staff of office. Nevertheless, the expression 'decently attended' could be interpreted in a number of ways and the funeral-furnishing fraternity saw this not as a restriction on their panoply, but as a possible recommendation for retaining the status quo.

Some of the funerals performed at this time were little short of a disgrace. William Chillingworth, the divine, died in 1644. 'He lies buried in the south side of the Cloysters at Chichester, where he dyed of the *morbus castrensis* after the taking of Arundel castle by the Parliament: wherin he was very much blamed by the King's soldiers for his Advice in military affaires there, and they curst *that little Priest* and imputed the Losse of the Castle to his advice. In his sicknesse he was inhumanely treated by Dr Cheynell, who, when he was to be buryed, threw his booke into the grave with him, saying, *Rott with the rotten; let the dead bury the dead.*'[20]

Arguably the most poignant funeral of the time was that 'performed' for Charles I himself, under the direction of Sir Thomas Herbert, his personal assistant. Immediately the execution had taken place on the morning of Tuesday 30 January 1649, the remains were placed into a coffin, covered with a black

156

velvet pall and taken into the Palace of Whitehall where the parliamentary surgeon, Thomas Trapham, sewed the head back on to the body and embalmed the whole. The corpse was then wrapped in cerecloth, soldered into an anthropoid lead shell and placed in a flat-lidded single-break wooden case upholstered with black velvet and *sans* depositum plate. It was then removed to St James's where it lay in state covered by a plain black velvet pall. Burial in Westminister Abbey was refused but Herbert's and Bishop Juxon's suggestion of St George's Chapel, Windsor, was accepted. The date was fixed for Tuesday, 6 February. Herbert relates that the coffin went to Windsor early on the morning of the 6th in a 'Hearse covered with black Velvet, drawn by Six Horses also covered with black; after which, Four Coaches followed ... in which were about a Dozen Gentlemen and others, most of them being such as had waited on his Majesty at Carisbrooke Castle and other places ... all of them being in black'.[21] On their arrival at Windsor the coffin was taken into the Deanery and placed on a long oak table[22] before being removed to the King's bedchamber within the castle. Meanwhile, Herbert and some friends were in St George's Chapel discussing the possibility of reopening Edward IV's grave, when the Duke of Richmond entered the chapel with a group of other noblemen and took charge of the burial, having being instructed so to do by Parliament. 'One of those Lords beating gently upon the Pavement with his Staff perceived a hollow sound, and ordering the Stones and Earth thereunder to be removed, discovered a descent into a Vault, where two coffins were laid.'[23] This was the vault of Henry VIII and Queen Jane Seymour.

While the grave was being made ready the party returned to the castle, a lead depositum plate with the inscription 'KING CHARLES 1648' was hastily made and fixed to the coffin, which was then carried on the shoulders of 'Gentlemen that were of some Quality in Mourning' towards the chapel, followed by the governor of the castle, Herbert's party, the Duke of Richmond and the other Parliamentary lords (*Col. 19*). Herbert recalled that 'the sky was serene and clear, but presently it began to snow, and fell so fast, as by that time they came to the West-end of the Royal Chapel, the black Velvet-Pall was all white being thick covered with snow. So went the White King to his Grave, in the 48th Year of his Age, and the 22nd Year and 10th Month of his Reign.' But this was not the end of the indignity for, on arrival at the vault, the governor of the castle refused to let Bishop Juxon read the funeral service from the now proscribed Book of Common Prayer: 'The Bishop of London stood weeping by, to tender that his service which might not be accepted. Then was [Charles I] deposited in silence and sorrow in the vacant place in the vault [the hearse-cloth being cast in after it] about 3 of the afternoon; and the Lords that night, though late, returned to London.'[24] Aubrey's record of the King's burial is more fanciful: 'Now as to the last part, I well remember it was frequently and soberly affirmed by officers of the army, &c. Grandees, that the body of King Charles the First was privately putt into the sand about White-hall; and the coffin that was carried to Windsor and layd in King Henry 8th's vault was filled with rubbish, or brick-batts. Mr Fabian Philips, who adventured his life before the King's Tryall, by printing, assures me, that the Kings Coffin did cost but six shillings: a plain deale coffin.'[25] Not so, as was proved when the coffin was examined by Sir Henry Halford, the Royal Physician, in 1813.[26]

During the Commonwealth it was not unusual for parish clerks to perform funerals, owing to absenteeism after the deprivation of livings in 1644. However, such had been the state of the Church during the previous fifty years that the parish clerk of the second quarter of the seventeenth century had many precedents to cite in support of his seeming usurpation. In 1621 Bishop Mountain of London was prepared to smooth the path of the vicar of Waltham Abbey, Essex, by licensing his clerk, Thomas Dickenson, to read prayers, church women and bury the dead, owing to the 'largeness of the parish and the excessive duties of the curate'.[27] At Selsey, Sussex, it was reported in 1625 that 'divers children had died unbaptised for want of a minister and divers corps have of necessity been buried by our parrish clerke' because the vicar, Robert Johnson, was such a notorious non-resident. Again, the churchwardens of St Mary Overy, City of London, replying to the bishop's article of the parish clerk, reported: 'Touching the Parish Clerk and Sexton all is well; only our clerk doth sometimes to ease the minister, read prayers, church women, christen, bury and marry, being allowed so to do.'[28] The parish clerk's presence at a funeral performed according to the directory was not required, though it was often the case that they did attend, if only to secure details on the deceased which enabled them to perform the chief object of their employ, namely the keeping of the parish registers. However, not all parish clerks were diligent in this duty. On 10 March 1651 the vicar of Carshalton, Surrey, penned the following apologia in his register:

> Good reader, tread gently: For though these vacant years may seem to make me guilty of thy censure, neither will I excuse myself from all blemish ... The truth is that besyde the miserys and distractions of these permitted years which it may be God in his owne wisdom would not suffer to be kept uppon record, the special grounds of that permission ought to be imputed to Richard Finch, the p'rishe Clarke, whose office it was by long pscrition to gather the ephemeris or dyary by the dayly passages, and to exhibit them once a year to be transcribed into the registry; and though I have often called upon him agayne and agayne to remeber his chardge ... I found to my great grief that all his accompts were written in sand, and his words committed to empty winds. God is witness to the truth of this apologie and that I made it knowne at some parish meetings before his own face, who could not deny it, neither do I write it to blemishe him, but to cleere my own integritie as far as I may, and to give accompt of this miscarriage to after ages by the subscription of my hand.[29]

Whatever the difficulties facing the parish clerks, the directory had little effect on furnishers of funerals; they might not have liked what went on at the graveside but they endeavoured to provide their clients with all that would make for the corpse to be 'decently attended from the house to the place appointed for public burial'. Ashton, in quoting from the *Life of the German Princess* – a notorious trickster who lived, and was hanged, in the second half of the seventeenth century – gives a glimpse of the provisions made for a funeral of middle quality in London. This 'princess' took a lodging at a house, in a good position, and told the landlady that a friend of hers, a stranger to London, had just died, and was lying at a 'pitiful Alehouse'. Might she, for convenience's sake, bring his corpse there, ready for burial on the morrow? The landlady consented, and

... that Evening the Corpse in a very handsome Coffin was brought in a Coach, and plac'd in the Chamber, which was the Room one pair of Stairs next the street and had a Balcony. The Coffin being cover'd only with an ordinary black Cloth, our Counterfeit seems much to dislike it; the Landlady tells her that for 20s. she might have the use of a Velvet Pall, with which being well pleas'd, she desir'd that the Landlady would send for the Pall, and withal accommodate the Room with her best Furniture, for the next Day but one he should be bury'd; thus the Landlady perform'd, getting the Velvet Pall, and placing on a Side-Board Table 2 Silver Candlesticks, a Silver Flaggon, 2 Standing gilt Bowls, and several other Pieces of Plate; but the Night before the intended Burial, our counterfeit Lady and her Maid within the House, handed to their Comrades without, all the Plate, Velvet Pall, and other Furniture of the Chamber that was Portable and of Value, leaving the Coffin and the suppos'd Corps, she and her Woman descended from the Balcony by Help of a Ladder, which her Comrades had brought her.[30]

In the event the coffin was found to contain only brickbats and hay and, to rub salt into the landlady's wound, the undertaker sued her for the loss of his pall to its full £40 value.

An idea of what the common Puritan funeral looked like during the Commonwealth can be gained from an engraving taken from the title page of *London's Lamentations*, a polemical tract on the plague published in 1641. Here a short-palled coffin is carried towards a churchyard on the shoulders of four bearers, neither priest, clerk nor beadle heading the procession. Behind follow the mourners, first six men in day dress with short cloaks and flat hats, then a group of women in Puritan dress. Each is shown holding a sprig of rosemary,[31] as well as a nosegay; these sprigs were cast into the grave at the close of the ceremony – this was especially useful where intramural burial was concerned, as the herb's sweetness helped to mark the odour of decay. Simple as they were, these processions had a certain dignity. Puckle was singularly sarcastic about them: 'The procession conducting the body to the grave has always offered a welcomed opportunity for the display of pomp, circumstance and ostentatious grief, so prized by the vulgar mind. The average man or woman can claim public attention only at marriage and burial, and on each of these occasions a nonentity becomes the centre of attraction in a ceremonial procession to and from the church.' (78)[32]

Cromwell's funeral exuded all the pomp and panoply denied that of Charles I. It was an extremely grand occasion though, like most of the emulated pageantry of his regime, a sham. The Lord Protector died on 3 September 1658 and the arrangements for the funeral, based on the style of that befitting a monarch, were placed in the hands of the College of Arms. There was a ritual lying-in-state at Somerset House from 18 October to 10 November with a life-size wax effigy robed in purple and ermine, a sceptre in one hand and the orb in another lying on top of the coffin; on the head was a purple cap of maintenance; and the Imperial Crown lay on a chair at the head of the coffin, though it is said that for a time the effigy was displayed erect rather than supine, wearing the crown. The cost of the funeral was estimated at £100,000, part of which was expended on 30,000 yards of black cloth for hanging Somerset House and Westminster Abbey. The diarist

78 *Photograph of the decorated cart used to transport the body of William Morris at his funeral on 6 October 1896. The wagon, with yellow body and bright red wheels, was wreathed in vine and strewn with willow, over a carpet of moss, and drawn by a roan mare.*

John Evelyn recorded the event: 'Saw the superb funeral of the Protector. He was carried from Somerset House in a velvet bed of state drawn by six horses ... the pall held up by his new lords; Oliver lying in effigy in royal robes and crowned with a crown, sceptre and globe like a king, the pennons and guidons were carried by the officers of the army and the imperial banners, achievements, etc. by the heralds in their coats, a rich caparisoned horse embroidered all over with gold, a knight of honour armed cap-a-pie, and after all, his guards, soldiers and innumerable mourners.'[33] It was a sham in as much as the body had been buried some weeks previously, it being rumoured that the embalming had gone dreadfully wrong. At best Cromwell's obsequies were fitting for a major military figure, though the streets lined with soldiers, the regimental bands and the remainder of the army bringing up the rear of the procession set the style for later royal funerals.

The restoration of the monarchy in 1660 also saw the return of an episcopal Church and, within a few months of Charles II's entry into London, almost 700 Puritan clergy had been ejected from their livings. Following discussions between representatives of the Church of England and the Puritans in 1661 – at which time the bishops were sorely tried by the Puritans' fundamentalism – agreement was reached for a revision of the Book of Common Prayer, and it was

160

reissued as part of an Act of Uniformity on St Bartholomew's Day, 1662. The Order for the Burial of the Dead was considerably extended, providing psalms and the alternative of a graveside or church service, with the latter becoming the more accepted habit. Meeting the corpse at the entrance to the churchyard, the priest led the cortège into the church whilst reading the Sentences, and the body was placed on two stools in front of the chancel steps. Alternatively, the bier would have been set down. With the mourners ensconced in their pews, one or both of Psalms 39 and 90 were said, followed by a long reading from the Epistle to the Corinthians. This done, the procession re-formed and the priest preceded it to the grave. Here, 'while the Corpse is made ready to be laid into the earth', further plenary Sentences were read prior to the Committal. Then, with the burial party standing round the grave, all joined in with a shortened *Kyrie* and then the Lord's Prayer. Finally came a short Commendation, the Collect and then the Grace. In this way the pattern of today's Order for the Burial of the Dead was established.

With an established liturgy, the funeral furnishing trade could now proceed to add their own embellishments to the ritual. In some instances the black hangings used in the home of the deceased (79) were reproduced within the body of the church, though as far as the street procession was concerned, simplicity tended to be the order of the day. The grand heraldic funerals of the early seventeenth century were on the wane, the College of Arms witnessed a noticeable drop in requests of their services and funeral furnishing became a trade in its own right. There was an early attempt on the part of the funeral furnishers to emulate the panoply of the College of Arms but this did not meet with popular approval. Certainly the College endeavoured to take out injunctions against offending funeral furnishers but it would be wrong to ascribe the dilution of street panoply to the College's success in litigation. The Puritans had campaigned against the expense and pomp of funerals, and such attitudes were in part still current at the close of the seventeenth century, regardless of the general rejoicing over the restoration of the old customs and usages. It was public restraint that gave rise to the reduction in overt pageantry. Nevertheless there were plenty of other outlets for one's cash: printed invitations, mourning rings, hatbands, scarves, gloves, complete suits of mourning for pall-bearers, plus as many mutes and attendants, feathers, plumes, lights and carriages as one would care to hire.

The nocturnal funeral made its appearance at the very beginning of the seventeenth century and lasted, in some quarters, until the middle of the eighteenth (80). Primarily they were performed for the lesser nobility and owe their innovation to the increasing backlash against the expensive pomp of the College of Arms, the accoutrements of which – including the number of mourners – were supplied against a sliding-scale related to the rank of the deceased. The fact of the matter was that these heraldic funerals were becoming too expensive and, whilst a family might have been able to afford the necessary public honour provided by the College of Arms for the holder of the title, they would have been straightened if required to repeat the performance for the deceased's widow and children. The nocturnal funeral allowed the nobility to take matters into their own hands and negotiate privately with a funeral furnisher of their own choice, thereby dispensing with the heraldic trappings, the compulsory crocodile of mourners – particularly the children of Christ's Hospital who had a virtual

161

79   *For certain funerals churches, as well as domestic interiors, were draped with mourning. A vignette of a draped church can be seen on the right of this funeral ticket issued by Kendall of London in 1720.*

monopoly on attending daytime obsequies organized by the College – the provision of mourning cloaks and the expensive banquet. Gone too was the necessity of a funeral sermon, arguably a welcome relief to some.

The College of Arms protested vehemently, blaming the funeral furnishers whilst at the same time taking up the cudgel on behalf of the 'many poor tradesmen and workmen that were wont to vend divers commodities as clothes for the furnishing of their solemn funerals which were heretofore used'.[34] But it was a shallow argument, bolstering their own grievances rather than those of the wider trade, which was able to offer its services to the funeral furnishers now undertaking such arrangements for the nobility. Whilst congratulating the peerage for having found a way of dispensing with the 'public' funeral and establishing a 'private' dimension, it would be incorrect to assume that all the old traditions of largesse were dropped. Aware of the loss that some institutions would suffer, many families made provision for private donations to charitable and philanthropic societies, as well as specific bequests to livery companies and, as numerous bequest boards extant in churches testify, to the poor of the parish.

The funeral furnisher was only too willing to be associated with the private mourning of the nobility and to provide the intimate nuances of his trade. Again, such a simplified ritual led to its emulation by those lower down the social scale for, 'Since the method of these undertakers have got a footing, persons of ordinary rank may, for the value of fifty pounds, make as great a figure, as the nobility or gentry did formerly with the expense of more than five hundred pounds ... the gaiety and splendour both of the nobility and gentry is hereby very much eclipsed so that not many of them do exceed the show of the common people.'[35]

Fees for attendants at a nocturnal funeral were graduated according to the hour – five shillings at 9 p.m., ten shillings at 10 p.m. and £1 at midnight – and as many as thirty men could be employed and as much as fifty-six pounds of candles.[36] These candles, especially the 'linkes' – three thick wax tapers twisted at the stem and then branching out – could be expensive, as can be seen from an advertisement placed in the *Daily Courant* on 30 September 1713:

> Riots and Robberies. Committed in and about Stepney Church Yard, at a Funeral Solemnity, on Wednesday the 23rd day of September; and whereas many Persons, who being appointed to attend the same Funeral with white Wax lights of considerable Value, were assaulted in a most violent manner, and the said white Wax lights taken from them. Whoever shall discover any of the Persons, guilt of the said Crimes, so as they may be convicted of the same, shall receive of Mr. William Prince, Wax Chandler in the Poultry, London, Ten Shillings for each Person so discovered.[37]

Not everyone jumped on to the bandwagon of simplicity. One minor member of the nobility, Thomas Howard of Ashtead, went to the other end of the scale and ordered from William Russell an elaborate daytime heraldic funeral in 1702 costing £229 14s.,[38] amongst which were the following four items:

ffor Ranging ye Roome where ye Esqr. lay in State in deep mourning
   & covering ye floore, a Rayle of State of Velvet & plumes of feathers

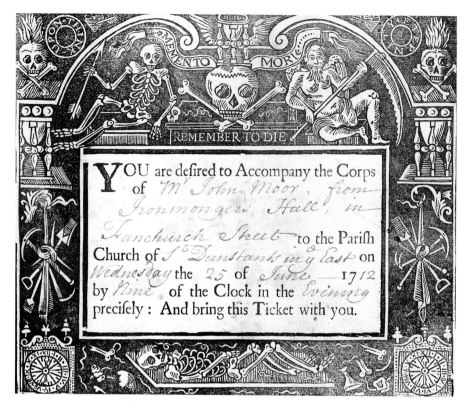

MEMENTO MORI

REMEMBER TO DIE

YOU are defired to Accompany the Corps of *Mr John Moor, from Ironmongers Hall in Fanchurch Street* to the Parifh Church of *St Dunstanks in ye East* on *Wednesday* the *25* of *June* 17*12* by *Nine* of the Clock in the *Evening* precifely : And bring this Ticket with you.

80 *Nocturnal funerals were performed between the early sixteenth and the mid eighteenth centuries. The College of Arms would not attend on nocturnal funerals, thereby making such events popular amongst those members of gentry unwilling – or unable – to pay for the full daytime pageantry.*

– round ye Roome large Silver Sconces round ye Body large Silver Candlesticks & Stands and The Hall with a Border	6	0	0
An Achievement for ye House	3	0	0
30 yds Bayes for ye Chancell & 4 yds for ye Pulpit	3	10	0
ffor Hanging my Ladys 2 Roomes in deep mourning for ye yeare and ye Passage with a Border	40	0	0

By the second quarter of the eighteenth century the panoply invented by the trade for the nocturnal funerals of the lesser nobility had become the standard pattern of their daytime ritual, soon to be enjoyed by all regardless of status, though the quality of the furnishings varied according to one's position in society. However, night-time funerals persisted in some outlying areas, such as that organized in Kent in 1760 for Dorothea Beckford who had left instructions in her will to be '... carried to my vault after twelve of the clock at night by as many men as may be necessary for that purpose ... attended by my servants and as many lights used as are necessary'.[39]

Of increasing anxiety to the socially concerned during the latter part of the eighteenth century were the solemnity and dignity attached to the burial of the poor. Burial clubs and societies, such as the Society for Burials based at

Whitechapel, had been in existence since Queen Anne's reign: 'This is to give Notice, that the Office and Society for Burials, by mutual Contribution of a Halfpenny or Farthing towards a Burial, erected upon Wapping Wall, is now removed into Katherine Wheel Alley in White Chappel, near Justice Smiths, where subscriptions are taken to compleat the number, as also at the Ram in Crucifix lane in Barnaby Street, Southwark; to which places notice is to be given of the death of any Member.'[40] Some funeral furnishers also ran their own clubs: Edward Evans, at the Four Coffins in the Strand, promised 'to perform 2s in the Pound cheaper than any of the Undertakers in Town or elsewhere',[41] whilst John Middleton, also based in London, promised for a twopence a week subscription 'a strong Elm Coffin, covered with fine Black, and finished with Two Rows all around close drove with Black Japanned Nails, adorned with rich ornamental Drops, a handsome Plate of Inscription, Angel above the Plate and Flower beneath, and pair of Handsome Handles with wrought Gripes ... For use, a handsome Velvet Pall, Three Gentlemen's Cloaks, Three Crepe Hat bands, Three Hoods and Scarfs, and Six Pairs of Gloves. Two Porters equipped to attend the Funeral, a Man to attend the same with Band and Gloves'.[42] All very 'handsome', no doubt. A few of the burial clubs were corrupt, especially those based at public houses in inner-city slum areas, but the majority assiduously executed their duties, occasionally branching out into other areas of personal finance, such as money-lending and life insurance. Nowadays the most common source of capital to meet funerary expenses is the personal insurance policy. Some funeral furnishers continue to provide 'pre-need' schemes – most notably the Co-Operative Society – and some have even ventured into life insurance through the established commercial firms, turning tables on the nineteenth-century burial clubs themselves.

In an age when success was measured by material possessions and monetary wealth, the nineteenth-century funeral was regarded as a public manifestation of one's acumen. The trade was aware of this and re-established the 'sliding-scale' system, itemizing the differences in class of funeral. This went down through all levels of society, but stopped short of the pauper class. A pauper funeral was, therefore, something to be avoided, not only because of its extreme simplicity but also for its significance in exhibiting one's failure to maintain a position, however lowly, in society. The covered hand-cart pushed by a hunched-up attendant, with the undertaker striding out in front and the mourners hurrying along behind, made a pathetic accompaniment to the children's rhyme, 'Rattle his bones over the stones; he's only a pauper who nobody owns.' J.H. Wick, an undertaker providing contract funerals at the beginning of the nineteenth century to the London Poor Law Union, agreed to provide a basic funeral for £1 15s. consisting of a plain pine coffin, four bearers and the hire of a baize pall. However, 'the poor would deprive themselves of the necessities of life for the sake of paying respect to the bodies of their departed friends', and an examination of Wicks's account book shows that many relatives took advantage of the union's caveat and contributed the additional six shillings which secured a depositum plate with painted inscription, together with the attendance of a mute and use of the best pall.[43] It is to be regretted that such augmentations are now no longer permissible where contract funerals are concerned.

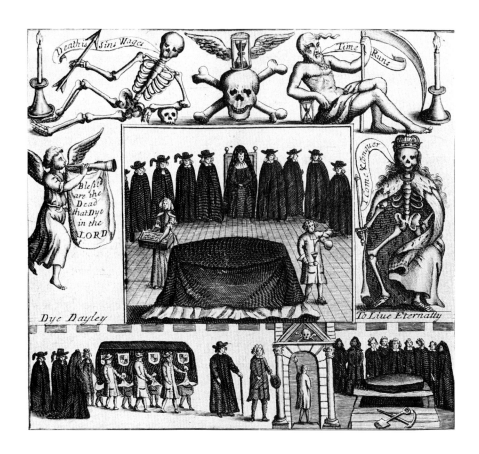

*81   The importance of this trade card is in the two figures aside
the coffin of the central panel. Here they are offering hippocras
and sweetmeats to the mourners, provided by Richard Innocent,
confectioner at Greenwich, whose c. 1725 advertisement this is.*

One abiding fear during the early nineteenth century was that of being buried
alive. The English never went quite as far as the Europeans, with their public
mortuaries and intricate devices allowing an interred 'corpse' to summon
assistance should he or she wake up. At a time when most coffins remained in the
home until the day of the funeral such continental precautions were
unwarranted. However, the fear should not be denied its space in this work.
Francis Douce, the antiquary and collector, who died in 1834, had the following
bequest in his will: 'I give to Sir Anthony Carlisle two hundred pounds,
requesting him either to sever my head or extract my heart from my body, so as
to prevent any possibility of the return of vitality.'[44] Whether or not Sir Anthony
Carlisle, the best-known surgeon of his day, performed this task has not been
recorded. Douce was not alone in asking for such a gruesome operation; his friend
Thomas Kerrick made a similar request. Douce's father, also named Francis,
desired that his body 'might be kept for two weeks before burial' to guard against
any premature actions on the part of his executors. Requests for the severance of
an artery or for the retention of the body for a protracted period were not
uncommon (*81*). Not all persons were afflicted with such fears, the majority being

166

content with the knowledge that medical science was quite capable of determining death without mutilation of the body.

By the close of the nineteenth century most funeral furnishers had their own mortuary chapels and were able to keep a weather eye out for signs of life. With the introduction of arterial embalming in the 1880s and 1890s premature burial was a thing of the past; if one was not dead on arrival at the funeral parlour, one certainly would be once the hygienic treatment had taken place. What we shall never know is the number of persons who counteracted their fears of premature burial through the purchase of above-ground mausoleums and public catacomb space (despite the fact that regulations for burial in such tombs stipulated the use of a lead shell). One of the most curious instances said to have been the result of a fear of premature burial refers to Clement Spelman of Narborough, Norfolk, who died in 1672. Rumour had it that he was deposited upright within his tomb. When the eight-foot pedestal supporting his monument was cut down in 1865 it was found that inside it Spelman's coffin stood upright. It is said that he insisted

82   Matthew Russell lying in state at Brancepeth Castle, County Durham, 1822. Oil on canvas. The funeral arrangements were probably by Dowbiggin & Holland of London. The hatchment and escutcheons indicate a surviving widow.

*83   Water-colour sketch for the lying-in-state of John, First Earl
of Brownlow, 1853. The society undertakers, Dowbiggin &
Holland, were responsible for the arrangements.*

on this position in order not to be trodden on.

Far worse than premature burial was the premature undertaker: it was not unknown for some tradesmen to mount a watch at the door of the home of an ailing member of the local society in anticipation of their patronage, though whether any went quite so far as invading the house itself, as shown in an 1807 caricature by Newton (*Col. 20*), is highly unlikely.

As the nineteenth century progressed, the number of in-house lyings-in-state amongst the landed gentry declined, and that of Matthew Russell at Brancepeth Castle, Co Durham, in 1822 (*82*) must have been one of the last of its kind. The nobility maintained the tradition well into the century – probably because it was expected of them by the trade – and a number of funeral furnishers were equipped to provide for the same (*83*). Certainly there were funeral furnishers outside the metropolis capable of hanging a house when the need arose, as shown from a surviving account submitted on 8 December 1864 by Maria Taylor of Coney Street, York, on account of the obsequies for George William Frederick Howard, Seventh Earl of Carlisle, at Castle Howard:

153½ yds black cloth for covering Domestic Chapel, Mausoleum &
  Chapel @ 6/6 pr yd   49   8   0

63 yds 8/4 domette for obscuring windows, cloth curtains &c, @ 3/9			
pr yd	11	16	3
Men's time fixing ditto up 21 days 9 hours	5	9	6
14 yds of fringe 14/– 1200 Tacks 12/–	1	6	0
1 paper of nails 3/9 10 yds of black cord 6/8		10	5
Twine 1/– Upholsterer's time 4 days 9 hours 1/9/6	1	10	6
32 side lights & 1 Hanging ditto for Mausoleum	2	10	0
Escutcheon frame covered with fine black cloth, Iron stays &c	4	10	0
Mr Wales account for painting ditto	17	6	0
Self & Men taking ditto over and fixing, Van and pair of Horses			
Expenses &c	3	8	0
15½ yds Black cloth for Welburn & Coneysthorpe Churches @ 5/6 pr yd	4	5	3
17 yds of fringe 17/– 4 large pulpit Tassels @ 3/9	1	12	0
Tacks & Thread 1/– 2 Men 3 days fitting up 18/–		19	0
Horse & Cart Tolls &c		11	0

For the landed gentry, the simple draped house catafalque replaced the elaborate draperies, though a more elaborate and richly embroidered variant was available for church use (*84*).

With a settled ecclesiastical formulary and an established secular ritual the funeral enjoyed a period of stability from 1662 (*85*) until the opening of the first private cemeteries in the 1820s and the necessary introduction of the horse-drawn glass-sided funeral car, adding to rather than replacing any of the entrenched customs. Thanks to the establishment of the private cemeteries (*86*)

84 Ecclesiastical velvet pall, from the c. 1890 catalogue of Ingall, Parsons & Clive. This highly embroidered item was available for purchase, though it was more usual to hire.

the undertaker was able to extend his attendance beyond the church service and subsequent burial in the churchyard, offering a secondary procession to the cemetery itself, perhaps even as far as the graveside. Floral tributes made their appearance in the late 1860s, and in 1889 Richard Davey commented, 'The fashion of sending costly wreaths to cover the coffin is recent, and was quite unknown in Paris twenty years ago as it was in this country until about the same period.'[45] Porcelain flowers beneath glass domes, mostly of imported German manufacture, were first seen in England in the late 1890s and gradually usurped the glazed earthenware type in popularity.

The 1890s witnessed the golden age of the Victorian funeral: the horse-drawn cortège, the flower-decked funeral car with its encased burden, and sable mourning coaches containing weeping ladies swathed in crape and black bombazine, supported in their grief by stiff-lipped husbands, brothers and uncles, resembling the top-hatted beetles in contemporary caricatures by Griset. On the road, two dreadful mutes led the way, harbingers of death itself (87),

85   Burying the Dead, *a pen-and-ink drawing of c. 1792 by Thomas Stothard. No attempt has been made to disguise the soil or to provide boards for the mourners to stand on in this country churchyard.*

*86 Kensal Green Cemetery opened in 1833. The purchase of
separate plots by Prince Augustus Frederick and Princess Sophia
in the 1840s ensured the success of the private cemeteries.*

whilst the tramp, tramp, tramp of the attendants' measured paces re-echo the clop, clop, clop of the horses' hooves. Too soon the 'I am the resurrection and the life ...'; and Lyte's hymn, 'Abide with me, fast falls the eventide'. Then the grave, and 'Man that is born of a woman ...'

David Cannadine argues that 'the Victorian celebration of death was not so much a golden age of effective psychological support as a bonanza of commercial exploitation'.[46] That may be so, but there were those within the trade who since the 1870s had embarked on a modified street ritual – such as a less elaborate funeral car, a reduction in the number of attendants and the abandonment of mutes, trays of feathers and prancing horses – which found favour with the upper and middle classes. It was those lower down the social scale who insisted on ostentatious display. The introduction of cremation in the 1880s brought in restrictions on account of the utilitarian specifications for the coffin itself. Spiritually, greater emphasis was being placed on the format of the church service, resulting in an embellished liturgy, and less attention being paid to the outward and visible accoutrements of the public face of private mourning.

However, the greatest influence on the simplification of the English funeral came as a result of the First World War. Primarily, there was a thinning-out of funeral operatives due to war service which, coupled with the requisitioning of non-essential work-horses, led to a reduction in both personnel and vehicles. Secondly, there was a particular undercurrent of public opinion to contend with: the morality of staging a grandiose funeral when those who had died for king and country on foreign fields were unable to be repatriated. At such a time of great national suffering and sorrow, individual displays of funerary pomp and panoply did not sit comfortably on the conscience.

*87 (Overleaf): Two mutes, photographed in 1901 by Sir Benjamin
Stone. 'Two more thorough specimens of the mourners of the
world you could not hope to find than in these dreadful mutes.'*

7

The Heraldic Funeral

A heraldic funeral was one marshalled by the College of Arms, who are part of the Royal Household. To put it crudely, the College of Arms represented the 'posh' burial guild. Although they arranged the funerals of monarchs, those of royal blood and other members of the nobility, they also acted for archbishops, bishops, knights and gentlemen-at-arms, together with those of armigerous status. Part of their role was, then, to act as the Crown funeral furnishers.

The College's role in the development of the English funeral – its complex panoply and order of precedence relating to those taking part in the street procession, together with the chivalric element of the service within the church building – was of paramount importance and should neither be disregarded nor underestimated. Their ruling was absolute, their decision final. But even Garter King of Arms would have been obliged to admit that the English heraldic funeral was, as with much of the College's early ritual, based on the extremely elaborate and complex proceedings of the public expression of homage paid at the French Court funerals of the late thirteenth century, a time when the crowns of England and France were conjoined. Be that as it may, the College did not adopt all of the formularies, particularly that relating to the public exposition of the apparelled remains of the deceased monarch during the funeral procession. The complicated preparations required in ordering the obsequies of a monarch precluded such a macabre spectacle.

The library at the College is weak in material prior to 1597; and though an attempt was made to rectify the matter in 1568, by bringing together those records kept by individual officers, this was delayed when the then Earl Marshal was beheaded for aspiring to marry Mary, Queen of Scots, so that it was not until 1597 that reform got under way. The College's records are fairly complete after this date, comprising eighteen volumes relating to funeral certificates of the sixteenth and seventeenth centuries. From these can be gleaned information relating to the achievements provided for each funeral, together with notes on the deceased and details of the 'official' mourners and those members of the College who were in attendance.

The street procession was of great importance, allowing for a grand display of heraldic pomp and civil pride, and taking many hours to perform. The mere fact that the Kings-of-Arms had to represent the College at all heraldic funerals within their province would have had some bearing on their frequency and this is but one reason why the funerals of the nobility were delayed, often by as much as a month or more after death had taken place. Another cause for delay rested with the availability of the 'official' mourners.[1]

Since the founding of Christ's Hospital in 1552, the boys and girls of the school paraded at the funerals of distinguished Londoners and shared in the feast afterwards. The poor men and women behind the crocodile of sable-clad children would have been as many in number as was the age of the deceased and, as they were provided with their 'black cotes' and an attendance fee from the estate of the deceased, there was something to be said for dying young. Neither the neighbours nor the parishioners would have minded being at the rear of the procession, secure in the knowledge that those who followed the official mourners were that much more 'important' than those who walked in front of the coffin; and a similar situation prevails today. In fact, the focus of attention was the palled coffin, those going before merely 'heralding' its approach.

It is only by looking in detail at the trappings provided that we can obtain an idea of the College's role and the purpose of the items provided. Social and civic rank dictated the order of the procession, with a city council and its officers taking precedence over the livery companies. Female relatives were allowed to attend, though they took second place to the men. The King-of-Arms walked immediately in front of the coffin, thereby leaving the prominent position in the procession to the chief mourner, whilst at the same time acting out an important role as the representative of the royal household.

The cloaks for the Christ's Hospital children were provided from the deceased's estate, but as these children were expected to attend the funerals of all distinguished Londoners it would not be unreasonable to suppose that the hospital had their own cloaks and preferred to accept an agreed fee in lieu. Conversely, it was the accepted norm for the poor to be provided with cloaks. Again, the Lord Mayor, the council and the livery companies would have worn their violet mourning unless they had been singled out as a special friend of the deceased to be provided with 'blackes' from the estate. In 'The order observed by the Lord Maior, the Aldermen, and Sheriffes for their meetings and wearing of their apparell throughout the whole yeere', printed in John Stowe's *Survay*, is the following instruction:

> For the buriall of Aldermen – the last love, duty and ceremony one to another. The Aldermen are to weare their violet gownes, except such as have (of their friends' allowance) blacke gownes of mourning. When an Alderman dieth, master Swordbearer is to have a blacke gowne, or three and thirty shillings and fourpence in money. And if the Alderman deceased doe give to the Lord

174

Maior mourning, then master Swordbearer is to have mourning also, or forty shillings in money as the value thereof, and so carry the Sword in blacke before the Lord Maior. Master Chamberlain is not to weare his tippet but when the Lord Maior or Aldermen do weare their scarlet or violet.[2]

There were special places in the procession for those aldermen 'having no blackes', though in all probability they would have been wearing their violet gowns rather than day-clothes. Stowe's account makes passing reference to the City of London mourning sword with its sable hilt and black leather scabbard.

The pattern of the cloaks acquired by the chief mourner and his supporters was determined by the College of Arms, according to their rank, the length of the chief mourner's train distinguishing him from his four associates. The six yeomen carrying the palled coffin, the four pall-bearers together with Clarenceux, the herald and the pursuivant would all have been in cloaks with hoods and tippets, the latter three sporting their heavily embroidered and highly colourful tabards over their cloaks (*Col. 21*); likewise the bearer of the penon and those carrying the coat-of-arms and the targe, as well as the bearers of the four lesser penons, would have been sporting cloaks and tippets.

At least nine heraldic items were provided by the College for the funeral of a knight: standard, penon, helm and crest, coat-of-arms, the four lesser penons and the targe. John Gough Nichols provides a complete description of the twelve qualities of items available from the College for the performance of funerals, as well as a short commentary on their use.

The *Banner* was originally oblong in form, that is, about twice the depth of its width ... It displayed the armorial coat of its owner, spread entirely over its surface.

The *Standard* was originally an ensign too large to be borne by a man into battle, [They were] graduated according to the owner's rank, from the duke's standard of seven yards and a half in length, to the knight's of only four.... Every standard and guydon was 'to have in the chief (that is, next to the staff) the cross of Saint George; next, the beast (the modern supporter) or crest, with his devise or word (motto); and to be slit at the end.'

The *Guydon* resembled the standard but was only two and a half or three yards in length; and it was allowed to esquires, or lieutenants.

At funerals banners and bannerols seem to have been allowed to all peers and their ladies; standards, but not banners, to all knights and their ladies; penons, but not standards, to esquires. Mere gentlemen had no penons, only scotcheons of arms.

The *Penon* displayed at funerals (at which we do not meet with guydons) also resembled the standard in form, but was of less size, and was rounded, instead of slit, at the end. It was also entirely different in its charges; as it bore the arms of the party, like the banner.

The *Bannerols* were banners of increased width, made to display impalements, representing the alliances of the ancestors of the deceased.

But, if banners of arms were confined to persons of high rank, there was another kind of banner which was probably allowed to all who were inclined to pay for it. During the prevalence of the rites of the church of Rome, we meet with *Banners of Images* which were square, and represented either the personification of the Trinity or the figures of saints. Their number is uniformly four, and they were carried about the corpse, 'at the four corners'.

Pensels, the diminutive of penon, or *penicillus*, were very small, like the vanes which sometimes terminate the pinnacles of pointed architecture, or the ironwork of the same period. They were supplied in large quantities; the pensels and scotcheons being chiefly, if not entirely, to deck out the hearse.

The *Helmet* is still seen lingering in some country churches; it is seldom found to be more than a fictitious helmet, made for the purpose to which it is applied. In early times a knight's real helmet was offered; but such have now almost entirely disappeared, having proved too tempting objects of antiquarian curiosity or cupidity. The *Mantles*, which used to be made of black velvet and the *Crest*, have now generally perished from decay.

The *Target* was a shield of the coat of arms of the defunct, the successor of the knight's real shield.

The *Coat-Armour* was made like a herald's tabard, worked or painted before and behind with the same arms, and which were also repeated on its short sleeves.

The *Sword* was generally of the same description as the helmet, made rather for show than for use.

The lowest description of heraldic ensign allotted for Funerals was the *Scocheon*. Mere gentlemen had no penon; but as many scocheons as were desired. But the funerals of the higher ranks were also provided with scocheons, in addition to their other insignia, and that sometimes profusely — to the extent of four, six, or eight dozen. These scocheons were the prototype of our modern hatchments. Originally made of some perishable material, and fastened up in the churches, they were required to be painted on panel, in order to last longer; and from these small achievements on panel (still to be found in some country churches) they have grown into the large and unwielding frames of canvas now spread on the front of modern mansions, or stretched on the roof of the chancel and aisles, the walls of which scarcely offer sufficient space for their accommodation.

It will be observed that peculiar rests of iron were made for the reception of these trophies, which were inserted in the wall of the church. Suspended on these, they were left to testify to the worldly grandeur of the defunct so long as their fragile materials might endure.[3]

John Gough Nichols is extremely helpful, since he lists the above items according to the order of their position in the procession – though he omits mention of the spurs and gauntlets which, with their own attendant heralds, came immediately behind the bannerols and in front of the helm and crest, so that the standard headed the procession with the sword bringing up the rear. Precisely who walked in between the achievements depended on the rank of the deceased and the attendant formulary of the procession. Returning to the mid sixteenth-century regulations for a knight's funeral, the standard was positioned immediately behind the 'preacher', whilst the penon and coat-of-arms followed the 'executors of the defunct', with the King-of-Arms strategically positioned between the coat-of-arms and the coffin.

Palls were to be had from the College and were usually of rich black Genoese or Utrecht velvet. Falling not much lower than the sides of the coffin (larger palls, about fourteen by ten feet, were also available, such as that provided in 1588 at the funeral of Sir Philip Sydney), they were decorated with nine 'scocheons', three along each broad side, one at each end and the ninth on the top at the central point of the coffin lid. These escutcheons, as they were later known, were provided by herald-painters and were little more than painted canvas rectangles some eight inches high and six inches wide, attached to the pall by tacking stitches so as to allow for their easy removal at the end of the funeral, thus allowing the College to reuse the pall at a later occasion should they so wish. Only in very rare instances were the arms of the deceased embroidered directly on to the velvet, such as happened with livery-company or family palls.

The number of bannerols allowed to be carried alongside the coffin generally depended on the rank of the deceased, so whilst a knight might be restricted to four, a duke might have a dozen. Yet Nichols tells us that bannerols could also be used to display the heraldic alliances of the deceased; therefore a well-connected ducal family could well have sported twelve, the same number as was used at the funeral of Queen Elizabeth I in 1603. However, it was rare to see the regulations of the College of Arms flouted, and the executors of Sir Philip Sydney chose to stay with four, as can be seen in a contemporary engraving by T. de Bry (*88*).

Nichols has already pointed out that the sword carried in procession was specifically made for the purpose. Mourning swords were in plentiful supply for the general public, though those used as part of the heraldic procession were somewhat larger than the average arming sword.

88   The funeral of Sir Philip Sidney, an engraving of 1586 by T. de Bray. In the case of knights, the College of Arms restricted the number of bannerols carried alongside the coffin to four.

The duties of the College did not stop at the church door. On the contrary, their ancient heraldic customs were about to begin. It was the accepted form for the 'mass penny' to be paid to the celebrant by the chief mourner at a small ceremony known as the Offering, which took place between the reading of the Gospel and the public recitation of the Creed. After the Reformation this act of public homage interrupted the office of the Burial of the Dead after the lesson from the First Epistle to the Corinthians. In the formulary for a knight's funeral, the chief mourner approached the altar twice; once alone and then with his supporters. At the first 'visit' a cash offering was made as his own private donation, the second approach being to make an offering on behalf of the deceased. Then came the heralds, followed by the other mourners according to their rank.

> After the gospel ... when the Earl of Warwick had offered the mass penny to the offertory, the King of Arms, proceeding to the offertory before the Earl of Worcester, delivered the coat of arms to him with due reverence. The Bishop then delivered it back to the Earl of Warwick, in token that it belonged to him as the heir, and he gave it back to the King of Arms, who then stood on the right side with it. In the same way the shield was borne by a King of Arms before Lord Montague, handed over to the heir and then back to the King of Arms. The sword and the helmet and crest were similarly dealt with by the heralds ... The other nobles made their offerings and then the Kings of Arms and heralds bore the coat of arms, shield, helmet and crest to the tomb and there laid the coat of arms in the midst, the helmet and crest at the head, the shield below the sword, hanging by the banner on the right side of the head, and the standard on the same side at the foot. This done they took off their coats of arms, but in token that the coat of arms of the deceased was handed over by his heir the Earl's herald stood before the hearse wearing it for the rest of the mass until the burial.[4]

This being done, the achievements were taken to the place of burial and laid up in the usual way until such time as the brackets had been affixed for their permanent display (*89*). As the majority of the surviving brackets in churches the length and breadth of this country are identical in form to those shown in the John Gough Nichols engraving, it can be presumed that these fittings were also to be had from the College of Arms, possibly being supplied by the armourers or the herald-painters.

Towards the end of the fifteenth century and the beginning of the sixteenth, an element of confusion was plaguing the heraldic funeral *vis-à-vis* the correct etiquette for 'mourning', the nomenclature ascribed to the 'blackes' worn by the official mourners. Regulations were drawn up during the reign of Henry VII but within thirty years of his death most of these orders had either been forgotten or conveniently abandoned, and far too often were the College of Arms hearing reports of families flouting the regulations and issuing mourning above that formally ascribed to the rank of the deceased. It seems unlikely that such waverings were deliberate attempts by families to undermine the College's ruling and accord themselves an elevated status – rather it came about through ignorance of the rules and an over-zealousness on the part of the supplying upholder, the herald-painters and the executors. To the College of Arms it was

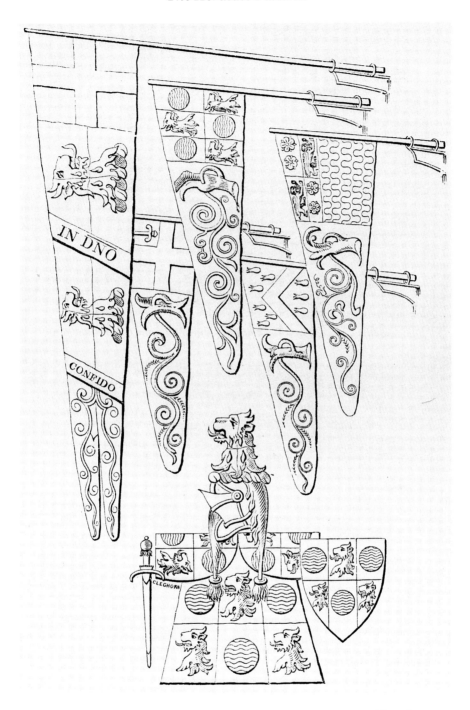

*89   The achievements of Sir John White in Aldershot Church,
Hampshire, engraved by Cleghorn in 1848. Standard and
penons are supported by brackets of the type provided by the
College of Arms.*

more a matter of 'by their clothes shall ye know them' and in 1541 they sought to control and reform these anomalies by issuing an order entitled 'The manner of the ordering and settyng forth of a corps, of what estate that he be of and how every manne shall goo in dew ordre after the estate and degrees that they be of.'[5] But it was short-lived, for within four years of its publication the spirit of the Reformation was influencing all ecclesiastical ritual and the first item to be dropped was the inclusion in the procession of the various religious followed by a decline in the use of the four great banners of the Trinity and Saints, though the flag of St George was to remain as part of the Standard.

As far as the mourning was concerned a baron or banneret, being a Knight of the Garter, was entitled to have for his gown and hood six yards of black cloth and livery for not more than eight servants. The lower down the pecking order, the simpler it became, so that none below the rank of esquire was allowed hoods: they had to be content with tippets.

The Kings-of-Arms acted as the representatives of the royal household and, unless it was ordered otherwise, only one honoured a heraldic funeral with his presence. Precisely which one depended on the location, for each had their own province, in much the same way as did the two archbishops. There were, however, occasions when all three did attend, ' ... at the beriall of a pier of the realme ·he being of the blod riall or alse in any of thes offices as constable and marshall, chaunceler, high tresorer, chamberlaine, steward, admirall or lord prevy sele,' when 'ther hath byne accustomed all the offycers of armes of the kynges' to be present and to wear 'the kynges coote of armes and to have their gownes and hoods and v li. in money to be devided amonge then and ther costs and in likewyse yef anny lord of the parlament chance to dye duryng the tyme of the paerlament the said officers to have as ys aforesaid.'[6]

The fees and perquisites, the '*droits et largesse*', received by the heralds made up a substantial contribution to their emoluments. Set down during the reign of Henry VII, it stipulates the amount of mourning to be provided for the attendance of a funeral, plus fees. Each member of the College attending the funeral of a baron received £2, at that of knight, captain or esquire £1, and ten shillings for being in attendance at the obsequies of gentlemen entitled to bear arms. The '*droits*' seem to have been the same for each funeral of whatever quality: 'Item all the blake cloth within the railes and apon the railis and the forsaid railes with the cloth of majeste shuld be ther fees.'[7] With there being a greater call on the herald's services during the first and second quarters of the sixteenth century, as the result of an increase in the granting of arms, a system had to be evolved in order to give each of the heralds a bite at the cherry. The situation was resolved in 1564/5 whereby the various officers would serve at funerals in rotation, each officer being made responsible to file at the College a certificate signed by both the executors and the 'official' mourners of the deceased, recording the details of the date of death, the place of burial, the marriage and issue of the union. Almost as soon as the system had been introduced it was discovered to have a serious flaw in as much as one could find a provincial King-of-Arms officiating at the funeral of a royal duke whilst a Garter King-of-Arms was down to attend that of an armigerous gentleman's widow. Further discussion ensued and in 1588 the Earl Marshal agreed to the following table: Garter King-of-Arms was to marshal the funerals of Knights of the Garter, peers temporal and the heirs apparent of dukes, marquesses and earls, those of their wives, and of the archbishops of Canterbury and York and the bishop of Winchester; Clarenceux and Norroy were to marshal those funerals of other noble and gentle persons within their respective provinces. Furthermore, each was to take with him his junior officers.

Sometimes it was impracticable for the King-of-Arms and his officers to attend a funeral; indeed it seems highly unlikely that they would have been willing to travel to Cumberland or Cornwall to officiate at the obsequies of, say, the elderly widow of a knight's youngest son. Nonetheless, funeral certificates were expected to be returned to the College whether or not a herald had been able to attend. A list of fees payable to the College for the entering of such certificates was issued by the Earl Marshal in 1618:

For a duke, duchess or archbishop: £45
For a marquess or marchioness: £40
For an earl or countess: £35
For a viscount or viscountess: £30
For a bishop: £25
For a baron or baroness: £25
For a baronet or banneret: £13 6s. 8d.
For a knight: £10
For an esquire: £6 13s. 6d.
For a gentleman: £2

To this had to be added not only the hire charge of the pall but also the cost of the work executed by the herald-painters. The College of Arms did not have the staff to produce such items as standards, bannerols, penons and escutcheons and their role in the production of the achievements was limited to researching the devices and quarterings to which the families had claim and then passing this information on to the herald-painters who would then provide the items in accordance with the traditional heraldic pattern and colours.

Items of armour had also to be provided. Up until the late sixteenth century some families did relinquish items and a few early tilt-helms and close-helms given over for this purpose survive in churches, cathedral treasuries and museums.[8] The funerary armour was not all that it tried to be, for often sets did not match and one comes across complete sets of funerary armour where helm, gauntlets and spurs are mismatched and not contemporary with another. Did families provide the bits and pieces, or did the College of Arms have its own stock? There is a fine *c.*1540 helm in the Museum of London from the tomb of Sir Nicholas Heron in Croydon parish church originating from the Greenwich Royal Armouries, and an equally magnificent creature, complete with crest, at Lydiard Tregoz, Wiltshire, adjacent to the tomb of Sir John St John (d.1594).

The two seventeenth-century painted helms at Great Bardfield, Essex, are fabrications, impossible to have been worn, and made of iron plates. Were these obtained via the College of Arms? From the large number of such 'symbolic' helms provided during the seventeenth century it appears that it was becoming increasingly difficult to locate original pieces of armour.

A further expense was the provision of the carved wooden crest to surmount the helm. Many of these survive – the helm at Lydiard Tregoz retains its gilded rising falcon crest and a *c.*1482 helm at Wethersfield, Essex, above the tomb of Henry Wentworth sports an elegant unicorn, though its horn has long since broken off. It is unfortunate that the helms had to be provided with a spike upon which the carved crest could be mounted. Not one funerary helm retains its black velvet mantling and even recent conservation of the more important examples has omitted to reinstate the same. One has to go to Henry VII's chapel at Westminster Abbey and the choir of St George's Chapel, Windsor, to see what mantled helms looked like, for the canopies above the stalls of the Knights of the Bath (Westminster) and the Knights of the Garter (Windsor) are surmounted with mantled and crested helms.

The two finest sets of funerary armour are those at Canterbury Cathedral to the Black Prince (d.1376) and Westminster Abbey to King Henry V (d.1422). The Black Prince's surviving shield is the one carried by him into war; the helm – similar to one of *c.*1375 in the Royal Scottish Museum, Edinburgh, from the Pembridge tomb in Hereford Cathedral – is of English manufacture and, with its gilded leather crest, would have been worn for battle; the padded velvet embroidered coat armour also comes from the Black Prince's armoury and is unique, likewise the pair of gilt copper and leather gauntlets; parts of the red leather scabbard and the halter strap of the shield also survive.

The Westminster achievements of Henry V are similar in style to those made forty-seven years earlier for the Black Prince. The shield is practically identical and was certainly for use in battle whilst the helm – *sans* crest – is of a type worn in peace-time, that is for tournaments and parades. No coat armour here, but instead a saddle. It was the custom to include an equipped horse as part of the Offering to the Church, as was recorded at the 1462/3 funeral of Richard Neville, Earl of Salisbury at Bisham Abbey: 'After the gospel the two Kings of Arms went to the west door of the church, where there was a man riding a horse which had on it a trapper of the arms of the deceased. The herald led him to the door of the choir, where he alighted and held the horse ... Then the rest of the heralds and pursuivants preceded the man of arms with the horse and trapper and Lords Hastings and Fitzhugh presented his arms and the horse to the church.'9

Considering the multitude of banners, standards, guydons, penons, bannerols, pensels and escutcheons provided by the College of Arms for royal funerals between the late fifteenth and the late eighteenth centuries it is astounding that, apart from the achievements of the Black Prince and Henry V, only one item appears to survive: a painted and gilded carved wood cartouche used at the funeral of Charles II in 1685 and now in the Museum of London (*90*).10 What, one wonders, happened to all the rest? Did they disintegrate in the course of time, were they taken down and disposed of once they became dishevelled or were they removed from Westminster Abbey and St George's Chapel, Windsor, during later restoration programmes?

Conversely, a surprising number of lesser achievements survive in parish churches. John Aubrey gives an eyewitness account of the scene in Lydiard Tregoz church in Wiltshire in the 1670s: 'The Chancell, and the aisle of the St Johns adjoining, are adorned with about 30 penons; over the altar doe hang two

*90   Wooden cartouche carried
at the funeral of Charles II,
1685. However, lack of the
Roman numerals 'II' between
the initials cause scholars to
question whether this item
should not be associated with
the funeral of Charles I.*

banners of St George, two guidons of Ulster, and on each side a Mandilion (tabard) beautified with all their quarterings, with shield, sword, helmet, and crest, made in manner of a trophie, with gauntletts, gilt spurs, and such like badges of Equestrian dignitie.'[11] Now only the helms and crests survive. But by far the most complete set is that of Sir William Penn (d.1670) in St Mary Redcliffe, Bristol (*91*), which, considering the number of restorations the church has undergone over the last 300 years, is a remarkable survival. The coat, complete with tassels, is above the memorial, then, in order of ascendency, the breast-plate with attached leg-guards, the helm and crest, and the painted wooden target behind which is tucked the sword. Flanking the coat are, at the bottom, the spurs with, above, the gauntlets. To the left of this suite hang the standard with bannerol above, whilst to the right are two penons, one above the other. As well as being the most complete set of funerary achievements it is also the only set displayed around a monument in the fashion suggested by the College of Arms, except that the 'flags' are set flat against the wall rather than at right-angles to it.

In the chancel of Staunton Harold, Leicestershire, are a number of disassociated standards and bannerols of the seventeenth and eighteenth

91   The achievements of Admiral Sir William Penn (d. 1670) in St Mary Redcliffe, Bristol, is the most complete set of seventeenth-century funerary achievements.

centuries to the Shirley family, whilst the achievements of Sir Robert Shirley (d.1656) are set above the chancel arch.[12] Here we have a coat with spurs and gauntlets below and a bracket bearing the helm and crest and supporting the sword, the whole flanked by two bannerols mounted at right-angles to the nave wall, though hard up to the chancel arch. An even larger series of standards and bannerols, mainly of seventeenth-century origin and of painted canvas, relating to the Earls of Dorset and the Earls De La Warr, provide a glorious burst of colour in the Sackville Chapel at St Michael's, Withyham, Sussex (*92*).

Above the impressive monument to Sir Roger Manwood in St Stephen's, Canterbury, rests an early wooden target of 1592 with, on an unusually long horizontal bracket, the helm and crest, a pair of gauntlets and the mourning sword. A similar situation exists at Bottesford, Leicestershire, above the 1591

Gerard Johnson tomb to the Fourth Earl of Rutland (d.1588). The rusty three-dimensional coronet to the left of the achievements once rested atop the coffin in the vault and was probably put in its present position when the coffins were transferred to the mausoleum in the grounds of Belvoir Castle in 1828.

The Museum of London possesses an emblazoned escutcheon from Cromwell's funeral car. It is a small object, not more than eighteen inches high and ten inches wide, painted on taffity. But the arms – Cromwell impaling Claypole – are of great interest in as much as they are surmounted by

92   *Four bannerols and a standard of late seventeenth and early eighteenth century date to various members of the Sackville family in the Sackville Chapel at Withyham, Sussex.*

the Lord Protector's 'crown' (*93*). Robert Uvedale, a Westminster scholar, impishly snatched an escutcheon from the hearse.[13] This item was presented to Westminster School in 1904 by his descendant, Miss Mary West.

The City Museum and Art Gallery at Bristol is fortunate to own one of the most beautiful targets to survive. It is of wood, painted and richly gilded, and of considerable size, measuring thirty-nine by 32½ inches, with the arms of the Bristolian philanthropist, Edward Colston, who died in 1721. The arms are shown on a convex oval cartouche within an elaborate rococo frame carved with stylized foliage, above which is a skull signifying that with Colston's death the lineage came to an end.[14] The target became part of the regalia of the charitable societies that administered Colston's will, and was carried in the annual procession commemorating the benefactor's birthday on 13 November. It is questionable whether the other items of heraldry ever survived the funeral, if we are to take the London *Weekly Journal*'s account in 1729 of the obsequies of another Bristolian, Cornelius Stevens, as the norm for the city when 'the mob, as was the custom, tore off the glittering panoply'.[15]

When the body had to be taken some considerable distance from the place of

93 *Painted canvas escutcheon used at the funeral of Oliver Cromwell in 1658.*

94   Carved wooden mitre,
painted and gilded, used at the
funeral of the Rt. Revd
Nathaniel Lord Crewe, Bishop
of Durham, in 1721. Until 1832
the bishops of Durham enjoyed
the title of Prince-Bishop, hence
the coronet encircling the mitre.

death to the place of burial, the College of Arms had to make separate
arrangements for the transport of the achievements. An eyewitness account
written almost immediately after the funeral of Archbishop William Juxon in
July 1663 tells us that, because of the inclement weather, only the minimum of
trappings were displayed during the journey from London. The cortège
approached the Divinity School, whose upper floor had already been hung with
mourning to receive the body for a two-day lying-in-state, and 'all the boxes that
contained the streamers, scutcheons, and other matters belonging to his body
were brought in'; once the obsequies were over, 'The mourning and the
escotheons remained in the chapel.'[16] This was the first archepiscopal funeral to
be organized by the College of Arms since the Restoration, an era in which the
College enjoyed an upsurge. Garter King-of-Arms was present, together with
Lancaster Herald (William Riley), Windsor Herald (Elias Ashmole), York Herald
(George Owen) and a further two unnamed heralds.

Bishop Fell's obsequies at Christ Church, Oxford, in 1686, were also attended
by the College of Arms. In the cathedral treasury at Christ Church is the head of
the pastoral staff and the mitre (*Col. 22*), items provided by the College of Arms
for use at Fell's funeral. Both are of carved and gilded wood, the head of the
pastoral staff re-echoing the baroque continental pastoral staffs of the period, the

95 Carved wooden pastoral staff, gilded, used at the funeral of the aforementioned bishop of Durham, in 1721. In ordinary circumstances this pastoral staff, together with the accompanying funerary mitre, would have remained atop the coffin in the burial vault.

mitre being gilt all over with raised gesso 'stones' and spandrils, painted proper, with the insides of the points painted red. There are no lappets on the mitre and it appears, by the absence of nail holes on the rim, that there never were any.

High up on the north wall of the north aisle at Steane, Northamptonshire, the mortuary chapel of the Crewes, is a reused capital upon which sits a dishevelled gilt gessoed wooden funerary mitre (*94*). The item has blackened with age and the gesso has a pronounced crackling yet it is still possible to see the raised 'stones' through the broken surface; despite being more than a mere shadow of its former self, it is far more important than the one at Oxford, for, in place of the apparelled headband there is a prince's coronet. This item relates to the Third – and last – Baron Crewe, 'The Right Rev[d] and Right Hon[ble] Nathaniel Crewe, Lord Bishop of Durham and Baron of Steane' who died in 1721 at the age of eighty-nine. As occupant of the See of Durham, Crewe was able to avail himself of the ancient title prince-bishop and, as such, was allowed the special distinction of a coronet encircling the mitre.

Near the monument to the Second Lord Crewe are two fragments of wood, carved with enfolding acanthus leaves; when pieced together they made the head of a pastoral staff (*95*). A further search brought to light the ebonized staff, propped up in the north-east corner of the chapel. This item was without doubt the bishop's funerary pastoral staff.

In York Minster, the pastoral staff on Archbishop Sterne's tomb is the one used at his funeral in 1683 but that held by Archbishop Lamplugh (d.1691) on his tomb is probably not, though it would be unwise to rule it out altogether purely because of its simplicity of design.

It was possible to by-pass the College and go direct to herald-painters to provide the necessary standard, bannerol, penons and escutcheons. The College was well aware of this and often negotiated all-in prices to cover the cost of their attendance and the provision of the achievements, thereby making their prices favourable. The College decided in 1624 to fix their fees so that 'for those turns which shall happen to be in London the kings of arms are contented to allow every herald and pursuivant in his course out of that sum £12, and if it shall happen to be less, then the herald or pursuivant to have the half or an equal share with the king of arms'.[17] Still the armigerous families were not content and found the basic attendance charges of £75 too high.

With the Restoration and a demand for a return to the panoply and pomp of pre-Commonwealth days, the College looked forward to a renaissance. This was not to be, and the number of funerals they were being asked to organize continued to decline to such an extent that in December 1660 they again dropped the price, this time to 'twelve pounds apiece and not under'.[18] But not even this was enough to tempt the nobility and gentry back into the fold, as the private undertaker was in a position not only to provide all that was customary with greater speed than the College, and at a lower price, but also had attendance charges of lesser magnitude. In a desperate bid the College of Arms made their final reduction in November 1699. It was agreed that, for the future, no funeral should be served under the sum of £10, besides the usual transportation fee of twelvepence per mile, out and home again, for each officer. But it was too late; and the College of Arms lost out to the trade. In 1682 John Gibbon, appointed Bluemantle Herald in 1671, wrote, 'It was my hard hap to become a member of the Heralds Office, when the Ceremony of Funerals began to be in the Wane ... In eleven years time I have had but five turns.'[19] They had only themselves to blame.

One item often associated with funerals from the early seventeenth century was the hatchment, derived by the herald-painters from the armorial escutcheons and targets of the heraldic funerals. First used as a pictorial announcement to passers-by that a death had taken place in the family, they were nailed up on the wall of the house, usually at first-floor level and, if possible, over the main entrance. In the Victoria and Albert Museum a water-colour of 1776 by James Miller depicting Cheyne Walk, Chelsea, shows a herald-painter or joiner balancing precariously on a first-floor window-ledge about to hang a hatchment (*Col. 23*).[20] Once over it was taken down and transferred to the church where the body had been deposited and offered up as a heraldic memorial. Quite often these hatchments were the only indication that a particular member of a family had been deposited in the dynastic vault.

Rules apply to the background against which the arms are painted and, once grasped, it is possible to tell at a glance whether the deceased was a bachelor, a spinster, someone married with a surviving spouse, a widow or widower. Where married couples are concerned, the gender of the deceased/survivor can be ascertained where the arms of the husband and wife are impaled, for the husband's arms are always shown on the dexter (the right-hand side of a shield when held from behind, the left side as one looks at it) and the wife's on the sinister (vice versa). The format is as follows:

Background painted all black, single coat-of-arms: the deceased was a bachelor.

Background painted all black, single coat-of-arms displayed on a lozenge: the deceased was a spinster.

Dexter half painted black, sinister half white: the deceased was a married man survived by his wife.

Sinister half painted black, dexter half white: the deceased was a married woman survived by her husband.

Background painted all black, impaled coat-of-arms: the deceased died a widower.

Background painted all black, impaled coat-of-arms displayed on a lozenge: the deceased died a widow.

In the case of a person entitled to impale official arms with his own, it is the sinister side, which bore his personal arms, that is painted black. So, in the case of a bishop, the dexter side with the arms of the diocese will have a white background, because his see survives him. An example of this type, to the Rt Revd William Ward (d.1838), rector of Great Horkesley, Essex, and subsequently Bishop of Sodor and Man, can be seen in the vestry of Great Horkesley church. Instead of a helm and crest is a bishop's mitre.

Hatchments rarely bear the name of the deceased, the personal identification being ascertained from the arms. Often the motto itself was changed, words of a more morbid nature being substituted, such as *Resurgam, In Coelo Quies* or even *Dread Shame*. Early hatchments, those produced during the seventeenth century, were little more than two feet square but by the early eighteenth century they had grown in size to four feet square and an uncommonly fine series of seventeen hatchments of the larger size to members of the Compton family can be seen at Compton Wynyates, Warwickshire (*96*). The wooden frames supplied for hatchments were a uniform black baguette with a narrow gilt moulding or slip abutting the canvas; sometimes these frames were covered with puckered black crape and occasionally surmounted by a bow of the same material. As they were not included in the official achievements, the College of Arms exercised little control over their manufacture apart, of course, from keeping a watchful eye over the herald-painters lest they began issuing bogus hatchments to non-armigerous families.

Funerary achievements were not limited to the street procession, for they also played an important symbolic role whilst the encoffined body remained in the home prior to the funeral. It was the custom, from the mid seventeenth century until the late nineteenth century, for the bodies of armigerous families to 'lie in state' in their own houses, the walls of the selected room being hung floor to ceiling with 'mourning'. The magnitude of this arrangement depended on the number of rooms included, which rarely seems to have been less than three: the hallway, a small withdrawing-room where visitors could be received, and the

96   Hatchments to the Compton family at Compton Wynyates
Chapel, Warwickshire. These late seventeenth- and early
eighteenth-century hatchments were probably suppled direct by
herald painters, rather than via the College of Arms.

chamber where the encoffined body lay on its catafalque surrounded by the implements and elements of heraldry. Some households retained their own mourning for this purpose, though from existing bills and receipts it appears that the majority were had on hire from the funeral furnisher's, and there are instances where the full mourning was replaced after the first stage of private mourning by grey cloth trimmed with white for the second stage – each stage lasting for about six months. Lunsingh Scheuvleer, in his *Documents on the Furnishing of Kensington Palace*,[21] makes reference to grey hangings in the king's apartment in 1697, doubtless left over from the court mourning for Queen Mary.

A full account by Francis Sandford of the funeral of General Monk, Duke of Albemarle, in 1670 pays particular attention to the hangings at Somerset House where the body lay in state. The accompanying trappings were of the highest quality, the funeral having been ordered by King Charles II and organized by the Royal Wardrobe. Two rooms were passed through until one came to the third and final room which 'was hung with Velvet, floored with Bays, adorned with Escutcheons, and Black Sconces, with White Tapers, and at the upper end upon a Haute-pass, a Bed of State of Black Velvet was placed with Black plumes at the Four corners of the Tester; at the Head a Majesty-Escutcheons, and another in the midst of the Tester. Upon the Bed was placed a Coffin covered with a fine Holland-Sheet of Eight bredths, and Eight ells long, and over that, a Pall of Black Velvet of Eight breadths, and Eight yards long, and thereupon the Effigies of the Duke'.[22]

Sandford's engraving (97) raises questions about his own description for, though the effigy is plainly to be seen (the armour survives in the Undercroft Museum at Westminster Abbey), the palled coffin is not, and one is led to conjecture that it must have been beneath the palled boards provided to support the effigy.

In an attempt to ascertain the reasons for the College's becoming less popular we need to focus on the complicated system of '*droits*' and lucrative perquisites, which it had been enjoying from public royal funerals since at least the second quarter of the sixteenth century. As part of the royal household, the gift of black cloth from the Great Wardrobe for mourning apparel was a legitimate action on the part of the Lord Chamberlain; so was the payment of the heralds' attendance fees and meeting the bills for the supply of the various and varied items of heraldry supplied by the College. More questionable was the College's right to the items of funeral furniture provided at the expense of the Lord Chamberlain's Office; what we might legitimately label 'purloining', the College preferred to call '*droits*'. In short, the heralds stripped Westminster Abbey almost bare within a few hours of a funeral's having taken place. Sir Anthony Wagner relates the following disgraceful incident:

> After James I's funeral in 1625 the heralds divided among them 601 yards of velvet, 68 yards of tissue, being one of the palls, 56¼ yards of purple satin, the lining of the pall, 32 black velvet chairs without elbows, 32 velvet cushions used on the chairs, 21 stools, taffeta that lined the roof of the hearse, the timber of the hearse, escutcheons and 'pencills' [penoncels]. Other items they sold and divided the proceeds; among them a desk, a table, black velvet cushions, a great black velvet chair, pile velvet, three things like andirons, a great chair with elbows, and a purple velvet cushion with gold fringe and great tassels of gold.

97   General Monk, Duke of Albemarle, lying in state, 1670.
Surrounded by the full emblems of chivalry, Monk's effigy lies
on a bed of state provided by the Royal Wardrobe.

The removal of these items was, however, delayed for some nine months, '... partly by reason of the contagious sickness of the plague immediately happening thereon and partly because some of the velvets as one of the palls and other things used about the representation [funeral effigy] rested in the hands of Mr Ireland Keeper of the Monuments at Westminster Abbey, who withheld them till now upon pretence that he had not had the robes delivered him from the Wardrobe for adorning his Majesty's Effigies, to be set up in the press provided for it.'[23] On this occasion the heralds also lost out to a Mr Grimes, who had stolen the plain holland pall from the chariot outside the Abbey whilst the funeral service was in progress! These *droits* vexed the Dean and Chapter, who believed theirs to be the stronger claim, the furniture and fabrics already being on their premises. Tension was not relieved until 1758 when the two parties agreed to share the proceeds, though Dean Pearce endeavoured to renege on some of the issues after the funeral of George II in 1760 and stepped down only when the College threatened legal action. Pearce might well have forced the issue had he known that he had been witnessing the last royal funeral at the Abbey. However, none of the foregoing reflected well on the College and it is not surprising that from the date of James I's funeral the nobility gradually turned away from the College of Arms, looking more towards the assistance of the herald-painters to furnish their funerals, where less pomp and more accurate costings could be obtained without the fear of *droits*.

The restoration of the monarchy in 1660 failed to attract a return to the situation as it existed prior to the Civil War. The immediate effect felt by the heralds was a serious drop in their revenue. The College of Arms tried, albeit unsuccessfully, to limit the herald-painters in their performance of heraldic funerals, though they did manage to get an agreement out of the Painters' Company in 1686 which forced their members to cease issuing bogus emblazons for funerals. Not all members conformed, for in the following year the College suppressed and prosecuted two painter-stainers, Henry Howell and Richard Wallis, for painting false arms and marshalling a funeral. This was a toothless bite on the part of the College of Arms and misdemeanours did not abate.

Arguably the most ingenious painter-stainer was William Russell, a herald-painter-*cum*-funeral furnisher, who entered into an agreement with the College of Arms in November 1689 that two heralds would attend in an official capacity at his funerals of armigerous families. This could be interpreted as capitulation on the part of the heralds, though the more plausible reason was that Russell was willing to pay £20 a time for this service, an increase of two-thirds above that charged by the College of Arms. In putting themselves at Russell's disposal the heralds were able to bank on a guaranteed fee of generous proportion without having to resort to *droits*. Russell, for his part, could guarantee to his clients that the heralds would be willing to attend for a flat fee, without any hidden extras. It was an ingenious system, in that it assured Russell of becoming a society funeral furnisher. Whether or not this agreement was fulfilled is not recorded, and if it did then it was short-lived, for no heralds attended at the funeral of the Hon. Thomas Howard, performed by William Russell at Ashtead, Surrey, on 13 April 1702 (*Col. 24*).[24]

By now even the Kings-of-Arms had to admit that the heyday was over, Clarenceaux having attended only three funerals in the whole of 1696. An attempt in 1699 to recommence prosecutions against erring funeral furnishers was a dismal failure.

The final nail in the coffin was hammered home in 1717 when, owing to a disagreement between the then Earl Marshal and the Lord Chamberlain over the heralds' right to attend at the baptism of the infant Prince William, the Lord Chamberlain decided that it would be he and his successors who would decide whether or not a royal occasion was deemed a 'public' ceremony within the jurisdiction of the Earl Marshal. From that day forward it was the tendency to make all royal functions 'private' – within the Lord Chamberlain's control – including funerals. The royal household made its intent abundantly clear in 1751 when the Lord Chamberlain employed the services of a Mr Harcourt, funeral furnisher, to attend to the obsequies of Frederick, Prince of Wales; this appears to be the first occasion at which an undertaker was used at a royal funeral.

Though the funeral furnishers tried hard to capture the array formerly provided by the College of Arms, they were unable to reproduce the colourful spectacle given to the occasion by the gloriously embroidered tabards of the heralds and the vibrant hues of the standard and bannerols, and all that survived from this elaborate and ancient ritual were the escutcheons on the pall (*Col. 25*). But the greatest loss was that moment when the coffin, swaying on the shoulders of the bearers, was taken down into the vault. At this point, hitherto, the King-of-Arms had stepped forward and pronounced in a stentorian voice the style and titles of the deceased. The funeral furnishers knew that they could never compete with this.

8

The Burial Vault:
The Eternal Bedchamber

It was a large room, much larger, I think, than the schoolroom where Mr Glennie taught us, but not near so high, being only some nine feet from floor to roof. I say floor, though in reality there was none, but only a bottom of soft wet sand; and when I stepped down on to it my heart beat very fiercely, for I remembered what manner of place I was entering, and the fearful sounds which had issued from it that Sunday morning so short a time before. I satisfied myself that there was nothing evil lurking in the dark corners, or nothing visible at least, and then began to look round and note what was to be seen. Walls and roof were of stone, and at one end was a staircase closed by a great flat stone at top – that same stone which I had often seen, with a ring in it, in the floor of the church above. All round the sides were stone shelves, with divisions between them like great bookcases, but instead of books there were the coffins of the Mohunes ... It was plain enough that the whole place had been under water: the floor was still muddy, and the green and sweating walls showed the flood-mark within two feet of the roof; there was a wisp or two of fine seaweed that had somehow got in, and a small crab was still alive and scuttled across the corner, yet the coffins were but little disturbed. They lay on the shelves in rows, one above the other, and numbered twenty-three in all; most were in lead, and so could never float, but of those in wood some were turned slantways in their niches, and one had floated right away and been left on the floor upside down in a corner when the waters went back.[1]

Without doubt J. Meade Falkner, the author of *Moonfleet*, from which the foregoing quotation is extracted, must have at one time glimpsed into a burial vault, for what he makes the young John Trenchard see conforms to the general pattern of the more grandiose subterranean sepulchres of the late seventeenth century. However, it is regrettable that Meade Falkner did not pay closer attention to the construction of the coffins, for the later incident in the story, involving a single-shell wooden coffin, could not have happened: such items were not used for vault deposit.

Examples of their appearance in vaults have been recorded but, on the whole, this was due either to unfamiliarity on the part of the undertaker in vault burial techniques or because of deliberate intrusions into the vaults of extinct families in the early nineteenth century, as will be seen later.

The large slab of stone with its integral lifting ring set into the floor of the chancel, the steep flight of steps leading down into the vault and the shelved recesses are correct and not the fantasy of Meade Falkner. In reality, the dank chamber pierced by needle-point rays of sunlight through partially blocked ventilation holes, the damp walls and chilly atmosphere, together with the sight of banks of neatly shelved coffins on either side of the intruder, can produce feelings of awe and suspense. Overall is the pervading smell of decay, a mixture of saturated timber and mouldy fabric. There is an instinct to tread lightly and speak softly, as though any sudden movement or loud noise could awaken the dead from their slumber.

'Beneath are deposited ...', 'Here lies Interr'd ...' and 'In a Vault near this place ...' are but three of the more familiar preambles to funerary inscriptions seen on countless sepulchral monuments in town and country churches. Yet how many have stopped to consider what appear to be unimportant geographical directives to conjure up a mental picture of what these subterranean chambers might be like? Indeed, what is a burial vault, why were they favoured, what quality of person commanded their construction and when were they in vogue?

Over the last ten years the author has visited and recorded the contents of nearly 100 vaults.[2] Most have felt welcoming, few hostile, yet all were bathed in poignant, chilling sadness. The small coffins of children, some little more than a few hours old at death, jockey for shelf space with the huge cases of long-dead ancestors; teenagers who, having survived the vagaries of childhood illness, succumbed at a time when their parents must have been confident of their surviving to adulthood; young mothers having died in childbirth; dutiful daughters and profligate sons; elderly spinster aunts and bachelor uncles. Generation upon generation of one family, divided by time yet joined through bonds of filial kinship, now trimmed, dressed and chested side by side in the same vault, mute and cold yet expectant of the Last Trump and their resurrection. One vault, beneath a now ruinous church in the Kent countryside, was particularly saddening. Here was a spacious chamber of the 1830s, expensively fitted with whitewashed brick loculi and slate shelves affording space for twenty-three people. The sole occupants were three adults – father, mother and spinster sister – and two children, one aged thirteen, the other but a few weeks old – both grandchildren of the vault's founder. All had died within a space of twenty-five years, an entire dynasty wiped out in a generation. 'And yet they think that their houses shall continue for ever: and that their dwelling-places shall endure from one generation to another; and call their lands after their own names.' (Psalm 49, v.11).

By way of introduction to the whole subject of burial vaults, their importance and the part they play in providing information for the funerary historian, we need only direct our attention to John Weever, the seventeenth-century antiquary, for a contemporary commentary.

> It was vsuall in ancient times, and so it is in these our dayes, for persons of especiall ranke and qualitie to make their own Tombes and Monuments in their life-time; partly for that they might haue a certain house to put their head (as the old saying is) whensoeuer they should bee taken away by death, out of their Tenement, the world; and partly to please themselues, in beholding their dead countenance in marble. But most especially because thereby they thought to preserve their memories from oblouion.[3]

So there we have it. Vaults, so says Weever, were the prerogative of the wealthy and usually constructed prior to requirement. Yet the vault, as a dynastic burial chamber, was a short-lived phenomenon, popular between the first quarter of the seventeenth century and the second quarter of the eighteenth. It was unusual, though not unknown, for a family to own more than one vault within a church building, since additional space was achieved either by a judicious clearance of the more decayed coffins or by extending the internal boundaries to the east and/or west, though north and south extensions – often little more than 'leading-off' chambers – are also known, such as at the Harvey vault in Hempstead, Essex.

The comparatively recent introduction of archaeology within churches in use, together with an increase in ecclesiastical archaeology in general, has opened new avenues for the social historian, the demographer and the funerary antiquarian. Our knowledge of burial practices, coffin types and undertaking techniques have been furthered due to practical vault examinations undertaken as a result of discoveries made during restoration programmes, reordering exercises and redundancy schemes, the latter usually entailing bulk vault clearance, especially in the inner cities, prior to the building's being handed over for its alternative use. This means not only that vaults are now more readily accessible to the specialist but also that opportunities have arisen to allow for greater time to record their contents and construction; beforehand, there was a time limit, usually one working day, placed on such examinations. This applies equally to brick-lined graves, a mode of intramural burial associated more closely with city and large town churches in the eighteenth and nineteenth centuries. Prior to these new opportunities it was virtually impossible to gain access to burial vaults, unless they had their own purpose-built entrance leading off from the churchyard, for to have entered via the church floor would have meant applying for a faculty (diocesan legal permission), which would have been granted only where there was a stronger reason for entry on the part of the appellant than mere curiosity. The only legitimate and trouble-free way of gaining entry was to wait until the vault was reopened for the reception of remains or to have been the subject of the funeral oneself.

As the majority of burial vaults are post-medieval in construction they have not excited much attention from the archaeological fraternity and have all too hastily been dismissed as 'nasty modern disturbances', an impediment to those seeking to reach earlier evidence of site occupation. Due to the pioneering zeal of a small band of historians and church archaeologists matters are being rectified, though it remains painful to reflect on the quantity of valuable source material which, until recently, has been denied examination, evaluation and the concomitant post-excavation analysis, interpretation and publication. However, the question remains whether every opportunity afforded for vault examination should be taken. Deliberately to disturb a vault on the strength of curiosity is unnecessary, for it should not be forgotten that such chambers were constructed as places of private sepulture whose occupants, at the time of purchase, probably never contemplated being disturbed by the inquisitive, and such sentiments should be respected. Nevertheless, curiosity has often proved too great a temptation, and numerous vaults have been entered. In these instances it is always better to err on the side of caution. It is, however, logical to incorporate an examination in instances of vault clearance under faculty; there the historian or archaeologist can liaise with the contractor, to work to an agreed methodology and satisfy the needs of research without disturbing the schedule of the contract. Unfortunately not all vault clearances have been accompanied by a watching brief; indeed, one could go further and state that many have been cleared unnecessarily over the last two decades when a more rational on-site disposition of the coffins would have been more appropriate. One such example of coping with this situation will be cited later.

The chancel at Thaxted, Essex (*Col. 26*), provides a good opportunity for the funerary historian to study at first hand the types of markers used in association with intramural burial from the sixteenth through to the mid nineteenth century. Thaxted escaped major restoration in the nineteenth century, for the community was too poor to finance such a venture and, since the patron's interests lay elsewhere, the chancel retains its delightful higgledy-piggledy seventeenth-century floor of large unglazed tiles, paviours and bricks, which affords more than the usual arrangement of black, white and grey fossil marble ledger stones. Whereas it is almost certain that the indented stone of *c.*1450 with its brass to Robert Wedow and an early seventeenth-century indented slab *sans* brass in the centre of the chancel floor are reset, the ledger stones at the east and west ends are not; dating from the early seventeenth to the early nineteenth century they remain *in situ*. Almost without exception these ledgers are nothing more than incised capping-off stones to brick-lined shafts with many chips showing around the edges, the result of crowbars having been used to facilitate the opening of the shaft for the reception of further deposits. Other depressions in the floor have been caused by coffin collapse in earth-cut graves. On the south side of the chancel is an area of early nineteenth-century glazed tiles covering a section of the floor some ten feet east to west and six feet north to south which was laid in 1817 following the construction of the Frye vault. It is identified by a small slab of stone, twelve inches square, set into the centre of the tiles and conveniently marked 'FRYE/1817'. At least a dozen further burials are marked by similar stones or light-coloured tiles, most of which have lost their inscriptions as a result of human traffic, others simply bearing the initials of the deceased and, in some instances, the year of death. Such items, interesting if only for their antiquity, would most certainly have been discarded during any nineteenth-century reflooring scheme.

198

Yet it is in the chancel south aisle where the most ingenious evidence at Thaxted might be found. Here are two single-width plots, each with an eroded identification tile, but whose boundaries have been defined by scribing the outline of a ledger stone directly on to the brick floor – less for the edification of the family of the deceased than as an indication to the sexton of the grave's area. A more macabre scribing can be seen at the west end of the north aisle on the raised platform behind the font; here, in place of a rectangle, is cut into the floor the outline of a single-break coffin. Indeed, there are at least twice as many intramural burials in Thaxted than the ordinary ledger stones imply. Yet Thaxted is not unique, as similar situations exist at Great Walsingham, Lavenham and South Creake in East Anglia and in other parts of the country. All go to prove that churches were put to excessive use for intramural burial.

In the south-east corner of Thaxted's sanctuary, to the right of the high altar, is a doorway leading on to a spiral staircase (*98*). 'Up' – though now infilled for structural reasons – led to the roof, whilst 'down' descended to a late fourteenth-century charnel or crypt, its entrance now bricked up. Outside, the three squat narrow square-headed openings towards the base of the east wall, originally giving illumination and ventilation to the vault, have been blocked in. Whether the charnel was cleared of remains on its appropriation is not known, but it was not unusual for such an act to take place, the bones being transferred to the churchyard whence they once came. John Aubrey relates the case of a charnel that certainly merited some revision, if not total clearance: 'Under the Cathedral-church at Hereford is the largest Charnel-house for bones that I ever saw in England. In A° 1650 there lived amongst these bones a poor woman that, to help out her fire, did use to mix deadmen's bones: this was thrift and poverty: but cunning alewives putt the ashes of these bones in their Ale to make it intoxecating.'[4] Whether the effect was equally efficacious if added to spirits, Aubrey does not say.

Interment within churches was frowned upon by the Church of Rome and Pierre Roger de Beaufort, Pope Gregory XI (1370–8), prohibited the practice as unwholesome. Unwholesome indeed, when intramural burial ranged from simple shroud burial to deposit in a stone coffin whose lid additionally served as the ledger stone; such shallowness of deposit together with poor cementation of stone coffin lids must have led to unpleasantness, foul air and nasal offence. Regardless of the prohibition, Europe continued the practice and monarchs, high-ranking clergy, founders and benefactors were afforded the privilege either as a result of their sacerdotal status or in recognition of their social standing and/or pious acts.

Not all of the best sites within the church were reserved for the high-ranking clergy – in some monastic institutions the favoured place was the chapter house – since the Church was well aware of the revenue such plots could command from a demanding nobility eager to secure burial within the wall of the building. And these sites were highly sought after, so much so that some families went so far as to enter into agreement with the religious communities to acquire grave space in advance, something now known as 'reservation' or, more crudely, 'pre-need selling'; in this way the patron was satisfied, for it provided him with the opportunity to commission and supervise the erection of a tomb, as was hinted by John Weever.

98   *The c. 1510 charnel steps in the south-east corner of the*
chancel at Thaxted, Essex.

In the parish churches the preferred location for intramural burial was in the chancel, as close to the high altar as possible, it being thought that the nearer one was to the altar the closer one came to God. In reality such a position had a simpler explanation. To have one's tomb adjacent to the high altar meant that it was always seen by the clergy, acolytes and worshippers during the mass, thereby continuing social status beyond the grave. In the cathedrals, abbeys and priories a similar attitude prevailed, though graves east of the pulpitum had a reduced chance of being seen by the laity. At Worcester Cathedral there are eight pre-Reformation tombs to the laity east of the pulpitum. That to King John occupies the most privileged position in front of the sanctuary steps – the effigial coffin-lid having been raised on to a tomb-chest in *c*.1529 – whilst the Chantry Chapel to Prince Arthur (Henry VIII's elder brother, d.1502) occupies a prime site on the south side of the sanctuary itself, incorporating the sedilia. The other six monuments are in the north and south retrochoir aisles. But was there anything to be gained in having one's body deposited in an area of the building inaccessible to the laity and where only members of the community would see them? Yes, there was; for in places where the shrines of saints were situated at the east end of the retrochoir, such monuments would have been passed by pilgrims on their circuit to and from the shrine. Looking at smaller foundations, Romsey Abbey has only one pre-Reformation secular monument east of the pulpitum, that to a lady of the thirteenth century: an appropriate gender, for Romsey was a nunnery.

Lesser spiritual benefit could be gained by purchasing a plot in the nave between the piers of the arcade. As the area west of the pulpitum was given over to the daily use of the laity, both the habitual worshipper and the itinerant pilgrim would have seen these tombs on their entry to the building. In themselves these tombs provided a moral essay to the onlooker on the attainments achieved in life through obedience, loyalty and service to one's monarch. It was also somewhat cheaper to be buried west of the pulpitum.

The earlier burial vaults were little more than stone-lined troughs capped off with substantial stone slabs which formed the bed for the funeral monument. Other cists were more elaborate, such as that to Henry III (d.1272) in Westminster Abbey. In October 1871, the effigy having been removed for cleaning, it was decided to open the tomb-chest to examine its construction and contents.

> The marble bed [on which the effigy lay] consists of one long and two short pieces, making up a length of 7 feet 11 inches, and a width of 3 feet 2 inches … The long piece lies on the north side, and at its north-east corner there is a slight fracture … but the piece is only very slightly dislocated. There are four cramps, one of them loose and corroded at one end; the others are sound, and have suffered but slightly from corrosion. The surface of the marble immediately under the metal [bed] is as perfect as it was at first, the small covering of dust which had insinuated itself, and was spread over it, having tended to preserve it from the action of the air. At the junction of the three pieces of marble there is a neatly cut rectangular hole or notch. On looking through this hole into the space beneath, a flat surface about a foot below the marble bed was observed. This surface was at first thought to be a leaden box or coffin of perhaps a quarter of an inch in thickness … The two short stones being lifted on to the long one on the north side, the whole chamber or grave, with its coffin, became exposed, the latter nearly filling the space … The wood of the lid, which is oak, is remarkably sound. Its upper surface is slightly decayed in some parts to the extent of about a quarter of an inch. The under surface appears to be quite sound, and this difference of the two surfaces seems to have caused the warping upwards so that there is an opening of an inch at the middle of the head, where the forefingers may be inserted, and the lid was therefore also loose, and only held in position by its own weight.

The iron chains at the head, foot, and sides, whereby the coffin was carried and lowered into its chamber, yet remain. They are neatly made of wrought-iron bar, about half an inch in diameter. They terminate with rings 4 inches in diameter, large enough for the hands or for poles to be passed through them, so as to carry and lower the coffin. These rings and a few links of the chain were lying loose between the sides of the coffin and the marble tomb. The rings, when drawn out, rise a few inches above the edge of the tomb. These had been coated with a black resinous substance, which remained tolerably bright and smooth.[5]

When Richard II's queen, Anne of Bohemia, died in 1394 the king fulfilled his wish to be buried as close as possible to the shrine of Edward the Confessor by transferring the monument and coffins of Humphrey and Mary de Bohun, grandchildren of Edward I, from their position in the Confessor's Chapel to the north side of the Chapel of St John the Baptist. This now gave him a prime site within the shrine area and he immediately instructed Henry Yevele and Stephen Lot to erect a tomb-chest whilst commissioning Nicholas Broker and Godfrey Prest to execute the effigies of himself and his late wife. Following the temporary removal of the effigies for conservation in August 1871, Sir George Gilbert Scott was asked to supervise the opening of the tomb.

The interior of the tomb consists of a chamber immediately under the marble slab [on which the effigies rested] about 6½ feet deep, having the floor of the grave 2 feet 6 inches below the floor of the Confessor's chapel, and about 1 foot 6 inches above that of the Ambulatory. The lower part of the chamber is the grave, which is about 7 feet long and 5 feet wide, over it is a space transversed longitudinally by an arch formed at about mid-height, so as to carry the two long slabs above, and dividing that space into two parts 8½ feet long and each about two feet wide.[6]

This, then, is the transitional link between the cist-type burial chamber of Henry III and the purpose-built vault of Edward IV.

Shortly before his death in 1483, Edward IV selected a site on the north side of the chancel of St George's Chapel, Windsor for his tomb. This allowed for the construction of a vault for the reception of his remains and the subsequent erection of a sumptuous two-storied chantry chapel. The vault itself is quite low, being not much more than six feet 6 inches at the apex of its arched roof, entrance being gained from the north choir aisle side via a crisp and elegant low-springing arch some four foot high at the centre, infilled with neatly cut irregular-sized blocks of stone, many of which bear masons' marks. An engraving of 1790 by James Basire after sketches taken by H. Emlyn (*99*), and published by the Society of Antiquaries, clearly shows the masons' marks on the stones. Nevertheless, this vault is not an entirely separate construction as it incorporates, through abutment, portions of the original substructure of the chapel itself.

The earliest accessible vault with its own distinct entrance can be found in St Alban's Abbey and, as with other unique examples of architecture, it had unusual

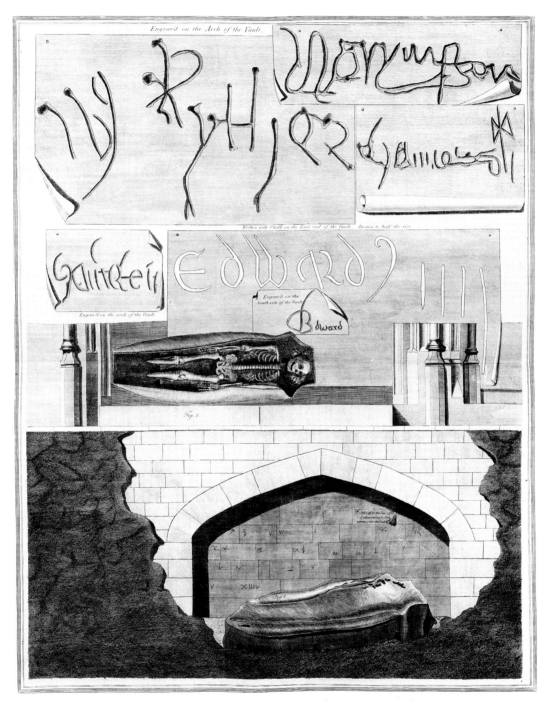

99   *Edward IV's vault in St Georges's Chapel, Windsor, constructed in c.1483 – from an engraving of 1790 by James Basire, after sketches taken by H. Emlyn on the vault's opening in 1788.*

203

beginnings. Humphrey, Duke of Gloucester (d.1477), the brother of Henry V, was a close friend and patron of the humanist scholar John Bostock of Wheathampstead, Abbot of St Albans (d.1465). Both were interested in the New Learning of the fifteenth century and, as the abbot of St Albans ranked in importance above all English abbots, Wheathampstead would have been a familiar figure to those at Court, his friendship with the Duke of Gloucester taking him into the royal circle itself. As a tribute to this friendship, Wheathampstead constructed a sumptuous chantry chapel for Gloucester occupying the entire south side of the shrine area, a pendant to the earlier fifteenth-century wooden watching loft on the north side. This was indeed a rare and choice gift, being not only the most expensive site available in the Abbey but also the most important. The chantry, which was probably erected in 1430 when Wheathampstead built his own (long-demolished) chantry chapel to the south of the south aisle, is magnificent – one of the most poetic essays in stone of the period. Prominently displayed in the decorative moulding is Gloucester's device of plants in a cup, a classical *memento mori* motif signifying the Garden of Adonis and probably introduced on the suggestion of Wheathampstead himself. So as not to obscure the shrine from the gaze of the pilgrims there is a large tripartite opening in the base of the chantry affording an uninterrupted view of the saint's feretory, screened off by a beautiful late thirteenth-century iron grille of rectangular panels constructed of alternating vertical, horizontal and diagonal bars. This grille originally filled the arched opening now occupied by the Gloucester chantry, and it remains a tribute to Wheathampstead's artistic judgement that it was saved and reused. Slightly to the north of the chantry, and set into the floor of the shrine area itself, is an iron grille affording access to a steep flight of eight steps leading down into the burial vault, the arched entrance of which is secured by an iron gate of somewhat later date. A single step leads into a panel-vaulted tomb-chamber not much more than seven foot high, seven foot east to west and five foot north to south. The interior walls and ceiling are rendered and the now recased anthropoid coffin rests on the floor rather than on a mortuary plinth. The unique feature of this tomb-chamber is a black-outline wall painting of the Crucifixion on the east wall. The central figure is flanked by two angels, the one on the right holding the lance which pierced Christ's side, whilst the one on the left holds out the Sangrail into which drops blood from the pierced side. The wall painting alone makes this tomb-chamber one of the most beautiful sepulchral settings in the country.

One of the earliest, if not the earliest, independent vaults was that constructed between 1503 and 1509 for Henry VII and Elizabeth of York beneath their magnificent Torrigiano monument in what is now known as Henry VII's Chapel in Westminster Abbey. Elizabeth of York died in childbirth on 11 February 1503, eighteen days after Abbot John Islip had laid the foundation stone of the Chapel; her remains were therefore deposited temporarily in a side chapel awaiting later transference to the intended vault. Henry VII died on 21 April 1509, the funeral taking place on 9 May when he was placed in his 'cavernous vault ... by the side of his Queen'.[7] Unfortunately 'cavernous' it was not! Was the body of Elizabeth of York moved from its temporary resting-place between the date of the King's death and his funeral, or at an earlier stage? During an investigative programme, mounted in February 1869, to search for the whereabouts of the coffin of James I, the vault beneath the Torrigiano monument was opened:

> Soon under the step and enclosure, a corbel was discovered, immediately under the panelled curb, evidently to form an opening beneath; and onward to the east the earth was cleared, until the excavators reached a large stone, like a wall, surmounted and jointed on the north side with smaller stones, and brickwork over all. This was evidently the entrance ... It was at once evident that the vault of Edward VI was only the continuation westward of the passage into the entrance of the Tudor vault[8] ... The mouth of the cavern was closed ... by a huge stone, which, as in Jewish sepulchres, had been rolled against the entrance.... The vault is partly under the floor of the west end of the enclosure of the tomb, and partly under the tomb itself; so that the western end of the arch is nearly coincident with the inside of the Purbeck marble curb above, and the eastern end above 2½ feet west of the eastern extremity of the tomb above. Thus the vault is not quite conformable with the tomb, but is so placed that the western face of it abuts against the thick bonding wall of the chancel. This want of conformity with the direction of the tomb doubtless arose from the circumstances that the vault was excavated before the tomb above was designed. The vault is beautifully formed of large blocks of firestone. It is 8 feet 10 inches long, 5 feet wide, and, from floor to apex, 4½ feet high. The arch is of a fine four-centred Tudor form; and the floor, which is stone, is about 5½ feet below the floor of the tomb. The masonry is very neatly wrought and truly placed. The stone exhibited hardly the least sign of decay, and, apart from its absorptive and porous nature, there was no appearance of dew-drops on the ceiling.[9]

Solid in construction, the internal dimensions are little more than those of the surface area of the effigial monument above (*43*). Nevertheless, this vault is important for three reasons: it marked the transition from burial within a tomb-chest to a separate chamber, isolated from but adjacent to the tomb; it introduced the convenience of steps to facilitate easy access for subsequent interments; and it established – apart from the rolling stone – the format for burial vault construction on a wider scale. Henry VII was determined to have a burial chamber capable of safely shielding his remains and those of his Queen 'as long as the world shall endure'. But was he worthy of it? His biographer, Bacon, did not think so, saying that '... he lieth buried at Westminster, in one of the stateliest and dantiest monuments of Europe, both for the chapel and the sepulchre. So that he dwelleth more richly dead, in the monument of his tomb, than he did alive in Richmond or any of his places. I could wish that he did the like in this monument of his fame'.[10]

Not all pre-need burial vaults were occupied by their patrons. Edmund Harman, one of Henry VIII's barbers and a gentleman of the Privy Council, erected 'a monument to the Christian memory of himself and his only and most faithful wife Agnes and of the sixteen children whom, by God's mercy, she bore him' at Burford, Oxfordshire in *c*.1540–3. Yet the accompanying vault is empty, for Agnes and Edmund Harman subsequently moved to nearby Taynton and both were eventually buried there rather than at Burford, Agnes dying in 1576 and Edmund in 1577, four months after he had married his second wife. Indeed, vault

100   *Burial vaults of the late seventeenth and early eighteenth
centuries within Barton-on-Humber Church, Lincolnshire.
Such vaults are quite common in England, being not much
more than double-width brick-lined graves.*

examinations have shown that those specifically mentioned on a mural monument as having been deposited in an adjacent vault were not necessarily so, and vice versa. Absence may be the result of periodic clearance.

It is not until the third quarter of the sixteenth century that we see an increase in the number of landed-gentry and noble families taking advantage of a more liberal and relaxed ecclesiastical system to construct for their exclusive and perpetual use places of subterranean sepulture within parish churches. With the dissolution of the religious houses complete there were no longer any particularly special buildings ranking high in the intramural burial stakes. Westminster Abbey was restricted, since Elizabeth I had limited burial within its confines to 'those especially who shall have well and gravely served about our person, or otherwise about the public business of our kingdom', and this tradition was rigorously maintained. The majority of the estate churches quickly became private mausoleums for the local leading family, even though their intended purpose was to cater for the spiritual needs of the community.

There were other advantages in choosing one's parish church. Had one been offered a place in Westminster Abbey the resulting plot would have been very small, whereas the patron of even the tiniest country living could command a greater area for his vault. If space did not permit the opening of a new vault, there was always the possibility of paying for the addition of a chapel if not an entire aisle, the foundations of which could be dug especially deep to provide for a burial vault, together with its own access steps, as did the Harveys at Hempstead, Essex (*49*).

For the purpose of definition, the burial vault is a subterranean chamber of stone or brick capable of housing a minimum of two coffins side by side, and with an internal height of not less than 1.74 metres (*100*). Anything narrower is a brick-lined grave (*Col. 27*). The wording on some mural monuments can be misleading, if not deliberately untruthful, for even the most perfunctory study of the floor of the church reveals that the wording 'In a Vault near this place ...' actually refers to a brick-lined grave capped-off with a ledger stone. Admittedly, such harmless pretentions were more commonly met in the eighteenth century. A vault need not necessarily have access steps and neither was there any compunction for its presence – nor, indeed, that of any burial – to be identified in the floor of the church. At Woodford in Essex, 'Sir Thomas Rowe, Lord of Mannour, was Buried in the upper end of the Chancell in the middle, his head lying part of hit lying vnder the Comunion Table, just soo far as against the Brasse that is on Mrs Mabs stone, and his feet lying against ye wall at the East end of the Chancell the eight day of November, 1644'[11] in an unmarked grave. George Herbert, the seventeenth-century divine, fared little better when he was interred at Bemmerton, Wiltshire, in 1633 in a brick-lined grave 'in the Chancell, under no large, nor yet very good, marble grave-stone, without any inscription'. However, as John Aubrey continues, 'He was buryed (according to his owne desire) with the singing service for the buriall of dead, by the singing men of Sarum. Francis Sambroke (attorney) then assisted as a chorister boy: my uncle Thomas Danvers, was at the Funerall.'[12]

Detailed notes in a church's register, such as those relating to Thomas Rowe's burial at Woodford, Essex, were necessary when vaults were not marked. On the other hand, some families provided distinct entrances to their vaults. In 1618 Thomas Rayner constructed a new vault beneath the north of the crossing at Thaxted, Essex, at which time he laid down a marker whose inscription not only recorded the position of the entrance and that the 'bricks laid on end' in the floor indicated the boundary of the chamber, but also informed the reader that he had taken the opportunity of gathering together from other sites within the building the known remains of his family for deposit in the new vault. Also at Thaxted, the Heckfords, relatives by marriage to the Rayners, appropriated an earlier fifteenth-century indented ledger to cover the entrance to their vault of *c*.1710 in the south of the crossing, inscribing the stone so that no one would be left in any doubt as to the precise location of the entrance. When John, Second Viscount St John, remodelled the western vault beneath the south aisle at Lydiard Tregoz, Wiltshire, in the 1740s he inserted steps in its north-east corner, access being gained via an unmarked stone with lifting rings immediately in front of the chancel screen.

The church of St John of Beverley at Harpham in the East Riding of Yorkshire is, rightly, famed for its magnificent collection of funerary monuments to the St Quentin family. Of lesser note is a ledger stone with iron lifting rings set into the floor of the St Quentin chapel, with the following legend: 'ENTRANCE/TO THE VAULT OF THE/S.T QUENTIN'S FAMILY/BUILT BY ORDER OF/WILLIAM S.T QUENTIN ESQ.R/LORD OF THE MANORS;/OF HARPHAM & LOWTHORPE/OCTOBER 15.TH 1827.' Further down is cut: 'THIS ENTRANCE CLOSED/MAY 1885.' Here we learn not only when a substantial family vault was constructed but also the duration of its use.

Interesting as these entrances are, the prize has to go to Davy Turner of South Creake, Norfolk. In the churchyard, hard up against the south wall of the church and to the east of the south porch, is a large ledger stone inscribed lengthways in huge letters with the legend 'THE MOUTH OF THE/VAULT', leaving no one in doubt – grave-robbers included – of the quickest way into the sepulchre. Turner died in 1825 aged seventy-five and his wife, Sarah, in 1826 aged sixty-seven, though the vault was in fact constructed in *c*.1811 to receive the remains of one of their adult children. All five children died before their parents, the youngest in 1811 aged twenty-two years, the eldest in 1825 aged forty-seven. Turner's wit reappears within the church: seven bodies were deposited in the vault – parents and five children – and seven plain flag stones, two large and five small, were used to cap the backfill in the church floor.

Exterior entry from the churchyard provides greater scope for the imaginative pen of the architect and has led to some ingenious means of access. The cavernous Sackville vault beneath the north chapel at Withyham, Sussex (*101*), was remodelled in 1673 and is entered via a single wooden door, reset from an earlier position and opening to steps down. At the bottom of the steps is a heavy iron gate opening into the vault. As these steps are somewhat steep, and little more than three feet wide, there exists a mid to late nineteenth-century wooden slide with integral iron rollers, so constructed as to lock on to the treads and down which the heavy lead-lined coffin could be slid, feet first, with retention tapes threaded through the handles allowing the bearers to control the speed of the descent. By contrast, the steps provided by Sir Jeffrey Wyatville in 1814 for his extension of the Poulett vault at Hinton St George, Somerset, are wide

101   *The Sackville Vault, Withyham, Sussex. Remodelled as a
tunnel vault in 1673 when the Sackville Chapel above was
rebuilt, the shelves were not inserted until the early nineteenth
century, at which time most of the then occupants were
transferred to the south side, leaving the north range free for
further deposits.*

enough and suitably shallow to allow the bearers to descend into the burial chamber with the coffin on their shoulders. At the top of the staircase is a small portico, entered from the churchyard via a pair of studded wooden doors, in a pseudo-Perpendicular style, painted sky-blue with black iron fittings, opening on to a landing seven feet 6 inches long and four feet 6 inches wide, affording space for the bearers to compose themselves prior to making the descent. This portico stands in a small stone-flagged courtyard enclosed within cast-iron railings, also painted sky-blue, whose double gates open opposite the doors into the vault.

When Sir George Gilbert Scott was approached by the First Earl of Ellesmere in 1846 to design St Mark's, Worsley, instructions were given for the provision of a burial vault beneath the east end of the south aisle and the sanctuary. The south aisle vault extends some six feet east into the churchyard and a pair of outward-opening iron doors lead on to a shaft some eight foot north to south, five foot east to west and eight feet deep, the whole closed off at ground level by an iron grid. To facilitate entry this grid had to be lifted, and the eight bearers descended by means of a ladder. The coffin was lowered on to their shoulders and the bearer party walked forward into the vault, the doorway being tall enough to allow for the passage of a shouldered coffin surmounted by a cushioned coronet.

An equally ingenious arrangement, this time by Sir Arthur Blomfield for the 1873 Baring vault at High Beach, Essex, is similar to the Worsley model but with the addition of access steps to the shaft. This large and impressive vault lies in the north-east corner of the churchyard, some feet away from the main building and, when not in use, is sealed with a canted steel cover secured by padlocks.

There is no strict pattern of vault construction. Whilst some remain bare stone or brick, others are rendered or lime-washed; some might have drainage and ventilation, others lit by natural daylight or not at all; some may have an integral charnel pit or cistern, whilst others make no provision whatsoever for decayed remains; and the neat arrangements of shelves or loculi space often conflicts with the earlier vaults, in which coffins were stacked on the floor one upon another.

The primary hurdle for any family wishing to construct a vault within a church lay in securing a faculty from the diocese, each application having to meet with the approval of the vicar and churchwardens, who were responsible for the fabric of the building and also better informed as to whether or not space was available. There were instances when the status of the petitioner outweighed the views of vicar and churchwardens: 'This October, 1681, it rang all over St Albans that Sir Harbottle Grimston, Master of the Rolles, had removed the Coffin [of Sir Francis Bacon, Viscount St Albans] to make roome for his owne to lye-in in the vault there at St Michael's church.'[13] Such despoliation was not unique. Two years previously, in 1679, the poet and dramatist Sir John Birkenhead had left instructions in his will that he be buried not in a vault but rather 'in St Martyn's churchyard-in-the-fields, neer the church ... his reason was because he sayd they removed the bodies out of the Church'.[14]

The most celebrated case of appropriation took place at Ketteringham, Norfolk, in 1853. The squire, Sir John Boileau, was determined to secure a prestigious site for himself and his family beneath the chancel of St Peter's Church. Having first ascertained that the existing Heveningham-Atkyns vault was incapable of extension, and having been reliably informed that it had not been used for at least fifty years, Boileau applied to the Bishop of Norwich for permission to transfer the remains to the churchyard in order that the vault might be released for his own use. The bishop replied on 26 October, 'Your legal right to remove the coffins would, I think, be questionable, if there were any to question it. This does not seem likely. I can only advise you as a friend, and my advice is, that you should first transfer to the churchyard all the coffins except that which has a name on it ... I doubt whether I could grant a faculty and think, on the whole, that the matter had better be conducted privately and quietly.'[15] Sir John took the bishop's advice and had the remains removed. Everything seemed in order until 23 November when he received a letter from a Mr Pemberton of Caxton, Cambridgeshire. It began, 'I learn this morning with the deepest surprise and indignation, that you have ventured to break open the family vault ... As one of those coffins contains the remains of my sister-in-law, I lose not a post in writing to request an immediate explanation of this most extraordinary proceedings ...' Consequently Boileau had to disinter the coffins from the churchyard and return them to the vault. A humiliating episode not only for Boileau but for the bishop and archdeacon too. To satisfy his sepulchral requirements Sir John commissioned Messrs Lofty of Heatherset to erect a mausoleum in the churchyard, it being thought more appropriate in this instance than a burial vault within the church.[16]

Intramural burial vaults of the period 1650–1850 fall in to four types:

1 The large dynastic vaults, either beneath a sidechapel or aisle, more usually associated with noble families.
2 The family vaults, often not much more than a double- or triple-width brick-lined grave with its own barrelled roof, usually for the landed gentry.
3 The single-width brick-lined grave, capped of by a ledger stone, a superior version of the family grave, patronized by the professional classes.

102   The east Poulett Vault at Hinton St George, Somerset, c. 1574–80. Stacking leads to the eventual collapse of the coffins on the lower register; here, those on the north have collapsed, leading to a general shift of the contents to the south. The vault was abandoned in 1814.

211

4 The extensive private and parochial vaults, specially constructed beneath some large town and city churches, generally erected between *c*.1725 to 1850.

Required size and site restrictions were the two main considerations to be accounted for prior to any excavation work. It has already been noted that not all of the family vaults were recorded, and it was not unusual for soundings to be taken in what the sexton thought to be an 'available' part of the church only to discover a previously unknown vault or earth-cut grave. Had such soundings been taken on 17 January 1800 at St Mary's, Chelmsford (now Chelmsford Cathedral), prior to work starting on a new vault, the nave roof and south arcade might not have collapsed.

The earlier burial vaults, those of the mid to late sixteenth century, are rarely larger than fifteen feet north to south and eight feet east to west, constructed either of stone blocks, brick or a mixture of both, with a gently curving roof somewhat similar to a flattened Perpendicular arch. The walls and roofs of these vaults are invariably lime-washed (often rendered too) to amplify any natural daylight afforded by the ventilation, and to reflect the artificial light provided by the lanterns of the bearers on entry. The eastern Poulett vault of *c*.1574–80 at Hinton St George, Somerset (*102*), is of this type, as is the western vault of the St John's at Lydiard Tregoz, built in *c*.1590. None of the early vaults has either shelves or loculi, the coffins being placed on the brick or stone floor with later occupants stacked on top of them and separated from their neighbours by wooden bearers. These bearers serve three functions: they distribute the weight of the coffin, allow air to circulate freely and enabled the undertakers' men to position the coffin without fear of trapped fingers. The illustration of the Hinton St George vault shows what can happen in adopting this stacking method. Here the combined weight of the two coffins at the top of the north stack has proved too great for the coffin at the bottom; the right-hand side of the latter caved in, so that the top two coffins fell over to the south, causing the coffins on the three remaining stacks to fall against the south wall of the vault. The western St John vault at Lydiard Tregoz, Wiltshire, is practically identical in size and construction to the early Poulett vault; again, the stacked coffins have collapsed under the weight of the later occupants. This type of collapse was common to all over-subscribed sixteenth-century vaults and might well have been the contributing factor for the almost immediate introduction of shelves and loculi in the early seventeenth century.

The large burial vault was not an overnight success, as most families preferred to remain with the small chamber adjacent to the wall monument. When Sir Henry Unton was buried at Faringdon, Berkshire, on 8 July 1596 his coffin was placed in a modest sepulchre beneath his monument. This is shown, together with his viscera chest, in a narrative painting almost certainly commissioned by Unton's widow, shortly after her husband's death, as a perpetual reminder of his achievement (*103*).

Elizabeth, Countess of Shrewsbury – better known as Bess of Hardwick – made elaborate preparations for her burial vault beneath the south chancel aisle of All Saint's, Derby (now Derby Cathedral), in 1600/01. This is an extremely luxurious chamber (*104*) and well reflects her interest in buildings of a commodious nature! The stone walls, floor and gently curving roof, together with the neat arrangement

103   *The burial vault of Sir Henry Unton (d. 1596) at Faringdon, Berkshire. The entrance to the vault is to the bottom left of the monument. Within the vault can be seen Unton's coffin (right) and viscera chest (left).*

213

*104   The Cavendish Vault in Derby Cathedral, c. 1605. An early
example of a burial vault with loculi compartments and venti-
lated by means of a grille in its north wall.*

of loculi, gives to this vault an air of spaciousness, although it is only fifteen feet east to west and twelve feet north to south. The coffins have been placed in the traditional manner with feet addressed to the east; hence those in the west range have their foot ends towards the central corridor and vice versa in the east range. At the top of the north wall is a ventilation grille through which came a constant change of air. This assisted in the dispersal of the obnoxious gases associated with decomposition. The outer wooden cases have all disintegrated, yet this was an occurrence well known to the undertaking trade – hence the provision of an additional depositum plate on the inner lead shell. Beneath the ventilation grille are two mid seventeenth-century viscera chests, from which we can deduce that at least two of the occupants of this vault were subjected to full embalming.

Less dramatic are the early seventeenth-century vaults. The east vault (1633) at Lydiard Tregoz, though equal in size to Bess of Hardwick's at Derby, has a somewhat untidy appearance, owing to the lack of loculi and shelves; nevertheless, some degree of dignity has been achieved through the introduction of a stone mortuary table, three feet in height and centrally placed on a west-east axis. This was inserted at the behest of Sir John St John (d.1648) for his remains and those of his two wives, Anne Leighton (d.1628) and Margaret Whitmore (d.1637), as we discover from his will, which was drawn up in 1645: 'And I will and ordaine that the remainder of my mortality shelbee interred in the new vault unde the new Isle lately made by me adioyning to the parish church of Liddiard Tregoze, aforesaid betweene my two wives that lye buried there.'[17]

Again, the 1638 vault beneath the Culpeper Chapel at Hollingbourne, Kent (*46*), is equal in ground area to that at Derby, though the barrelled brick roof, springing from a rendered rubble plinth three feet from the floor, gives the impression of cramped quarters with little space for further deposits. This is emphasized by the existence of twelve-inch brick runners supporting the coffins.

Lydiard Tregoz provides us with an indication of the costs borne by families for the upkeep of vaults. Under an agreement executed in June 1645 a rent charge of £10 per annum in perpetuity was made to the church – later ratified in 1685 – in order that

> the Isle and vault in the Church of Lydyard Tregoze … called the new Isle and vault and alsoe the other Isle in the same Church then called the old Isle … and the vault under the same Isle and all the monuments … might be from time to time … well and sufficiently repaired and maintained … without any charge to the said parish.[18]

Vaults did not come cheaply, either then or at any other time.

For those unable to afford the outlay required for intramural vault burial the next option was to solicit a site in the churchyard as close to the church as possible. This is precisely the course of action taken in the 1650s by the Campbells at Barking, Essex, whose vault abuts the south aisle wall at its west end. In construction it is similar to that at Hollingbourne, though here the roof springs from the walls at a height of four feet thereby giving a less exaggerated curve. Almost every available material was used: brick, flint, stone blocks and rubble, the whole rendered and lime-washed. Against the north wall are four niches, probably for the founder and his most immediate family, though the rest

*105   A tunnel vault of c. 1629 in south-east Leicestershire with
an early eighteenth-century west extension added on later. Beyond
the easternmost range of coffins is a charnel cistern of c. 1660.*

of the vault is devoid of fittings. Be that as it may, this vault is quite spacious,
capable of housing thirty-eight coffins.

One of the longest tunnel vaults in the country is in south-east Leicestershire.
Originally constructed in *c.*1629 it has been twice extended westwards and is
now thirty-eight feet long and twelve feet wide, containing twenty-three coffins
but with room for twenty-nine more (*105*). High up in the east wall is a
ventilation shaft of appreciable size which also acts as a source of light, though
the installation of electric light some fifty years ago now renders this obsolete.
The entire construction is of brick, including the access steps and side plinths for
the coffins, unrendered but lime-washed; scorch-marks on the walls indicate
where flambeaux and candles were positioned to illuminate the vault either for
depositum or maintenance purposes. Yet the chief feature is to be found at the
east end where the farthest three feet are taken up by an early
eighteenth-century brick cistern running the entire width of the vault. Into this
have been placed various times the more decayed coffins. It should be
remembered that these sepulchres were constructed for perpetual use, so it was

the practice periodically to remove the most decrepit coffins from the main chamber to make room for others, and the provision of such cisterns allowed for the displaced remains to be kept within the vault. Sometimes this was done by way of a charnel pit sunk into the floor and covered with an easily removable trapdoor, as was provided in the Roper vault of *c.*1590 at St Dunstan's, Canterbury.[19] Smaller brick bins exist in the west St John vault at Lydiard Tregoz, introduced in the 1740s, and at the west end of the north-west chamber in the 1621 Maynard vault at Little Easton, Essex, during its remodelling in 1746 (*106*). The Creswick family were not so concerned with such matters in their vault at Bitton, Gloucestershire, of *c.*1720, and had stacked any displaced bones in the south-east corner of the burial chamber, farthest away from the entrance. Neither archaeologists nor funerary historians should dismiss charnel cisterns as they invariably contain metal coffin furniture from the vault's earliest occupants.

Vault construction within churches in use must have caused considerable upheaval as well as disruption to the schedule of divine service. Having first selected the site all fixed furniture had to be removed and the floor carefully raised prior to the excavation, and it was not uncommon for earlier earth burials to be disturbed. Having prepared the soil, the floor and the springer walls were laid, after which came the erection of wooden shuttering, providing for the barrelled roof to be constructed from the outside. Once the mortar had dried, the shuttering was removed[20] and the two end walls were built up from the inside, the access trap or staircase being inserted at the same time. The bonding of the brickwork is usually very fine, though little attention was paid to finishing off the bonding of the roof once the shuttering had been removed (*Col. 28*). With the basic construction complete, and the sealing stone set, the trench was backfilled, the floor relaid and the furniture restored to its original position. Optional extras, such as rendering, lime-washing, shelves, loculi, brick runners and charnel cisterns could be provided according to the patron's requirements.

By the close of the seventeenth century space for new vaults in some of the city churches was becoming extremely limited. When John Graunt died in 1674 a place was found for him '... in St Dunstan's church in Fleetstreet in the body of the same church under the piewes (alias hoggsties) of the north side of the middle aisle. What pity 'tis,' wrote Aubrey, 'so great an Ornament of the Citty should be buried so obscurely!'.[21] But there was no alternative. What else could have been done, knowing that the prime sites had been allocated many years previously? The only available area was that beneath one's pew, and better to be under your seat in church than out in the churchyard, where security of grave tenure could not be guaranteed. However, it was possible to obtain space within an existing family vault provided one knew the family and they were willing to have you. Against the north wall of the outer lobby of the east Poulett vault at Hinton St George is the lead-lapped coffin of Bernard Hutchins. Hutchins, who died in 1733, was secretary to John, First Earl Poulett, and a close friend of the family – so close that he bequeathed property leased from the estate to various members of the Poulett clan.

It was the custom in some city churches to have a vault reserved for the sole use of the incumbent. During his enjoyment of the living he could put whoever he

*106   When in 1746 the First Viscount Maynard remodelled his
family vault at Little Easton, Essex, provision was made at the
west end of the north-west chamber for a brick charnel cistern.*

wanted into this vault, augmenting his stipend from the fees he charged.
Between the date of rebuilding St Alphage, Greenwich, in 1718 and up to 1810 a
total of 400 coffins had been let into Vault No. 16, the rector's vault. Amongst
these was deposited on 30 April 1795 the body of a twelve-year-old girl called
Sarah Moulton who, though born at Cinnamon Hill, Jamaica, was at the time of
her death on 23 April 1795 a pupil at a boarding school in Greenwich. Rather
than send her body back to her father's plantation the rector of St Alphage's, Dr
Andrew Burnaby, allowed for the coffin to be placed in his vault. Dead she is, but
she lives on as the sitter in Sir Thomas Lawrence's painting, popularly known as
Pinkie.

Not all deposits in such vaults were subject to a fee. When Nell Gwyn died in
1687 the good people of St Martin-in-the-Fields refused her burial space within
the church; immediately the rector, exercising his prerogative, afforded her space
in his own vault, something the parish was powerless to prevent. There are also
accounts of charitable burial elsewhere in the country. Aubrey relates the story of
the Revd Dr John Pell, who held the Essex plurality of Fobbing and Laindon at
the time of his death in 1685. He enjoyed an income 'of the value of two hundred
pounds per annum (or so accounted) but the Doctor was a most shiftless man as

218

to worldly affaires, and his Tenants and Relations cousin'd him of the Profits and kept him so indigent that he wanted necessarys, even paper and Inke, and he had not 6d in his purse when he died, and was buried by the Charity of Dr Richard Busby and Dr Sharp, Rector of St Giles-in-the-fields and Dean of Norwich, who ordered his Body to lye in a Vault belonging to the Rector (the price is X pounds)'.[22]

With space at such premium it is not surprising that some people commandeered the remaining available space in the vaults of extinct families. When Sir Robert Atkyns, formerly one of the Justices of the Court of Common Pleas, Lord Chief Baron of the Exchequer and Speaker of the House of Lords, restored and refitted the church of St Kenelm at Sapperton, Gloucestershire, between 1696 and 1707, he constructed for himself and his wife a small burial chamber, some eight foot square, beneath the south transept. Atkyns died without issue at this Westminster house on 29 November 1711 and was deposited in the Sapperton vault a few days later. Lady Louise, his wife, followed him in 1716. For just over 100 years they enjoyed sole occupancy of the vault, but some time in the early nineteenth century three single-shell wooden coffins of earth-burial type found their way into the vault, space at the south end having been provided by shifting Robert Atkyns to the north side of the vault, hard up against the lowest tread of the access steps. All three usurping coffins were later covered with soil, probably to counteract the odour of decomposition.

Some of the noble and landed families were able to cope with the lack of space either by providing for or increasing the use of a charnel cistern, by interior remodelling or extending those vaults beneath their private chapels. In 1737 Smart Lethieullier of Aldersbrook erected a funerary chapel eighteen feet square against the west end of the north wall of his parish church at Little Ilford in Essex, with a vault of similar dimensions beneath. Therein he placed the remains of his more immediate ancestors from various parts of the building, having them recased in identical coffins as he went along.

At Little Easton, also in Essex, the First Viscount Maynard refurbished his extensive vault beneath the south chapel in 1746. Having broken through a new entrance in the outer south wall he transferred all of the coffins to the south end of the west chamber and bricked them in. This left a totally clear space for him to work on. Next came a new floor, the rendering and lime-washing of the walls and the insertion of a charnel cistern at the west end of the remaining third of the west chamber. Subsequently, the space in the west chamber was used first, then the east vault and, finally, the central space. In this way Maynard was able to retain the earlier coffins as well as provide space for thirty-eight additional ones; there is still room for a further fifteen.

One of the largest conversion works took place in 1810 when George III shelved out a crypt beneath the Wolsey Chapel (now the Albert Memorial Chapel) at Windsor, the vaults at Westminster having become relatively full. Until 1898 the coffins rested on a stone plinth running the length of the vault, with the cases of George III, Queen Charlotte, Princess Amelia, Prince Alfred and Prince Octavius (the latter two moved from Westminster) on a stone dais at the east end (*107*). Queen Victoria transferred all the remains to the side shelves, placing monarch with consort, before positioning a bronze grille along the entire range of openings.

219

*107   The Royal Mausoleum, Windsor. In 1810 George III had the
crypt beneath the Wolsey Chapel at Windsor shelved to provide
space for eighty-one coffins. Remodelled by Queen Victoria in
the late nineteenth century, the shelf space was reduced to sixty.
More than thirty of the spaces remain vacant.*

This new arrangement reduced the original number of spaces from eighty-one to
sixty-one. At the same time a small stone altar was installed at the east end and
a stone mortuary table for temporary deposits at the west end. The vault is
connected by a small passage to the area beneath the hand-operated catafalque
of *c*.1908 in front of the sanctuary steps of St George's Chapel. The list of contents
was last published in 1910,[23] at which time only twenty-two of the available sixty
spaces were occupied.

   During the same year in which George III was attending to matters sepulchral
at Windsor, the Earl of Derby was negotiating for an extension to his dynastic
vault beneath All Saints, Derby. A faculty was issued and work began. The new
vault is identical in all respects to that constructed 200 years previously, with the
exception that loculi were built against the west wall only, the east being left
clear for future expansion. As events worked out only seven of the twelve loculi
were used; the other five remain empty.

   If one wanted to award a prize for the best-constructed vault in the country
then that erected in 1814 for John, Fourth Earl Poulett, at Hinton St George,
Somerset, would be one of the finalists. Wyattville, having been commissioned to

extend vault accommodation, began with a fifteen-foot-square chamber of two bays, the centre space having quadrapartite vaulting to the roof. Next came spacious double-depth York stone shelving in three tiers on each side, affording space for a total of twenty-four coffins; unshelved it is possible that sixty coffins could have been stacked into the available space. But Wyattville knew about vault construction, the importance of ventilation and damp-proof courses and this, together with the neat stretchered placement of the coffins on the shelves, have been contributory factors to the immaculate appearance of the vault today (*108*). It continues to be used by the Poulett family.

One family constructed their burial vault as the result of personal tragedy. When the teenage heir of Thomas, Fourteenth Baron De La Warr, died in 1677 his parents decided to add a funerary chapel to the recently rebuilt church at Withyham, Sussex. The work was completed by 1680 and included a vault beneath the entire thirty-foot-long and fifteen-foot-wide structure. Approached from the churchyard via a staircase at its west end, this enormous tunnel vault is naturally lit at the east end by an externally covered opening six feet in width, making it the widest window in any burial vault. Some of the coffins predate the 1677–80 construction, indicating that there must have been an earlier Sackville vault on the site. At some time in the mid nineteenth century the vault was shelved, the earlier coffins being placed on the south side, which thereby left the range on the north side free for later deposits. Two mortuary tables, one in the centre capable of taking four coffins and one at the far east end for a single coffin, have been added since the nineteenth-century modifications.

On a smaller scale, the brick-lined shaft (*109*) was the most popular method of intramural burial within city and town churches during the late seventeenth and the whole of the eighteenth century. This came about for two reasons: first, there was a heavy demand from the middle classes, owing less to the general overcrowding of the churchyards than to a disgust at the rising trend of the lower classes erecting headstones; second, space within churches was at a premium by the end of the eighteenth century, having already been over-subscribed by parishioners of previous generations. St Augustine-the-Less, Bristol, provides an excellent example of such over-subscription: when the church was excavated in 1983–4 the area beneath the floor was found to be a honeycomb of eighty-three instances of intramural burial, fifty-nine of which were brick-lined graves (*Col. 27*).

In London and other conurbations there was often not the space for large churchyards, yet such mercantile centres attracted the professional middle class and, as the tradition of burial within one's own parish was still deemed desirable, provision had to be made to cope with the demand for intramural burial. Thomas Archer, James Gibbes, John James and Nicholas Hawksmoor were the four architects involved in the 1711 Fifty New Churches Act for London. Their brief, in part, instructed that though the new churchyards could be used for burial there was to be no interment within the churches themselves. Not one of the completed thirteen churches obeyed this rule, however. Indeed one can state categorically that the churches erected under the Act provided for intramural burial on a scale never seen before in England. Each church was raised upon a plinth – good for dramatic effect and for providing a grand entrance – but these

108 The west Poulett Vault at Hinton St George, Somerset was constructed by Wyatville for the Fourth Earl in 1814. The three coffins on the shelves in the south-west range are by the nineteenth-century London undertakers, Dowbiggin & Holland.

plinths allowed for a semi-subterranean reproduction of the floor plan of the main body of the church. Though it was suggested that an income could be derived by letting out these basements for storage purposes, it was not long before they became host to a silent, lead-lapped and supine congregation with no intention of quitting the building. The bays beneath the side aisles were usually portioned off for private freehold vaults, the space below the chancel being given over to the incumbent's use, and the remaining areas under the nave and portico were not partitioned and were designated to general-purpose deposits under the title of public or vestry vault.

The prices charged for deposit in these vaults varied according to the grandeur of the area in which the church was situated in addition to the type of vault space required. The following prices, taken from a list of burial fees published by Turner of Farringdon Street in 1838,[24] reflects what one could be asked to pay in London at that time.

109 The single-width brick-lined shaft was the more popular mode of intramural burial from c. 1650–1850. On average twelve feet deep, they could accommodate six coffins, separated one from another by horizontal iron bars. The shaft was capped off with an inscised ledger stone.

St Mary-le-Strand

Church service	9s	0d
Vault	£6 0s	0d
Ditto – under 14	£4 0s	0d

St Pancras New Church

Vault	£18 5s	6d
Ditto – from 7 to 14	£11 5s	6d
Ditto – under 7	£7 5s	6d
Vaults to contain 4 persons	100 Guineas	

St Peter-le-Poor, Broad Street, City of London

Vault	£1 15s	2d

Of course, there were 'extras'. St Mary-le-Strand included bearers in the price, and at St Peter-le-Poor they were an additional 2s. 6d. each. Tolling the bell at the Pentonville Chapel was 5s., as against the 12s. asked by St Paul, Shadwell. Shadwell expected a fee of £6 for each lead or iron coffin buried in the churchyard; St Peter-le-Poor was far more expensive with their £50 extra. All churches charged double for non-parishioners whereas St Peter-le-Poor wanted £20 in addition to the double fee. It was expensive but these churches were offering security of tenure. However, since such charges were prohibitive to all but the well-to-do, deposit in these vaults was infrequent. Between 1729 and 1865 about 1,000 coffins were introduced to the vaults in Christchurch, Spitalfields, an average of one every seven weeks. Often those going into the public vault wanted to be placed next to a relative, in which case a professional searcher was employed to seek out the relevant coffin and guide the bearers to it on the day of interment; for rarely did the officiating minister, let alone the mourners, go further into the vault than the main doors leading off the churchyard, the Committal being read as the coffin was carried in. Some vaults, however, were crammed to capacity (*110*), whilst others could have welcomed more.

By the 1820s concern about the continuation of intramural burial in city churches was being voiced and, with the establishment in the same decade of privately owned cemeteries based on the Père-Lachaise model in Paris, Parliament paid greater attention to those campaigning for reform. In August 1850 the Metropolitan Interments Act put an end to intramural burial within the City of London; this was later strengthened by the 1852 Metropolitan Burial Act empowering vestries of any metropolitan parish to set up, at the request of ten or more ratepayers, a parochial cemetery. In August 1853 these arrangements were extended to the rest of England and Wales.

Not all vaults were closed and one could continue to enjoy their use provided that the terms of the Public Health Act were not infringed. Many vaults continue to be used today, both for the deposit of coffins and for cremated remains. However, some families preferred to opt out of the dynastic vault system to take advantage of the private cemeteries or to erect mausoleums on their own estates, as had been happening in Britain since the early eighteenth century, for example at Blickling, Norfolk, and Trentham Park, Staffordshire.

In 1726 Nicholas Hawksmoor, the high priest of funerary architecture, was

*110   Cheaper than a brick-lined shaft was deposit in a
communal vault. That beneath St Thomas's Hospital Chapel,
Ilford, Essex was constructed in the 1820s and was scarcely
one-third full when closed in 1850.*

commissioned by the Third Earl of Carlisle to design a mausoleum in the grounds
of Castle Howard to replace, as a family vault, the former Henderskelfe church
which had been demolished to make way for Castle Howard itself. Although
undoubtedly an enthralling commission for Hawksmoor, both on account of the
patron and the particular choice of building, it was dogged with trouble from the
outset because of the incessant interference of Sir Thomas Robinson – the Third
Earl's son-in-law – and Lord Burlington: the mausoleum was not completed until
1744. The rotunda houses the chapel, the podium and extensive burial chamber
lit by eleven large windows, and affords space for sixty-three coffins in the
radiating chambers and adjacent loculi. The irony lies in the fact that neither
patron, architect nor clerk of works lived to see the fruits of their labour. William
Etty, clerk of works, died in 1734, Hawksmoor two years later in 1736 whilst
Charles Howard, Third Earl of Carlisle, died at Bath on 1 May 1738. His body
was brought back and interred in the neighbouring church at Bulmer before
being transferred in 1744 to what is certainly Hawksmoor's finest creation. It is,
indeed, a ravishing building (*Col. 29*); as Horace Walpole said after his visit to
Castle Howard, it is 'a mausoleum that would tempt one to be buried alive'.

Appendix 1

'Non-trade' Funeral Performers: 1720–1830

List of London tradesmen, apart from coffin-makers and undertakers, performing funerals between 1720 and 1830, extracted from Ambrose Heal, *The London Furniture Makers from the Restoration to the Victorian Era* (Batsford, London, 1953)

Date	*Name and location*	*Main trade*
*c.*1830	Allen, Little Eastcheap	Upholsterer and cabinet-maker
*c.*1760	Philip Bell, St Paul's Churchyard	Cabinet-maker and upholder
*c.*1770	Charles Blyde, Knave's Acre	Cabinet-maker and upholder
*c.*1760	John Boothby, Norfolk Street	Upholder and appraiser
*c.*1820	William Bonella, Whitechapel	Chair-maker and upholsterer
*c.*1760	John Boothby, Norfolk Street, Strand	Upholsterer and appraiser
*c.*1730	George Browning, Cornhill	Upholder, appraiser and auctioneer
*c.*1760	Peter Burcham, Fleet Market, Strand	Chair and cabinet-maker
*c.*1760	Samuel Burton, St Mary Axe	Upholder and cabinet-maker
*c.*1730	David Cario, Moorfields	Cabinet-maker and appraiser
*c.*1730	William Clarkson, Moorfields	Upholder, appraiser and cabinet-maker
*c.*1720	Thomas Cloake, Lower Moorfields	Upholder, cabinet-maker and appraiser

*c.*1790	Cross, 57 Barbican	Cabinet-maker, auctioneer and appraiser
*c.*1740	William Darby, Aldermanbury	Upholder and appraiser
*c.*1780	Fall, St Paul's Churchyard	Beds, bedding and upholder
*c.*1770	Charles Grange, Snow Hill	Upholder and appraiser
*c.*1770	John Hatt, Aldersgate	Cabinet- and chair-maker
*c.*1780	Hawkins, New Bond Street	Upholder, cabinet-maker and appraiser
*c.*1820	Higgs, Whitechapel	Cabinet-maker, upholsterer, appraiser and auctioneer
*c.*1800	Anthony Hilke, Husband Street	Cabinet-maker
*c.*1750	William Hunter, Royal Exchange	Upholder and appraiser
*c.*1740	William Jellicoe, Fleet Street	Upholsterer and appraiser
*c.*1770	Lauders, Chandos Street	Cabinet-maker and upholder
*c.*1770	John Lawrence, Spital Square	Upholder and appraiser
*c.*1760	Robert Legg, Southampton Street	Upholder and appraiser
*c.*1790	Jonas Macklane, Leicester Square	Cabinet-, chair-maker and upholder
*c.*1800	Peter Marchant, Fleet Bridge	Upholsterer and appraiser
*c.*1750	Robert Maxwell, Great Pultney Street	Cabinet-maker and upholder
*c.*1810	J. Medhurst, West Smithfield	Cabinet-maker and upholder
*c.*1810	Morris & Cupiss, St Paul's Churchyard	Cabinet- and chair-maker
*c.*1740	Henry Newton, Leadenhall Market	Upholsterer
*c.*1805	William Perry, Chiswell Street	Upholstery, cabinet- and chair-maker
*c.*1770	Thomas Porter, New Round Street, Strand	Upholder and cabinet-maker
*c.*1770	John Potts, King Street, Covent Garden	Upholder
*c.*1740	John Prince, Catherine Street, Strand	Upholder and appraiser
*c.*1780	Godwin Prince, Durham Yard, Strand	Cabinet-maker and upholsterer
*c.*1750	Francis Pyner, George Yard, Lombard Street	Upholder and cabinet-maker
*c.*1815	G. Reynolds, Oxford Road, Dean Street, Soho	Cabinet-maker and appraiser
*c.*1740	Francis Say, Ludgate Hill	Upholsterer and cabinet-maker
*c.*1725	Henry Sidgier, Great Shere Lane, Temple Bar	Carpenter and joiner
*c.*1730	Thomas Silk, St Paul's Churchyard	Cabinet-maker, upholder and appraiser
*c.*1740	George Smithson, Holborn	Broker and appraiser
*c.*1740	John Taylor, Limehouse	Furnisher and auctioneer
*c.*1790	Vickers & Rutledge, Conduit Street, Hanover Square	Upholder and cabinet-maker
*c.*1810	William Wade, Leadenhall Street	Picture-frame maker, carver, gilder and printseller

c.1770	Richard Wallin, Newgate	Upholder and appraiser
c.1740	Christopher Wallis, Drury Lane, Long Acre	Cabinet-maker and appraiser
c.1760	John Whitcomb, Princes Street, Soho	Cabinet-maker and upholsterer
c.1750	William Whitton, St Margaret's Hill, Southwark	Upholder and appraiser
c.1740	Jane Woodroff, Gracechurch Street	Upholder and appraiser

Appendix 2

An Undertaker's Bill –
Field v. *Robey*

Not all undertakers were strictly honest in their dealings with clients and it was not unknown for them to disobey instructions and provide a funeral according to the social rank of the deceased. A request for a funeral exhibiting decency without excess panoply was made in 1859 by a Mr Robey, a sail-maker of St George's-in-the-East, London, when he ordered a funeral for his late wife from Mr Field, an undertaker of Charlotte Street, Shadwell. Negotiations between the two parties settled on the provision of a £50 funeral for £25. The final bill came to £22 but Mr Robey, dissatisfied with the services provided by Mr Field, was only willing to pay £20. Mr Field entered into litigation to recover the outstanding £2. At the end of the day the judgement was in Field's favour; however, the court got more than £2 in entertainment value from Field as the following account of the court proceedings shows. Mr Field might have won the day but he had to endure the incredulity of the jury. The details highlighted during the hearing provide an insight into the finer nuances of the trade and help us to understand why the funeral furnishing industry was held in such contempt.

COURT OF EXCHEQUER: before Mr Baron Channell.

This was an action to recover £22, the amount of an undertaker's bill. The defendant had paid £20 into court and had denied his liability to the £2. The plaintiff is an undertaker carrying on business in Charlotte Street, St George's East, and the defendant is a sail maker. On the 1st March last the defendant met the plaintiff in Watney Street and informed him of his wife's death and gave directions to make a case for his wife's leaden coffin and conduct the funeral. After the funeral the defendant expressed his satisfaction at what had been done and desired him to send in his bill the next morning and he would give him a cheque for the amount. In a conversation with the defendant the plaintiff, who has a peculiarly solemn cast of countenance, said he smiled and told the defendant the funeral would cost £50. Defendant replied, 'I did not think half of it'; upon which plaintiff said, 'Well, it will be about £25'. The plaintiff said his charges were fair and reasonable. In his cross-examination by Mr Huddlestone, the plaintiff said he did not publish handbills headed 'Respect to the departed', 'Decency and pomp combined for £10', with 'a hearse, prancing horses, &c.' (laughter). He had charged £5 for the elm shell, which was french polished. He presented the minister with a silk band and gloves, which he informed Mr Robey was the usual at respectable funerals, and the defendant did not object to it. He had charged half-a-guinea for himself attending the funeral with silk fittings (laughter). He had charged for six horse hearse velvets, three hammer cloths, and two mourning coaches, and for ten men including two mutes, described in the bill as 'two porters, with robes and silk fittings'. Mr Morsley and Mr Adam Springfield were called to prove the charges were fair and reasonable. In cross-examination the latter said there were prices for mutes (laughter). Mr Huddlestone – 'What is the usual charge for a mute with a dark, good melancholy physiognomy?' (laughter). Mr Springfield – 'There are various prices. It depends whether he is a good-looking fellow.' (laughter). Mr Baron Channell – 'Then you charge according to their looks?' Mr Springfield – 'Yes, certainly.' (laughter). Mr Baron Channell – 'When returning from a funeral they are generally merry-looking fellows?' Mr Huddlestone – 'They are then off duty; and, as my friend near me, Mr Hawkins, observed, they are no longer mutes, but liquids.' (laughter). To witness – 'What is a fair price for a good melancholy mute?'. Mr Springfield – 'That depends entirely on how he looks.' (laughter). Mr Huddlestone – 'That is when he has got a white choker on, and well pulls down the corner of his mouth?' (laughter). Mr Springfield – 'Yes; just so. (renewed laughter). The ordinary price of a mute was three halfcrowns. He had never heard of them being had for a soverign.' (laughter). Several other undertakers were called, who proved that the charges were fair and reasonable; some of them were too small; none of them too high. Mr Huddlestone said that this action was defended on principle, the plaintiff having supplied many of the articles against the defendant's consent, and that some of the charges were too high. The defendant was called. He denied the conversation spoken to by the plaintiff. Instead of ten men and two mutes, as charged for, being at the funeral, there were but eight men and two mutes. He objected to the minister's scarf and gloves, informing the plaintiff that having many bills to pay in consequence of his wife's illness, he must be just before he was generous, and could not afford to give anything to the parson; at the same time he objected to all pomp and foolery, and told the plaintiff it should be a plain funeral. He particularly told him he would have no mutes, and if he had not been prevented they would not have remained long at the door (laughter). When the plaintiff was making the coffin, he (defendant) called at his shop, and, seeing what he was about, told him he would not have a parcel of ornaments about it – angels, and such trash. (laughter). Several witnesses were called to show the charges were too high, one of them, Mr Holley, in his cross-examination, said it was usual for undertakers to charge according to the condition in life of the parties who employed them. The evidence with reference to the actual order was conflicting. Mr Baron Channell, in summing up, left it to the jury to say whether, under all the circumstances, they considered the funeral was conducted in a decent manner without pomp. The jury returned a verdict for the plaintiff and the amount claimed.

The Moufussilite ((pub. Meerut), 26 July 1859, p. 462 and quoting from *The Weekly Dispatch* (pub. London) of 5 June 1859.

Notes and References

1 THE TRADE

1   ed. Steele, *The Funeral or Grief à la Mode*.
2   D. Defoe, *The Complete English Tradesman*, 1645.
3   R. Campbell, *The London Tradesman*, 1747.
4   Willelmi de Dene, 'Historia Rossensis' in Wharton (ed.), *Anglia Sacra*, vol.I (1691), pp.375–6.
5   P. Ziegler, *The Black Death* (Penguin, Harmondsworth, 1970) and; R. Foster, *Discovering English Towns* (BBC Pubs, London, 1981).
6   Geoffrey Chaucer, *The Prologue to the Canterbury Tales*, ed. R.T. Davies (London, 1953), p.53.
7   D.M. Meade, *The Medieval Church in England* (Churchman, Worthing, 1988), p.81.
8   G.H. Cooke, *Medieval Chantries and Chantry Chapels* (Phoenix, London, 1947), p.39.
9   G.H. Cook, *English Medieval Parish Churches* (Phoenix, London, 1954), pp.127–30.
10   G.H. Cook, *Medieval Chantries*, p.38.
11   Sometimes the maintenance of a chantry and its priest was laid by the deceased on the shoulders of his successors: the priest resided with the family, probably doubling up as tutor to the children. Other times the responsibility was placed upon the administrative body of the church. Attached to the Hospital of St Mark, Bristol – known as Gaunt's Hospital – is a small chantry chapel founded by Sir Robert Poyntz of Iron Acton in 1520. His will of 1520 directs that

The master of the house of the Gaunts is to take issues [of certain named manors] to provide an honest and considerable priest to sing mass at the altar of the said chapel of Jesus ... the said priest to have for his salary £6. A solemn obit to be kept for my soul in the said church of the Gaunts on the day of my departing; in the evening placebo and dirige by note, and on the following day a mass of requiem by note. And four tapers of wax, every one of them a pound weight be brenning upon my herse about the Crucifix at all times during the said dirige and mass, and 6s 8d sterling to be distributed in alms to the poor. The said priest shall always be tabled and lodged within the house of the Gaunts.

12   A map showing the positioning of the medieval London city churches is in

A.E. Daniell, *London City Churches* (Constable, London, 1896), p.394.

13   These advowsons, or rights of patronage, are dispersed throughout the country in the following dioceses: Bath & Wells, Birmingham, Chelmsford, Chichester, Ely, Exeter, Gloucester, Hereford, Leicester, Lichfield, London, Norwich, Oxford, Peterborough, Rochester, St Albans, St Edmundsbury & Ipswich, Sheffield, Truro, Wakefield, Winchester and Worcester.

14   The Fayrey Pall: red cloth-of-gold brocade with embroidered figures of the Fayrey family at prayer and St John Baptist. The gift of Henry Fayrey who died in 1516. Currently (1990) on loan to the Victoria and Albert Museum, London.

15   These are; fishmongers, *c*.1490 (with figures of God the Father and St Peter surrounded by angels); brewers, *c*.1516; saddlers, dated 1520; merchant taylors, early sixteenth century; and vintners, two of the early sixteenth century. Two Post-Reformation/Pre-Commonwealth palls survive: one dated 1582 belonging to the Parish Clerks (on loan to the Museum of London in 1990) and one of embroidered purple velvet dated 1628, known as the Lucas Family Pall, and in Colchester Castle Museum from the redundant church of St Giles, Colchester.

16   *Loan Exhibition Depicting the Reign of Queen Elizabeth*, 22 & 23 Grosvenor Place, London, 26 January to 31 March 1933, No.73. Lent by F.H. Cripps-Day. Subsequently published by F.H. Cripps-Day, 'A Herald's Mourning Hood', in *Connoisseur*, XCIII (1934), pp.155–7.

17   The hood was later presented by Cripps-Day to the College of Arms shortly after 1934. R.C. Yorke, Archivist of the College of Arms (letter of 29 March 1989 to author), records that the College has never been entirely convinced of its authenticity. In 1988 it was examined by Miss Natalie Rothstein of the Department of Textiles at the Victoria and Albert Museum, London, and shown to be of pure silk velvet of early nineteenth-century manufacture, possibly dating from the 1830s. Mr Yorke's suggestion that the item is an imitation, possibly made for the Eglinton Tournament, seems the most likely.

18   The illustration of the funerary hearse of Abbot John Islip is taken from the Islip Roll. It was not unusual for religious houses to make confederations with each other, amongst which included an agreement to pray for each other's deceased brethren. On the death of a member of the community his name was inscribed on a mortuary roll, which was taken around the confederated houses by a monk from the monastery from which the brother had died. In the main these rolls were quite plain, being nothing more than a list of names; those for an abbot or bishop were more elaborate, often richly illuminated. That for Abbot Islip falls into the last category. It was the practice for the mortuary roll to be returned to the monastery once it had done the rounds.

19   A link was a torch made of pitch and tow carried to light the way in the streets, the more popular funerary nomenclature being 'flambeaus'.

20   John Weever, *Ancient Funerall Monuments, &c.* (Thomas Harper, London, 1631), pp.17–18.

21   *The Graphic*, June 4 1898, p.710.

22   Ambrose Heal, *London Tradesmen's Cards of the Eighteenth Century* (Batsford, 1925), pp.1–3.

23   Ambrose Heal, *The London Furniture Makers: 1660–1840* (Batsford, London, 1953). *See*: Appendix 1.

24   Ambrose Heal, *Sign Boards of Old London Shops* (Batsford, London, 1957), pp.45 and 174–5. The undertakers mentioned are as follows:

c.1680   William Boyce, at ye Whight Hart & Coffin, in ye Grate Ould Bayley, near Newgeat.

1764 Edward Chandler & Son, at the Naked Boy & Coffin, in the corner of Turnagain Lane by the Fleet Market, near Holborn Bridge.

1725 John Clarke, at the Four Coffins, in Jermine Street, near St James's Church.

*c.*1750 John Friday, at ye sign of ye Four Coffins, in St Martin's Lane, the corner of Burying Passage.

*c.*1720 Arthur Granger, at the Crown & Coffin, in Whitechapel.

*c.*1730 William Grinly, at ye sign of ye Naked Boy & Coffin, at ye Lower Corner of Fleet Lane.

*c.*1732 Alexander Horrocks, at the White Bear, against Gray's Inn Gate, in Holborn.

*c.*1720 John King, at the Four Coffins & Hart, in Little Earl Street, near the Seven Dials.

*c.*1770 Robert Low, at the Coffin & Crown, in Pater Noster Row, Spitalfields.

*c.*1700 Eleazor Malory, at the Coffin, in White Chapel, near Red Lion Street end.

*c.*1790 Richard Middleton, at the sign of The First & Last, in Stonecutter Street on the West Side of Fleet Market.

1752 George Page, at the Four Coffins, St Margaret's Hill, Southwark. (Succeeded by Robert Green.)

*c.*1740 Isaac Whitchurch, removed from Fleet Lane to the Three Coffins, by the Ditch side, near Holbourn Bridge.

*c.*1760 William Whitchurch, at ye Four Coffins, on Holborn Hill.

25 Victoria and Albert Museum (Department of Design, Prints and Drawings), London.

26 E. Chadwick, *A Supplementary Report on the Results of a Special Inquiry into the Practice of Interment in Town* (House of Lords, London, 1843), p.51.

27 E. Chadwick, op.cit., p.51.

28 A.F.J. Brown, *Essex at Work 1700–1815*, Chelmsford (Essex County Council, Chelmsford, 1969).

29 Hon. Christopher Lennox-Boyd Collection.

30 B. Puckle, *Funeral Customs* (Werner Laurie, London, 1926), p.128.

31 Hon. Christopher Lennox-Boyd Collection.

32 Ibid.

33 Charles Dickens, *The Adventures of Oliver Twist; or, The Parish Boy's Progress*, (Bradbury & Evans, London, 1846), Chapter 5.

34 Guildhall Library, London.

35 E. Chadwick, op.cit., p.267.

36 Ibid.

2 TAINTLESS AND PURE: EMBALMING TECHNIQUES

1 Kirkpatrick, *Reflections on the Causes that May Retard Putrefaction of Dead Bodies* (A. Millar, London, 1751), p.25.

2 William Hunter, *The Art of Embalming Dead Bodies*, 1796. Ms in the Library of the Royal College of Surgeons, London.

3 The full inscription of the wall monument to Lethieullier in the family mausoleum at Little Ilford, Essex, reads: 'In memory of SMART LETHIEULLIER Esq ͬ, a gentleman of polite literature and elegant taste, an encourager of art and ingenious artists, a studious promoter of literary enquiries and a friend of

learned men, industriously versed in the science of antiquity, but who modestly desired no other inscription on his tomb than what he had made the rule of his life to do justly, to love mercy and to walk humbly with his God.'

4   Letter written in 1734 by Smart Lethieullier from his Bond Street house to Dr Mortimer, Secretary of the Royal Society. Reproduced in part by C.H. Iyan Chown, 'The Lethieullier Family of Aldersbrook House', in *Essex Review*, vol.XXXVI, No.141 (January 1927), pp.3–4.

5   E.F. Scudamore, *Embalming*, 2nd edition (British Institute of Embalmers, Bristol, 1966), p.135.

6   Warton, *The History of English Poetry*, vol.II, p.98. Cited in 'Instances of Extraordinary Preservation of Dead Bodies in their respective graves', in *European Magazine*, vol.X (June 1786).

7   Dr Southwood Smith, 'Uses of the Dead to the Living', *Lancet* (1832).

8   An invitation ticket dated 8 June 1832 is in BM.Add Mss.34661, p.32. For a fuller account of the Bentham auto-icon see R. Richardson, *Death, Dissection and the Destitute* (Routledge & Kegan Paul, London, 1987), pp.159–61.

9   H.G. Ramm, *et al.*, 'The Tombs of Archbishops Walter de Gray (1216–55) and Godfrey de Ludham (1258–65) in York Minster, and their Contents', in *Archaeologia*, vol.CIII (1971), pp.101–48.

10   H.F. Hutchison, *Henry V* (Eyre & Spottiswoode, London, 1967), pp.214–15.

11   John Weever, op.cit., p.30.

12   M.H. Bloxham, *A Glimpse of the Monumental Architecture of Great Britain* (J.B. Nichols & Son, London, 1834), p.56.

13   C. Collingnon, 'Some Account of the Body Lately Found in Uncommon Preservation Under the Ruins of the Abbey of St Edmundsbury, Suffolk, &c.', *Philosophical Transactions of the Royal Society*, vol.LXII (1772), p.465.

14   'Ceremonial of the Funeral of K Edward IV. From a MS. of the late Mr. Anstis, now in the possesssion of Thomas Astle, Esq', *Archaeologia*, vol.I, 2nd edition (1779), pp.350–7.

15   P.M. Kendall, *Richard the Third* (Allen & Unwin, London, 1955).

16   C.J. Polson and D.J. Gee, *The Essentials of Forensic Medicine* (Oxford University Press, 1973), which quotes the 1471 Issue Roll in full. For a full commentary on the embalming and lying-in-state, see W.J. White, 'The Death and Burial of Henry VI', *The Ricardian*, vol.VI, no.78 (September 1982), pp.70–80 and vol.VI, no.79 (December 1982), pp.106–17.

17   ?James Prior, 'Report of the Committee appointed by the Council of the Society of Antiquaries to investigate the circumstances attending the recent Discovery of a Body in St Stephen's Chapel, Westminster', in *Archaeologia*, vol.XXIV (1852).

18   J. Strype, *Ecclesiastical Memorials Relating Chiefly to Religion and the Reformation of It*, vol.II (London, 1721). Appendix.

19   W.J. White, 'Changing Burial Practice in Late Medieval England', *The Ricardian*, vol.IV, no.63 (December 1978), pp.23–30.

20   J. Strype, op. cit.

21   J. Strype, op. cit.

22   J.C. Brooke, 'On the great Seal of Queen Catherine Parr', *Archaeologia*, vol.V (1779), p.234. The Cotton Mss are now in the British Museum, Department of Western Manuscripts.

23   Ibid.

24   Treadway Nash, 'Observation on the Time of the Death and Place of Burial of Queen Katherine Parr', in *Archaeologia*, vol.IX (1789), pp.1–9.

25   Ibid.

26   Ibid.

27   A.P. Stanley, 'On the Depositions of the Remains of Katherine de Valois, Queen of Henry V., In Westminster Abbey', in *Archaeologia*, vol.XLVI (1881), pp.281–96.

28   John Dart, *Westmonasterium*, 2 vols (James Cole, London, 1723), vol.II, p.39.

29   John Weever, op. cit.

30   Samuel Pepys, *The Diary of Samuel Pepys*, R. Braybrooke (ed.), 5 vols (London, 1848). Entry for 23 February 1688–9.

31   Comments on these observations can be found in A.P. Stanley, op. cit.

32   R. Gough, *Sepulchral Monuments in Great Britain, &c.*, (J.B. Nichols & Son, London, 1796), vol.II, p.115.

33   C. Gittings, *Death, Burial and the Individual in Early Modern England*, London (Croom Helm, London, 1984).

34   J. Manningham, *Diary of John Manningham 1602–3*, J. Bruce *et al.* (eds) (Camden Society, London, 1868), vol.XCIX, p.159.

35   John Clapham, *Elizabeth of England*, E.P. and C. Read (eds) (University of Pennsylvania Press, Philadelphia, 1951), p.110.

36   W.J. White, 'Changing Burial Practice in Late Medieval England', op. cit.

37   Olivia Bland, *The Royal Way of Death* (Constable, London, 1986), p.29.

38   A.P. Stanley, *Memorials of Westminster Abbey* (Murray, London, 1869), pp.668–70.

39   *Historical Manuscripts Commission, Buccleuch and Queensbury*, i. A fuller account of the embalming can be found in C. Gittings, op. cit., p.167.

40   C. Gittings, op. cit., pp.87–9, 92, 167.

41   Ibid., p.190.

42   T. Nashe, *Martins Months Minde* (London 1589).

43   Thomas Greenhill, *Nekpokh△eia: or, The Art of Embalming* (London, 1705).

44   Royal Society, *Proceedings* (London 1662 and 1663).

45   S. Mendelsohn, 'Embalming from the Medieval Period to the Present Time' in *CIBA Symposia*, vol.VI, no.2, May 1944, p.1805.

46   J.G. Adami, *Charles White of Manchester (1728–1813)* (Liverpool, 1922).

47   E.M. Brockbank, *Sketches of the lives and work of the honorary medical staff of the Manchester Infirmary from its foundation in 1752 to 1830 when it became the Royal Infirmary* (Manchester, 1904).

48   Jesse Dobson, 'Some Eighteenth Century Experiments in Embalming', *Journal of the History of Medicine*, vol.8 (1953), pp.431–3.

49   Gabriel Clauder, *Methodus Balsamandi* (Florence, 1679).

50   William Hunter, op. cit.

51   It was not at all unusual for sculptors to be asked to make a death-mask. One was taken for effigial purposes of Edward II in 1327 – probably by Stephen Hadley – whilst Pietro Torrigiano took that of Henry VII in 1509 and Maximilian Colt one of Elizabeth I in 1603. Most of the well-known sculptors of the eighteenth and nineteenth centuries – Roubilliac, Rysbrack, Nollekens and Chantry – are known to have based commemorative portraiture on death-masks. Albert Bruce-Joy took one of Edward VII in 1910.

52   A copy of the memorandum written by Martin van Butchell is preserved in one of the Donation Books in the Library of the Royal College of Surgeons, London.

53   Memorandum written by Martin Van Butchell himself, a copy of which is preserved in one of the Donation Books of the Museum of the Royal College of Surgeons, London.

54   W. Hunter, 'The Art of Embalming Dead Bodies', ms. 18pp., dated 13 January 1776, in Royal College of Surgeons Library, London.

55   Jesse Dobson, op. cit., p.434. My quotations are taken from the mss of 13 January 1776 in the library of the Royal College of Surgeons, London.

56   Ibid. A further epitaph, in Latin, appeared in the *Gentleman's Magazine* in January 1793. It commences, 'In reliquas Mariae Vanbutchell novo miraculo conservatas et a marito suo superstites cultu quotidiano adoratus', with William Hunter referred to as 'Vir egregius, artificii, prius intentati inventor idem, et perfector.'

57   C. Cobbe, *Burning the Dead; or Urn Sepulture* (London, 1857).

58   Fauja Saint-Fond, *Travels in England, Scotland and the Hebrides, undertaken for the purpose of examining the state of the arts, the sciences, natural history and manner*, Eng. trans. (London, 1799).

59   Pennant, *Tours in Wales*, vol.III and S. Baring Gould, North Wales.

60   M. Misson, *Memoirs and Observations of His Travels over England*, trans. J. Ozell (London, 1719).

61   Letter of 4 April 1789 from T. White to the editor, *Gentleman's Magazine* (April 1789), p.377–8.

62   John Aubrey (ed. O.L. Dick), *Brief Lives* (Penguin, Harmondsworth, 1972), p.229.

63   Dottridge Brothers, 'Catalogue &c', issued in London, 1902.

3   DRESS'D AND TRIMM'D: WINDING-SHEETS AND SHROUDS

1   A.J. Dezallier-D'Argenville, *Travels et Tours* (Paris c.1731). London, Victoria and Albert Museum (National Art Library), mss., Press Mark 86 NN 2. Transcript unpublished, but with mss.

2   Paris, Bibliothèque Nationale, Lat. 1156 ^{A}

3   London, British Library ms (*Bedford Hours*, c.1423), 08, Add. 18850, f.120.

4   Sold as Lot 1 in the John R. Gaines Collection Sale, Sotheby's (New York), 17 November 1986.

5   H. Macklin, *Monumental Brasses* (Swan Sonnenschein, London, 1905), p.83.

6   A somewhat similar rendition can be seen on the John and Sarah Latch monument at Churchill, Somerset. Here John Latch, in day-clothes, reclines on his right elbow and contemplates the shrouded body of his wife Sarah (d.1644) in top- and bottom-knot shroud.

7   N. Pevsner, *Buildings of England: Hertfordshire* (Penguin, Harmondsworth, 1977), p.163.

8   Isaac Walton, 'The Life of Dr John Donne' in A. Pollard (ed.), *The Compleat Angler and the Lives of Donne, Wotton, Hooker, Herbert and Sanderson*, (Macmillan, London, 1901).

9   Dulwich Picture Gallery, Bourgeois Bequest 1811. A version in the Spencer Collection at Althrop was formerly believed to be the original, but is now catalogued as 'after Van Dyck'.

10   Oxford, Ashmolean Museum; presented by Elias Ashmole, 1683. Cat:

Tradescant 8.

11   For further extracts from this will, see M. Girouard, *A Country House Companion* (Century, London, 1987), p.178.

12   Ibid.,p.178.

13   C. Gittings, op. cit., p.112.

14   Samuel Pepys, op. cit. Entry for 6 July 1661.

15   Lead seals from the reign of Pope Gregory XI (1370–8) found in burials at St Botolph's Church at Billingsgate, London, can be seen in the Museum of London.

16   Oxford, Ashmolean Museum. Evans Collection, inv. no. 1927.6476.

17   The vault clearances were carried out under faculty for the rector and churchwardens in 1983. The author visited the site on a number of occasions at the invitation of the Rector.

18   The vault clearance was approached as an archaeological project for the vicar and churchwardens under the direction of Jez Reeve during 1984–6, with the author as consultant on funerary practices. See: Reeve & Adams, *Across the Styx: The Spitalfields Project. Volume 1 – The Archaeology* (CBA, York, 1993).

19   M. Misson, op. cit., especially pp.88–93 and pp.212–15.

20   A.-J. Dezallier-D'Argenville, op. cit.

21   Burial in woollen was made compulsory by the Acts 30 Car. ii. c. 3 and 36 Ejusdem c. i.

22   John Aubrey, op. cit.

23   Chelmsford, Essex County Record Office. Parish Records, High Ongar, D/AEW 39.

24   Information from the written and oral archive of the author.

25   Information from Revd Anthony D. Couchman of Walthamstow, great-nephew of the deceased.

26   Private Collection.

27   Both Lydia Dwight stoneware portraits are in the Dept of Ceramics, Victoria and Albert Museum, London.

28   The design by Pierce for this monument is in the Victoria and Albert Museum, London (Department of Design, Prints and Drawings), inv. no. 3436.421. See: J. Physick, *Designs for English Sculpture 1680–1860* (HMSO, London, 1969), Cat. no.1.

29   L. Taylor, *Mourning Dress* (Allen & Unwin, London, 1983), p.29. A. Briggs, *How They Lived* (Blackwell, Oxford, 1969), vol.III, pp.9–10, citing R.S. Fitton and A.P. Wadsworth, *The Strutts and Arkwrights* (Manchester University Press, 1958) pp.129–30.

30   A.-J. Dezallier-D'Argenville, op. cit.

31 Priced catalogue issued by J. Turner, 'Coffin Maker, Plate Chaser, Furnishing Undertaker and Funeral Featherman' (Cunningham and Salmon, London, *c*.1838).

32   Anon., *The Workwoman's Guide* (1838; reprinted, Bloomfield Books, New York, 1975).

33   For a full account of the circumstances surrounding the production of this photograph see: M. Hallett, 'A Rite of Passage', in *British Journal of Photography* (5 May 1988), pp.24–5, illus.

34   Dottridge Brothers, 'Catalogue &c.', issued in London, 1922, p.38.

4 LAPPED IN LEAD, ENCASED IN WOOD: THE COFFIN

1   John Aubrey, op. cit.
2   I am grateful to Sir Thomas Hare, Bart., of Stow Bardolph, Norfolk for bringing this Ms will to my attention.
3   Chelmsford, Essex County Record Office. Ms.
4   Ms quoted by courtesy of the City of Bristol Record Office.
5   Anglo-Saxon wooden coffins were found in earth graves during the 1978–81 excavations at Barton-on-Humber, Lincolnshire, and a group of fourteenth-century encoffined burials were discovered at St Augustine-the-Less, Bristol, in 1983–4 (Eric J. Boore, 'Excavations at St Augustine-the-Less, Bristol, 1983–84', in *Bristol and Avon Archaeology*, vol.IV (1985), pp.21–33, illus.). Instances of medieval intramural shroud burial were recorded in a trial trench in the south aisle at Thaxted, Essex, in 1989, though it has been suggested by David Andrews that they were churchyard burials later built over when the aisle was constructed.
6   London, British Library, Add. ms. 18850.
7   London, British Library, Egerton ms. 1070.
8   London, Victoria and Albert Museum, 3581–1856.
9   The outer cases of the coffin of Lady Augusta Lovelace (d.1852) in the Byron vault at Hucknall Torkard and that of Admiral Sir Elias Harvey (d.1830) in the Harvey vault at Hempstead, Essex are identical. Both died in London, and their funeral arrangements were undertaken by Messrs. Dowbiggen and Holland, the society undertakers of the time. They also officiated at the funeral of the Duke of Wellington.
10   W.H.B. (initials only), 'Barnardiston Vaults in Kedington Church', in *Proceedings of the Suffolk Institute of Archaeology and Natural History*, vol.XVI, (1918), pp.44–8, illus.
11   Constance Whitney (d.1628) in St Giles, Cripplegate (destroyed in the Second World War); Mary Salter (d.1631) at Iver, Bucks.; Sara Colville (d.1631) in All Saints, Chelsea; Temperance Brown (d.1635) at Steane, Northants, and Mary Calthorpe (d.1640) at East Barsham, Norfolk.
12   M. Redknap, 'Little Ilford, St Mary the Virgin, 1984' in *London Archaeologist*, vol.V, no.2 (spring 1985), pp.31–7, illus.
13   Not all coffins were tailor-made. An examination of the outer cases at Christchurch, Spitalfields, revealed markings on the base giving the length and shoulder width, indicating that they were drawn from stock. Similar markings continue to be used today.
14   A section of veneered side plank from an inner coffin was discovered at St Augustine-the-Less, Bristol, in 1983–4, the veneer having been used to mask the kerfing which had been cut too deep.
15   M. Girouard, op. cit., p.181.
16   A. French, *John Joseph Merlin* (GLC, London, 1985), p.116, Cat.D9, illus. Exhibition Catalogue.
17   I am indebted to Stuart Campbell-Adams for this quotation, said to have come from the journals of an Italian noblewoman who had spent some time at Wanstead House, Essex. His information is that these notes were rescued from the Tylney papers either by a maid or a relative of Catherine Tylney Long (Hon. Mrs Long Wellesley) prior to many of the records being burnt.
18   London, Victoria and Albert Museum (Dept Design, Prints & Drawings): 1783 catalogue by 'J.B.' issued through Tuesby & Cooper of Southwark Acc.

No. E.997 to E.1011–1903 (M 63e); *c*.1821–4 catalogue by 'A.T.' Acc. No. E.994 to E.1021-1978; 1826 catalogue by 'E.L.' Acc. No. E.3096 to E.3132–1910.
19   Victoria and Albert Museum (Dept Design, Prints & Drawings), London. 1783 catalogue by 'J.B.' issued through Tuesby & Cooper of Southwark, Acc. No. E.997 to E.1011–1902 (M 63 e), title page.
20   London, Victoria and Albert Museum (Dept of Furniture and Woodwork): Acc. No. W.27–1954.
21   Beckford's coffin was deposited within the pink granite table tomb in Landsdowne Cemetery, Bath. This tomb sits on a small knoll within a circular 'moat' eight feet wide and six feet deep.
22   London, Victoria and Albert Museum (National Art Library): The Hardman Registers give the following information on the Earl of Shrewsbury's coffin:

A Spanish Mahogany Coffin, long, wide at top, deep, covered with rich crimson Genor silk velvet	21	00	0
Gilt Coffin Furniture as under			
6 Handles, with eyes and back plates, with Lions on Cap of 8 side clips Maintenance & twisted wires @ 67/6	20	5	0
A Plate for Lid, of Cross, supported at bottom by Talbots			
A Plate with Inscription for Head			
A Plate with Shield & Coronet for Foot			
Edging all round			
1150 Large Pins			
800 gold heades screws	78	15	0
Men's Time fixing above furniture on Coffin	2	16	
(The whole Engraved, Beaten and Saw pierced)			

23   London, Victoria and Albert Museum (National Art Library); Philip Webb Commonplace/Sketchbook, Press Mark 35 M 170.
24   Chelsmford, Essex Record Office: Dunmow Union Minutes, G/DM 11.
25   Castle Howard Archives: F7/29. I am grateful to Richard Robson for bringing this item to my attention.
26   *The Times*, 12 January 1875.
27   London, GLC Record Office: Kensington Borough Council vol.LVIII.

5   FUNERARY TRANSPORT

1   *Daily Telegraph*, 7 September 1984.
2   Bristol, County Record Office: will of Nathaniel Houlton, drafted 26 May 1767, proved 23 October 1767.
3   H.J. Wilkins, *Edward Colston* (Arrowsmith, Bristol, 1920), p.81.
4   Ibid., p.82.
5   These observations are based on the examination of various illuminations in Books of Hours and Missals in the British Library, the British Museum (Department of Western Mss) and the National Art Library at the Victoria and Albert Museum.
6   J.C. Cox, *Churchwardens' Accounts* (Methuen, London, 1913).
7   E.R. Wodehouse *et al.* (eds) *The Manuscripts of Rye and Hereford Corporations* (Historic Manuscripts Commission, London, 1892) 13th Report, Appendix pt.4, gen.

8   J.C. Cox, *The Parish Registers of England* (Methuen, London, 1910).
9   Chelmsford, Essex County Record Office: Lindsell Parish Record, D/P 110/1/1. Ms.
10   T. Cranmer *et. al.* (trans. and ed.), The Boke of Common Prayer and Administracion of the Sacraments, and other Rites and Ceremonies in the Churche of England (Edward Whytchurche, London, 1552), i: Preface.
11   1558 Act of Uniformity.
12   F. Tate, 'Of the Antiquity, Variety and Ceremonies of Funerals in England' in T. Hearne (ed.), *A Collection of Curious Discourses by Eminent Antiquarians upon Several Heads in out English Antiquities* (London 1771), 2 vols., vol.I, pp.215–21.
13   Currently (1990) on loan to Colchester Castle Museum, Essex.
14   Chelsmford, Essex County Record Office: Matching Parish Records, D/ABW 90/30. Ms.
15   E. Chadwick, op. cit.
16   *London's Lamentation; or a Fit Admonition by EP for John Wright Junior wherein is described certain causes of this affliction and visitation of the plague year 1641*, London 1641, Thomason Tracts E, 166.10.
17   Daniel Defoe, *A Journal of the Plague Year*, 1722.
18   Hon. Christopher Lennox-Boyd Collection.
19   Hon. Christopher Lennox-Boyd Collection.
20   A. Gordon, *Death if for the Living* (Paul Harris, Edinburgh, 1984), pp.77–8, illus.pl.13.
21   John Gay, *Trivia; or, The Art of Walking the Streets of London* (Bernard Lintott, London, 1716) Bk.3.
22   Hon. Christopher Lennox-Boyd Collection.
23   Hon. Christopher Lennox-Boyd Collection.
24   *The Flying Post and Medley*, 27 July 1714. A longer extract from this will can be found in J. Ashton, *Social Life in the Reign of Queen Anne* (Chatto & Windus, London, 1883), pp.44–5.
25   M. Misson, op. cit.
26   E. Chadwick, op. cit., pp.83–4.
27   J.C. Loudon, *On the Laying Out, Planting and Management of Cemeteries and on the Improvement of Churchyards* (London, 1843).
28   *Ecclesiastical Art Review*, February 1878.
29   Dottridge Brothers, Catalogue …, London 1923.
30   J. Clarke, *The Brookwood Necropolis Railway* (Oakwood, Headington, 1988), 2nd ed., p.10.
31   A series of engravings of the funeral car of Nelson are in the archives of the National Maritime Museum, Greenwich.
32   C.E. Radcliffe, *Round the Smoking Room Fire* (J. Murray, London, 1933).

6   THE COMMON FUNERAL

1   M. Misson, op. cit.
2   *The Booke of the Common Prayer and Administracion of the Sacraments, and other Rites and Ceremonies of the Churche after the Use of the Churche of England* (Edward Whitchurche, London, 1549).
3   As a person was dying the 'passing bell' was chimed for about an hour in order to solicit prayers from those who heard it; the sanctus bell was used for

241

this purpose or, if the church did not possess one, the treble. The tolling bell – the tenor – chimed for fifteen or thirty minutes prior to the burial. The custom was generally discontinued during the Commonwealth but revived at the Restoration, though most churches had abandoned it by the mid eighteenth century; it persisted in more rural areas until the late nineteenth century, surviving in certain parts of Devon, Somerset and Sussex until 1939 when all bell-ringing stopped on account of the Second World War. At this time bells were to be used only as a warning of invasion. The countrywide custom was the chime in the following way:

3 × 3 strokes for a man, followed by a stroke for each year of his age.
3 × 2 strokes for a woman, and ditto.
3 × 1 strokes for a child (under seven years of age), and ditto.

4   This Office consisted almost entirely of psalms, namely, 116, 120, 121, 130 and 138, with appropriate anthems or antiphons.
5   The author attended the funeral of Elizabeth Scott Bowman at Appleton Roebuck, Yorkshire, on 30 January 1987 after which the following refreshments were provided: shortbread, spiced brandy cake and champagne.
6   J.G. Nichols (ed.), *The Diary of Henry Machyn* (Camden Society, London, 1848), p.2.
7   Ibid., p.xii.
8   Ibid., p.ix.
9   Ibid., p.91
10   Ibid., p.193.
11   John Aubrey, op. cit.
12   J. Christie, *Some Account of Parish Clerks* (privately printed, London, 1893), p.153.
13   P.H. Ditchfield, *The Parish Clerk* (Methuen, London, 1907), pp.118–19.
14   C. Gittings, op. cit., pp.49–50.
15   G. Dix, *The Shape of the Liturgy* (Dacre, London, 1945), p.417.
16   John Aubrey, op. cit., p.478.
17   J.H.R. Moorman, *A History of the Church in England* (A. & C. Black, London, 1963), p.221.
18   State Papers. Solemn League of Covenant, 1642. (London, PRO)
19   Directory of Public Worship, 1644.
20   John Aubrey, op. cit., p.223.
21   T. Herbert, *Memoirs of the Last Two Years of the Reign of Charles I*, (1650), p.199.
22   This table can still be seen in the Deanery; the inset is a brass inscription plate recording the fact that Charles I's coffin temporarily rested on it.
23   T. Herbert, op. cit., p.203.
24   Thomas Fuller, The History of the Worthies of England, J. Fuller (ed.) (IGWL and WG, London, 1662) Vol III, p.504.
25   O.L. Dick, op. cit.
26   An account of the opening of the coffin in 1813 written by Sir Henry Halford was reproduced in *Chamber's Book of Days*, 1869.
27   P.H. Ditchfield, op. cit., p. 83.
28   Ibid., p.80.
29   T.F. Thiselton-Dyer, *Old English Social Life as Told by the Parish Registers* (E. Stock, London, 1898), p.57.
30   J. Ashton, *Social Life in the Reign of Queen Anne* (London, 1883), p.39.

31 Peter A.T.I. Burman tells me of a large and beautiful rosemary bush growing next to the lich-gate at Freshwater, Isle of Wight.

32 B. Puckle, *Funeral Customs, Their Origin and Development* (Werner Laurie, London, 1926), p.112.

33 J. Evelyn, *Letters*, William Bray (ed.) (Henry Colburn, London, 1818), p.260.

34 Cited in C. Gittings, op. cit., p. 197.

35 T.T. Merchant, 'Some General Considerations offered relating to our present trade ...' (1698), pp.6–7, cited in J.S. Burns, *The History of Parish Registers in England* (London, 1862), pp.109–10.

36 A.J. Jackson (ed.), *Ashtead* (Leatherhead & District Local History Society, 1977), p.76.

37 R. Davey, *A History of Mourning* (Jay's, London, 1889), p.110.

38 A.J. Jackson, op. cit., p.76.

39 A.J. Jackson, op. cit., p.77.

40 R. Davey, op. cit., p.110.

41 J. Ashton, op. cit., p.38.

42 From an advertisement issued by John Middleton in Funeral Box 3, The John Johnson Collection, Bodleian Library, Oxford. Cited in T. Laqueur, 'Bodies, Death and Pauper Funerals', in *Representations* vol.1, no.1, University of California (February 1983), pp.109–31.

43 T. Laqueur, op. cit., p.114.

44 *Gentleman's Magazine*, August 1834.

45 R. Davey, op. cit., p.111.

46 D. Cannadine, 'War and Death, Grief and Mourning in Modern Britain', in J. Whaley (ed.), *Mirrors of Mortality: Studies in the Social History of Death*, (Europa, London, 1981), p.191.

7   THE HERALDIC FUNERAL

1 The College's 1541 regulations stipulated the number of 'official' mourners allowed for an emperor (15), king (13), duke (11), marquess or earl (9), viscount or baron (7), knight, banneret or bachelor (5), and esquire or gentleman (3).

2 J. Gough Nichols, op. cit., p.xxiv.

3 J. Gough Nichols, op. cit., pp.xxvi–xxxii.

4 Funeral of Sir Rd Neville, Earl of Salisbury, and his son, Sir Thomas at Bisham Abbey, 15 February 1462. Sir A. Wagner, *Heralds of England* (HMSO, London, 1967), p.107.

5 Sir A. Wagner, op. cit., p.107.

6 Ibid.

7 Ibid., p.109.

8 Claude Blair, *European Armour: c.1066 to 1700* (HMSO, London, 1958).

9 Sir A. Wagner, op. cit., p.107.

10 J. Gough Nichols, op. cit., p.193. Although traditionally associated with the funeral of Charles II, its overall style suggests a date earlier than 1685. The lack of the Roman numerals 'II' between the C and R of the monogram again suggest that this cartouche could be associated with the 1649 funeral of Charles I. Thomas Herbert, Charles I's valet, records in his *Memoirs of the Last Two Years of the Reign of Charles I*, that the coffin was taken to Windsor on the morning of Tuesday 6 February 1649 in a 'Hearse covered with black

Velvet, drawn by Six Horses also covered with black'. There was no heraldic display but it seems highly unlikely that every vestige of funeral symbolism was done away with. Is it possible, therefore, that the cartouche in the Museum of London was affixed to the funeral car?

11   A.R. Dufty, 'The Church', in *Lydiard Park and Church*, Swindon (Borough of Thamesdown, Swindon, *c*.1980), p.21.

12   John Aubrey, op. cit. The unusual siting of Sir Robert Shirley's achievements was probably a tribute to him as founder of the church. An inscription over the west entrance reads, 'In the yeare: 1653 when all things sacred were throughout ye nation Either demollisht or profaned Sr Richard Shirley Barronet Founded this Church whose singular praise it is to have done the best things in ye worst times And hoped them in the most callamitous. The Righteous shall be had in everlasting remembrance.'

13   *Gentleman's Magazine*, lxii, pt.1, p.114.

14   K. Eustace, *Michael Rysbrack* (City Museum and Art Gallery, Bristol, 1982), Cat. No.7.

15   K. Eustace, op. cit. p.71.

16   A. Wood, *The Life and Times of Anthony Wood, Antiquary, of Oxford 1632–1695*, Clark A. (ed.), 5 vols., Oxford Historical Society, vols. XIX, XXI, XXVI, XXX and XL (1891–95). Entries for 7–7 July 1663.

17   London, College of Arms: Chapter Book I, folio 2.

18   Ibid., folio 59.

19   London, College of Arms: Chapter Book II, pp.60–1.

20   Cheyne Walk, Chelsea, Watercolour. Signed and dated *James Miller Del. 1776*. 40.9 x 62.8 cm. London, Victoria and Albert Museum. 731–1893.

21   Th. H. Lunsingh Scheuvleer, 'Documents on the Furnishing of Kensington Palace', *Walpole Society* vol.XXXVIII, p.24.

22   F. Sandford, *The Order and Ceremonies Used for and at the Solemn Interment of ... George Duke of Albermarle ...* (London, 1670).

23   Sir A. Wagner, op. cit., pp.113–14.

24   A.A. Jackson (ed.), *Ashtead: A Village Transformed (Leatherhead & District Local History Society, 1977), p.76.*

8   THE BURIAL VAULT: THE ETERNAL BEDCHAMBER

1   J. Meade Falkner, Moonfleet, London (Arnold & Co, London, 1947), pp.39–40.

2   Where not indicated otherwise, the information on the individual burials and their occupants were collected on site.

3   John Weever, op. cit., p.18.

4   O.L. Dick, op. cit. p.187.

5   A.P. Stanley, 'On an Examination of the Tombs of Richard II and Henry III in Westminster Abbey', *Archaeologia*, vol.XLV (1880), pp.309–22.

6   A.P. Stanley, op. cit.

7   A.P. Stanley, *Memorials of Westminster Abbey* (Murray, London, 1869), p.172.

8   A.P. Stanley observes in a footnote 'that the regular approach to the vault, though afterwards disturbed by the grave of Edward VI, may have been intended to have given a more public and solemn access, especially at the time when the translation of the body of Henry VI was still meditated'.

9 A.P. Stanley, op. cit., pp.678–9 and p.683.

10 Bacon, *Henry VII* (W. Stansby, London, 1662), vol.III, p.417.

11 J.W.S. Litten, *St Mary's Church, Woodford* (Passmore Edwards Museum, London, 1978), p.15.

12 O.L. Dick, op. cit., p.295.

13 O.L. Dick, op. cit., p.179.

14 O.L. Dick, op. cit., p.186.

15 Owen Chadwick, *Victorian Miniature* (Hodder and Stoughton, London, 1960) p.135.

16 Ibid., pp.132–46.

17 B. Carne, 'The St John Vault', in *Report of the Friends of Lydiard Tregoz*, no.18 (1985), p.30.

18 B. Carne, op. cit., p.30.

19 T. Tatton Brown, 'The Roper Chantry in St Dunstan's Church, Canterbury', in *Antiquaries Journal*, vol.LX (1980), pp.227–46, pls.xxv-xxviii.

20 A.P. Stanley, op. cit., p.659, states that the shuttering provided for Elizabeth Claypole's vault in 1658 'had been left in it and had fallen down'.

21 O.L. Dick, op. cit., pp.274–5.

22 O.L. Dick, op. cit., p.395.

23 *Illustrated London News*, vol.CXXXVI, no.3709 (21 May 1910), pp.772–3.

24 J. Turner, *Burial Fees of the principal Churches, Chapels and New Burial-Grounds, in London and its Environs, with List of Searchers, Hours of Burial, Early Dues, &c., and all Necessary Information for Undertakers: Arranged, with an Alphabetical Index* (Cunningham and Salmon, London, 1838).

Bibliography

During the course of preparation for this work, I have made recourse to the following books in my own collection:

Aries, Philippe, *The Hour of Our Death* (Allen Lane, London, 1981).
——, *Images of Man and Death* (Harvard University Press, Cambridge, Mass., 1985).
Ashton, John, *Social Life in the Reign of Queen Anne*, London 1883.
Avery, Gillian and Reynolds, Kimberley (eds), *Representations of Childhood Death* (Macmillan, London, 2000).
Bailey, Brian, *Churchyards of England and Wales* (Robert Hale, London, 1987).
Bailey, Conrad, *Famous London Graves* (George Harrap & Co, London, 1975).
Baker, Richard, *London: A Theme with Variations* (Jarrold, Norwich, 1989).
Bakewell, Joan and Drummond, John, *A Fine and Private Place* (Weidenfeld & Nicolson, London, 1977).
Ball, Mog, *Death* (OUP, Oxford, 1976).
Barker, Felix, *Highgate Cemetery: Victorian Valhalla* (John Murray, London, 1984).
Bartram, Felix, *Tombstone Lettering in the British Isles* (Lund Humphries, London, 1978).
Beattie, Owen and Geiger, John, *Frozen in Time: the Fate of the Franklin Expedition* (Bloomsbury, London, 1987).
Benham, William, *The Prayer-Book of Queen Elizabeth* (John Grant, Edinburgh, 1911).
Bentley, James, *Restless Bones: The Story of Relics* (Constable, London, 1985).
Berry, James, *The Glasgow Necropolis Heritage Trail* (City of Glasgow District Council, Glasgow, 1987).
Besant, Walter, *London in the time of the Stuarts* (A. & C. Black, London, 1903).
Binski, Paul, *Medieval Death: Ritual and Representation* (British Museum Press, London, 1996).
Bland, Olivia, *The Royal Way of Death* (Constable, London, 1986).
Bloore, Peter D., *Bank Street Wesleyan Methodist Chapel, Brierley Hill, Staffordshire: Burial Entries and Pew Rents 1833–1884* (Birmingham & Midland Society for Genealogy and Heraldry, 1980).
Bogle, Joanna, *Who Lies Where?* (Lamp Press, London, 1989).
Bond, Francis, *The Chancel of English Churches* (Milford, London, 1916).
Boore, Eric J., 'Excavations at St Augustine the Less, Bristol, 1983–84', in *Bristol and Avon Archaeology*, no.4 (1985), pp.21–33.
Brewer, Clifford, *The Death of Kings: A Medical History of the Kings and Queens of England* (Albion, London, 2000).
Bridgman, Harriet & Dury, Elizabeth (eds), *The Last Word* (Andre Deutsch, London, 1982).
Brooks, Christopher (ed.), *Mortal Remains: The History and Present State of the Victorian and Edwardian Cemetery* (Wheaton, Exeter, 1989).
Brown, A.F.J., *Essex at Work 1700–1815* (Essex CRO, Chelmsford, 1969).
Burgess, Frederick, *English Churchyard Memorials* (SPCK, London, 1979).

Burman, Peter (ed.), *The Churchyards Handbook,* 3rd edition (Church House Press, London, 1988).

Bushway, Robert, *By Rite: Custom, Ceremony and Community in England, 1700-1880* (Junction, London, 1982).

Cannadine, David & Price, Simon (eds), *Rituals of Royalty* (CUP, Cambridge, 1987).

Cantor, Norman, *In the Wake of the Plague: The Black Death and the World it made* (Simon and Schuster, London, 2001).

Caraman, Philip, *Henry Morse, Priest of the Plague* (Longmans, London, 1957).

Cautley, H. Munro, *Royal Arms and Commandments* (Boydell, Ipswich, 1934).

Chadwick, Owen, *Victorian Miniature* (Hodder & Stoughton, London, 1960).

Claoue-Long, Anne, *Mourning, Memorial & Sentimental Jewellery: The Franks Collection* (Tudor House Museum, Southampton, 1984).

Clarke, John, *The Brookwood Necropolis Railway* (Oakwood, Oxford, 1995) 3rd edition.

Collinson, Hugh, *Country Monuments* (David & Charles, Newton Abbot, 1975).

Conner, Patrick (ed.), *The Inspiration of Egypt* (Brighton Borough Council, Brighton, 1983).

Cook, G.H. *Mediaeval Chantries and Chantry Chapels* (Phoenix, London, 1947).

——, *English Monasteries in the Middle Ages* (Phoenix, London, 1961).

Cox, Margaret, *Life and Death in Spitalfields 1700–1850,* (CBA, York, 1996).

Cox, Margaret (ed.), *Grave Concerns: Death and Burial in England 1700–1850* (CBA, York, 1998).

Crichton, Ian, *The Art of Dying* (Peter Owen, London, 1976).

Cruz, Joan Carroll, *The Incorruptibles* (Tan, Rockford, Ill., 1977).

Curl, James Stevens, *The Victorian Celebration of Death* (David & Charles, Newton Abbot, 1972).

——, *The Victorian Celebration of Death* (Sutton, Stroud, 2000) revised and expanded 2nd edition.

——, 'Scotland's Spectacular Cemeteries', in *Country Life,* 3 October 1974.

——, 'Saving a Victorian Burial-Ground: Nunhead Cemetery, South London', in *Country Life,* 17 July 1975.

——, 'Nunhead Cemetery, London' in *Transactions of the Ancient Monuments Society* (AMS, London, 1977).

——, *A Celebration of Death* (Constable, London, 1980).

——, 'Northern Cemetery Under Threat: Jesmond, Newcastle-upon-Tyne' in *Country Life,* 2 July 1981.

——, 'Neo-Classical Necropolis in Decay: York Cemetery' in *Country Life,* 28 January 1982.

——, 'John Claudius Loudon and the Garden Cemetery Movement', in *Garden History,* The Journal of the Garden History Society, vol. XI, no. 2 (Autumn 1983).

——, 'Architecture for a Novel Purpose: Death and the Railway Age', in *Country Life,* 12 June 1986.

Daniel, Evan, *The Prayer-Book*: *Its History, Language, and Contents* (Wells, Gardner, Darton & Co, London, 1892).

Daniell, Christopher, *Death and Burial in Medieval England 1066–1550* (Routledge, London, 1997).

Davey, Richard, *A History of Mourning* (Jay's Mourning Warehouse, London, 1889).

Dick, Oliver Lawson, *Aubrey's Brief Lives* (Secker & Warburg, London, 1949).

Dickens, A.G., *The English Reformation* (Batsford, London, 1964).

Dickens, Charles, *Oliver Twist* (OUP, Oxford, 1966).

Ditchfield, P.H., *The Parish Clerk* (Methuen, London, 1907).

Dix, Gregory, *The Shape of the Liturgy* (Dacre, London, 1945).

Drake-Carnell, F.J., *Old English Customs and Ceremonies* (Batsford, London, 1938).

Druitt, Herbert, *A Manual of Costume as Illustrated by Monumental Brasses* (Tabard Press, London, 1970).

Duffy, Eamon, *The Stripping of the Altars: Traditional Religion in England 1400–1580* (Yale, London, 1992).

Earle, Peter, *The Making of the English Middle Class* (Methuen, London, 1989).

Enright, D.J., *The Oxford Book of Death* (OUP, Oxford, 1983).

Esdaile, Katherine A., *English Church Monuments 1510–1840* (Batsford, London, 1946).

Etlin, Richard A., *The Architecture of Death* (MIT Press, Cambridge, Mass., 1984).

Falkner, J. Meade, *Moonfleet* (Edward Arnold, London, 1947).

Ferro, Robert, *The Family of Max Desir* (Arrow, London, 1987).

Bibliography

Fletcher, Ronald, *The Akenham Burial Case* (Wildwood, London, 1974).

——, *In a Country Churchyard* (Batsford, London, 1978).

Ford, Colin, *Sir Benjamin Stone, 1838–1914* (National Portrait Gallery, London, 1974).

Gavaghan, Michael, *The Story of the Unknown Warrior* (M&L Publications, Preston, 1995).

Gibson, E.C.S., *The First and Second Prayer Books of Edward VI* (Dent, London, 1910).

Gittings, Clare, *Death, Burial and the Individual in Early Modern England* (Croom Helm, London, 1984).

Gordon, Anne, *Death is for the Living* (Paul Harris, Edinburgh, 1984).

Gordon, Bruce and Marshall, Peter (eds), *The Place of Death: Death and Remembrance in Late Medieval and Early Modern Europe* (CUP, Cambridge, 2000).

Greenwood, Douglas, *Who's Buried Where in England* (Constable, London, 1982).

Gresty, Hilary & Lumley, Mark (eds), *Death* (Kettle's Yard, Cambridge, 1988).

Gunnis, Rupert, *Dictionary of British Sculptors 1660–1851* (Abbey, London, 1951).

Harthan, John, *Books of Hours* (Thames & Hudson, London, 1977).

——, *An Introduction to Illuminated Manuscripts* (HMSO, London, 1983).

Harvey, Anthony and Mortimer, Richard (eds), *The Funeral Effigies of Westminster Abbey* (Boydell and Brewer, Woodbridge, 1994).

Heal, Ambrose, *London Tradesmen's Cards of the XVIII Century* (Batsford, London, 1925).

——, *Sign Boards of Old London Shops* (Portman Books, London, 1988).

Hole, Christina, *English Custom and Usage* (Batsford, London, 1941).

——, *English Shrines and Sanctuaries* (Batsford, London, 1954).

Houlbrooke, Ralph, A., *The English Family 1450–1700* (Longman, London, 1984).

——, *Death, Religion and the Family in England 1480–1750* (OUP, Oxford, 1998).

Ilmonen, Anneli (ed.), *Synty Ja Kuolema* (Tampereen Taidemuseo, Tampereen, 1989).

Jackson, Alan A. (ed.), *Ashtead: A Village Transformed* (Leatherhead & District Local History Society, Leatherhead, 1977).

Jalland, Pat, *Death in the Victorian Family* (OUP, Oxford, 1996).

James, E.O., *Christian Myth and Ritual* (John Murray, London, 1933).

Jones, Barbara, *Design for Death* (Bobbs-Merrill, New York, 1967).

Jones, Jeremy, *How to Record Graveyards* (CBA and RESCUE, London, 1979).

Joyce, Paul, *A Guide to Abney Park Cemetery* (Save Abney Park in association with the London Borough of Hackney, London, 1984).

Jupp, Peter & Gittings, Clare (eds), *Death in England: An Illustrated History* (MUP, Manchester, 1999).

Jupp, Peter and Howarth, Glennys (eds), *The Changing Face of Death: Historical Accounts of Death and Disposal* (Macmillan, London, 1997).

Kelke, W. Hastings, *The Churchyard Manual* (Cox, London, 1851).

Kemp, Brian, *English Church Monuments* (Batsford, London, 1980).

Kent, William, *The Lost Treasures of London* (Phoenix, London, 1947).

Kingsley Ward, G. & Gibson, Edwin, *Courage Remembered* (HMSO, London, 1989).

Knipsel, Franz, *Zur Geschichte des Bestattungswesens in Wien* (Wiener Stadtwerke Städtische Bestattung, Vienna, 1982).

—— *Zur Geschichte des Sarges* (Wiener Stadtwerke Städtische Bestattung, Vienna, 1985).

Laqueur, Thomas, 'Bodies, Death, and Pauper Burials', in *Representations*, no. 1, vol. 1, University of California (1983).

Linnell, C.L.S. & Wearing, Stanley J., *Norfolk Church Monuments* (Adlard, Ipswich, 1952).

Litten, J.W.S. & Clark, F.R., *St Mary's Church, Woodford, Essex* (Passmore Edwards Museum, London, 1977).

Litten, J.W.S., 'The Public Face of Private Mourning: The London Funeral 1695–1945', in *Victoria and Albert Museum Album*, No.1 (Templegate, London, 1982).

——, 'The Poulett Vault, Hinton St George', in *Somerset Archaeology and Natural History*, Taunton 1988.

——, 'Journeys to Paradise: Funerary Transport 1600–1850' in *Genealogists' Magazine*, March 1990.

——, 'The Funeral Effigy: Its Function and Purpose' in Harvey, Anthony and Mortimer, Richard (eds), *The Funeral Effigies of Westminster Abbey* (Boydell and Brewer, Woodbridge, 1994).

248

——, 'The Funeral Trade in Hanoverian England 1714–1760' in Jupp, Peter and Howarth, Glennys (eds), *The Changing Face of Death: Historical Accounts of Death and Disposal* (Macmillan, London, 1997).

——, 'The English Funeral 1700–1850' in Cox, Margaret (ed.), *Grave concerns: Death and Burial in England 1700–1850* (CBA, York, 1998).

——, 'Tombs fit for Kings: Some burial vaults of the English Aristocracy and Landed Gentry of the period 1650–1850', in *Church Monuments – Journal of the Church Monuments Society*, vol. XIV, 1999.

Llewellyn, Nigel, *The Art of Death: Visual Culture in the English Death Ritual c.1500–c.1800* (V&A/Reaktion Books, London 1991).

Llewellyn, Nigel, *Funeral Monuments in Post-Reformation England* (CUP, Cambridge, 2000).

Lowther Clarke, W.K., *Liturgy and Worship* (SPCK, London, 1932).

McDannell, Colleen & Lang, Bernhard, *Heaven: A History* (Yale University Press, London, 1988).

Macklin, H.W., *Monumental Brasses* (Swan Sonnenschein, London, 1905).

Matson, Katinka, *Short Lives* (Picador, London, 1981).

May, Trevor, *The Victorian Undertaker* (Shire Publications, Princes Risborough, 1996).

Meade, Dorothy M., *The Medieval Church in England* (Churchman Publishing, Worthing, 1988).

Meara, David, *Victorian Memorial Brasses* (Routledge & Kegan Paul, London, 1983).

Meller, Hugh, *London Cemeteries* (Avebury, Amersham, 1981).

Metken, Sigrid (ed.), *Die Letzte Reise* (Hugendubel, Munich, 1984).

Milne, Gustav, *St Bride's Church, London: Archaeological research 1952–60 and 1992–95*, (English Heritage, London, 1997).

Mitford, Jessica, *The American Way of Death* (Hutchinson, London, 1963).

Molleson, Theya and Cox, Margaret, *The Middling Sort: The Spitalfields Project. Volume 2 – The Anthropology* (CBA, York, 1993).

Morley, John, *Death, Heaven and the Victorians* (Studio Vista, London, 1971).

Morris, Richard, *The Church in British Archaeology* (CBA, London, 1983).

Murdoch, Tessa (ed.), *The Quiet Conquest: The Huguenots 1685–1985* (Museum of London, London, 1985).

Nichols, John Gough, *The Diary of Henry Machyn* (Camden Society, London, 1848).

Nicol, Robert, *In Memoriam, The Victorian Way of Death* (University of South Australia, Flinders, 1985).

Office of Fair Trading, *Funerals: A Report* (HMSO, London, 1989).

Opie, Iona & Tatem, Moira (eds), *A Dictionary of Superstitions* (OUP, Oxford, 1989).

Packard, Jerrold, *Farewell in Splendour: The Death of Queen Victoria and Her Age* (Sutton, Stroud, 2000).

Palmer, Richard, *The Pest Anatomized* (Wellcome Institute, London, 1985).

Parsons, Brian, *The London Way of Death* (Sutton, Stroud, 2001).

Penny, Nicholas, *Church Monuments in Romantic England* (Yale University Press, London, 1977)

——, *Mourning* (HMSO, London, 1981).

Perham, Michael, *Liturgy Pastoral and Parochial* (SPCK, London, 1984).

Pinnell, P.M., *Village Heritage* (Alan Sutton, Gloucester, 1986).

Platt, Colin, *The English Medieval Town* (Secker and Warburg, London, 1976).

——, *King Death: The Black Death and its aftermath in late-medieval England* (UCL, London, 1996).

Plume, Sable, *Coffins and Coffin Making* (Undertakers' Journal, London, c.1920).

Procter, F. & Frere, W.H., *A New History of the Book of Common Prayer* (Macmillan, London, 1911).

Puckle, Bertram, *Funeral Customs* (Werner Laurie, London, 1926).

Rahtz, Philip & Watts, Lorna, *Wharram Percy: The Memorial Stones of the Churchyard* (York University, York, 1983).

Randall, Gerald, *Church Furnishing and Decoration* (Batsford, London, 1980).

Rayment, John L., *Monumental Inscriptions* (Federation of Family History Societies, Plymouth, 1981).

Reeve, Jez & Adams, Max, *Across the Styx: The Spitalfields Project. Volume 1 – The Archaeology* (CBA, York, 1993).

Rennell, Tony, *Last Days of Glory: The Death of Queen Victoria* (Viking, London, 2000).

Richardson, Ruth, *Death, Dissection and the Destitute* (Routledge & Kegan Paul, London, 1987).

Rodwell, Warwick, *The Archaeology of the English Church* (Batsford, London, 1981).

Routh, Pauline E., *Medieval Effigial Alabaster Tombs in Yorkshire* (Boydell Press, Ipswich, 1976).

Schorsch, Anita, *Mourning Becomes America* (Penn Memorial Museum, Harrisburg, 1976).

Scudamore, E.F., *Embalming* (British Institute of Embalmers, Bristol, 1966).

Selwyn, Bernard, *The Brompton Cemetery* (Friends of Brompton Cemetery, London, 1988).

Shaw, D., *Beneath This Stone* (Clewer (D. Shaw) *c*.1980).

Spiegl, Fritz (ed.), *A Small Book of Grave Humour* (Pan, London, 1971).

Stamp, Gavin, *Silent Cities* (RIBA, London, 1977).

Stanley, A.P., *Historical Memorials of Canterbury* (John Murray, London, 1865).

——, *Historical Memorials of Westminster Abbey* (John Murray, London, 1869).

Stokes, Gwyneth (ed.), *Nunhead Cemetery* (Friends of Nunhead Cemetery, London, 1988).

Suffling, Ernest R., *English Church Brasses* (Tabard Press, London, 1970).

Summers, Peter (ed.), *Hatchments in Britain*, vol. VI (Phillimore, London, 1985).

Sumner, Ann (ed.), *Death, Passion and Politics: Van Dyck's Portraits of Venetia Stanley and George Digby* (Dulwich Picture Gallery, Dulwich, 1995).

Swete, H.B., *Church Services and Service Books before the Reformation* (SPCK, London, 1896).

Taylor, Lou, *Mourning Dress* (George Allen & Unwin, London, 1983).

Temple, Nigel, *Seen and Not Heard* (Dial Press, New York, 1970).

Times, The, Hail and Farewell: The Passing of King George V (*The Times*, London, 1936).

Timpson, John, *Timpson's England* (Jarrold, Norwich, 1987).

——, *Timpson's Towns* (Jarrold, Norwich, 1989).

Tindal Hart, A., *The Man in the Pew* (John Baker, London, 1966).

Waugh, Evelyn, *The Loved One* (Chapman & Hall, London, 1948).

Weaver, Lawrence, *Memorials and Monuments* (Country Life, London, 1915).

Weever, John, *Ancient Funerall Monuments* (Thomas Harper, London, 1631).

Werner, Alex (ed.), *London Bodies: The changing shape of Londoners from Prehistoric times to the Present Day* (Museum of London, London, 1998).

West, Jack, *Jack West: Funeral Director* (Stockwell, Ilfracombe, 1988).

Whaley, Joachim (ed.), *Mirrors of Mortality: Studies in the Social History of Death* (Europa, London, 1981).

White, Lesley, *Monuments and their Inscriptions* (Society of Genealogists, London, 1987).

White, William, *Skeletal Remains from the Cemetery of St Nicholas Shambles, City of London* (London & Middlesex Archaeological Society, London, 1988).

Whistler, Laurence, *The English Festivals* (Heinemann, London, 1947).

Wilkinson, Theon, *The Two Monsoons* (Duckworth, London, 1976).

Williamson, R.P. Ross, 'Victorian Necropolis', in *Architectural Review*, vol. XCII, no. 550 (1942).

Wilson, David, *Aweful Ends: The British Museum Book of Epitaphs* (British Museum Press, London, 1992).

Winter, Gordon, *A Cockney Camera* (Penguin, Harmondsworth, 1975).

Wolfston, Patricia S., *Greater London Cemeteries and Crematoria* (Society of Genealogists, London, 1985).

Wood, William, *A History of Eyam* (Bell & Daldy, London, 1859).

Woollacott, Ron, *Nunhead Notables* (Friends of Nunhead Cemetery, London, 1984).

Wyatt, E.G.P., *The Burial Service* (A.R. Mowbray, London, 1918).

Young, David, *Bats in the Belfry* (David & Charles, Newton Abbot, 1987).

Ziegler, Philip, *The Black Death* (Collins, London, 1969).

Index

251